Business Owners' Wisdom

Business Owners' Wisdom

Great business owners share their stories

Brett Kelly

CLOWN
PUBLISHING

Clown Publishing
PO Box 1764, North Sydney NSW 2059, Australia
Telephone: (02) 9923 0800 Facsimile: (02) 9923 0888
Email: brett@brettkelly.com.au
www.brettkelly.com.au

National Library of Australia
Catalogue-in-Publication data:

Author	Kelly, Brett, 1974–
Title	Business Owners' Wisdom: Great business owners share their stories / Brett Kelly.
ISBN	978-0-9807765-2-2 (hbk.)
	978-0-9807765-3-9 (pbk.)
Series:	Business Owners' Wisdom ; No.1.
Subjects:	Entrepreneurship–Australia.
	Businesspeople–Australia.
	Entrepreneurship–Australia–Anecdotes.
	Businesspeople–Australia–Anecdotes.
Dewey Number:	338.04

Editorial Management Filtered Media
Editor Megan Drinan
Sub-Editor Dan Stojanovich
Copy-Editor/Proofreader Ella Martin

Design/Print Management Reno Design, Sydney R31025
Designers Graham Rendoth, Ingrid Urh | Reno Design
Photography Simon Carroll, Kurt Sneddon (Harry Triguboff), Louise Smit (Lorna Jane).
Images not credited are from the individual's files. All reasonable efforts have been
made to correctly reference images and contact relevant copyright holders.
Printing Toppan Security Printing Pte. Ltd., Singapore

10 9 8 7 6 5 4 3 2 1

For Rebecca, Thomas, Nicholas and Audrey

Contents

'There is also a part of me still today that enjoys creating new businesses ... You know, what are people going to want, what's happening out there that's not being delivered that people would want? Some people call that entrepreneurship.'

– Brett Blundy

Preface

It never ceases to amaze me just how generous busy people can be with their time and wisdom. This book is the first in a two-part compilation of interviews I conducted with Australian business owners between June and September 2012. I approached thirty-four business owners, and the first sixteen conversations appear in these pages.

Each person not only carved out time from their busy schedules to sit down with me, some even met me twice. I learned plenty of valuable new lessons about running a private business, and in the process made some new friends.

I also confirmed a little understood discovery. When people become successful in business and life, they're also happy to share their insights with others. And I don't think it's an ego thing. Business owners genuinely want to see other people succeed. There's an old saying that 'no man is an island'. Well in this case, I've discovered the spirit of business in Australia: No company is an island.

It's no secret that for many businesses the past few years have been tough. In fact, I still believe many parts of the economy are in recession. The road to recovery won't be quick for everyone.

With that in mind, I've been very deliberate in the way I approached these interviews. Yes, I asked people about their business strategies. But I also asked them about their personal lives. In my experience business owners live a unique existence. Their personal and professional lives become financially and emotionally intertwined.

There's simply no way to escape this reality because the buck stops with you. At the same time, business owners are doing something completely remarkable. They're living with passion, with intent, they're doing something they love and often helping thousands of people improve their lives. Running a business isn't just a job. It's your life.

It's a tough road sometimes, but pursuing your dreams is the only way to live. I've personally made a commitment to live a conscious life because I could think of nothing worse than being unconscious and disconnected from the world around me. This book reflects that pursuit, and I hope the stories of sixteen remarkable people ignite a similar passion in you to go somewhere and be the person you told yourself you would be when you grew up!

'Do I wake up some days wondering how it all happened?
Absolutely! Would I change a thing? Absolutely not!
Are my dreams for Lorna Jane bigger and better? You bet!'

– Lorna Jane Clarkson

Acknowledgements

Business Owners' Wisdom is the product of hard work by many people. First and foremost, I want to thank the business owners who generously gave up their time to speak with me and share their wisdom. This is wisdom gained through the hard work, persistence and passion that comes from working on your own business.

This book simply would not have happened without the following sixteen business owners and their personal assistants: Andrew Simmons, Bill Bridges, Brett Blundy, Collette Dinnigan, Harry Triguboff, Imelda Roche, James Stevens, James Erskine, John Cutler, Lorna Jane Clarkson, Mark Carnegie, Matt Moran, Mike Cannon-Brookes, Nicola Cerrone, Peter Stutchbury, Tom Waterhouse, Jessica Kelly, Cheryl Griffiths, Anna De Paoli, Nikki Andrews, Fiona Fraser, Christina Papa, Ardleigh Matthews, Donna Hills, Danielle Ross, Loreto Escobar and Renee Lord.

Simon Carroll from Living Image Photography walked the journey with me. Thoughout the interviews he provided objective comment, encouraged the project and took incredible photographs.

Thanks also to my talented production team who turned thousands of transcribed notes into the tightly edited stories featured in the following pages.

Graham Rendoth of Reno Design worked with me to design and print my previous books *Collective Wisdom* and *Universal Wisdom*. Then, as now, he's brought experience and design sensitivity to produce a book that looks fantastic.

Ella Martin has also returned to work with me on this book. She's a first class copy-editor/proofreader, and her incredible attention to detail is a rare talent. Dan Stojanovich likewise returned to help me turn some very tough transcripts into readable text. Your hard work under pressure made all the difference.

I'm grateful for the work of new members of the editing team. Megan Drinan is a seasoned book editor and she worked under a tight deadline to make each chapter sparkle. Thank you to Mark Jones and Heather Jones at Filtered Media for their ideas, insistence on excellence and assistance in writing matters.

Finally, to my immediate and extended family. My in-laws make our lives so much better. Rebecca, my wife, is the strength, wit and intelligence who runs the real business, our family. Thomas, Nicholas and Audrey get me up early and keep me going late into the night because I want to be the best I can for them.

Introduction

'Die you will, but only regret can kill you.'

In 1997 I had my wake up call. I was twenty-two and watching people in their fifties grappling with having just been made redundant like me. Their whole world was collapsing as they lost their business card, and with that their identity.

I decided never to go back to sleep. Never live with regret.

Not knowing what I should do with my life, but knowing I had nothing to lose, I decided to write a book, which became a bestseller. Not your average response to a situation like mine.

Every seven years since, I try to take stock. I look at my life, the world around me, and how I've been spending my time. What am I learning, and what impact am I making on people's lives? How can I consolidate my knowledge about one area of life? Am I happy? What meaning is there in my life?

The job I'd lost in merchant banking at twenty-two was supposed to be the glamour career job that set you up for life, but the reality was I was miserable. And looking back, many of the people I worked with didn't strike me as happy either.

The experience changed my life. It forced me to stop and think about changes I needed to make. I wanted to know what it meant to live a meaningful life.

At the time, my father gave me two books which really got me thinking: Dale Carnegie's *How to Win Friends and Influence People* and Napoleon Hill's *Think and Grow Rich*. Together, these books offered two valuable insights I've never forgotten. First, your ability to deal with people is more important than anything else. Second, success in business and life comes when you model successful ideas that build great habits.

I'm a person who doesn't ignore good advice, so I took the authors' advice and took control of my situation. The first book I wrote was called *Collective Wisdom*. It was a compilation of thirty-four interviews I conducted with prominent Australian achievers – people who, in meeting with them, changed me.

Seven years later – in keeping with my new seven-year review discipline – I published *Universal Wisdom* in which I examined the lives of seven people who changed the world, including Nelson Mandela, Warren Buffet and Martin Luther-King.

And now you're holding *Business Owners' Wisdom*, a book that chronicles my latest round of interviews with successful business owners. Seven years comes around quickly, but in this case not quickly enough. This is the first of two books to exclusively focus on what makes business owners tick, and you can expect the next instalment next year.

So, why the focus on business owners, you ask?

Firstly, my family has grown to three young children: two boys aged seven and five and a new baby girl. My kids are reason enough to make me stop and reflect on life: where I've been and where I'm going. They grow so quickly and seem to emphasise the need for considered and deliberate living.

Secondly, our business. I have been building Kelly+Partners chartered accountants from scratch to five offices and a hundred-plus staff over the last six and half years with an exclusive focus on helping private business owners achieve their goals. And I want to keep learning in order to help my clients and my business.

Thirdly, the combination of my experience in family and business has helped me find my passion: what I call 'helping people get somewhere'. Whether that's a client, a friend or a team member, I'm driven by a desire to help people improve their situation.

And lastly, I'm inspired by the example of successful private business owners. These are independent thinkers, people who are driven and determined to change the world. They challenge me to push my standards higher and demand more of myself.

These thoughts inspired and shaped the way I approached the business owners interviewed in this book. Every interview is different in that every person has a unique story. I asked them to share a story with me that would change my thinking or challenge my assumptions.

The result is a collection of profoundly moving and inspiring stories. Here are a few examples:

- Brett Blundy built retailers Sanity, HMV, diva, Bras N Things, and Dusk with a relentless focus on doing the best for the customer;

- Collette Dinnigan and Lorna Jane Clarkson both started completely different fashion companies but started from the same place – other people wanted what they made for themselves;

- In contrast, Mike Cannon-Brookes is a young man who in the space of eight short years has, together with his co-founder Scott Farquhar, built a company that employs more than five hundred people and attracted this accolade from Fortune: 'Atlassian is to software what Apple is to design';

- Then we have Mark Carnegie, a successful man who's made millions of dollars and thinks deeply about how to improve society; and

- John Cutler, a fourth generation bespoke tailor who operates a family business in Sydney that's continued for more than a hundred and twenty-five years.

I'll let you discover all the other stories in this book for yourself, but if there's a common thread that's captured me it's that these are people who have found what they love and dedicated their life to being the best they can be at that endeavour.

To me, there's nothing more inspiring than spending time with entrepreneurs, game changers, deep thinkers, and people who never stop dreaming about a better tomorrow.

I found myself walking out on the street after meeting these business owners and feeling completely overwhelmed, literally on a high. I've been challenged to constantly raise my standards, to think of new ways to innovate and help my own clients achieve their goals.

I've come to realise that for me, there's no excuse for living an unconscious life. I want to live consciously and very deliberately. In my travels I constantly talk with business owners such as these and wider afield, addressing audiences of business people at conferences and private events. It's taught me the value of constantly seeking to grow in wisdom and understanding.

In my mind, there are few things worse than turning fifty and realising you still don't know much more about life than when you were twenty.

Brett Kelly

Brett Blundy

Retailer – BB Retail Capital (BBRC)

'If it's worth doing, do it well, do the best you can.
If you can do it, you ought to do it.'

Brett Blundy's story started with a small record store in Pakenham, outer Melbourne, in 1980. His private investment company, BB Retail Capital (BBRC), is currently one of Australia's biggest retail groups, investing in a variety of concept enterprises and properties. Some of the retail ventures along this colourful journey have included Adairs, Bras N Things, diva, Dusk, Lovisa, Sanity, HMV, Virgin and even BridgeClimb on the Sydney Harbour Bridge.

www.bbretailcapital.com.au

Interview

BRETT KELLY: Brett, you've built an amazing business while managing to keep a low profile. Tell me, where did you grow up and how did you get started?

BRETT BLUNDY: I'm a country boy, I grew up in South Gippsland, Victoria. My father was a farmer – carrots, cabbages and potatoes. At the age of twenty, I decided it would be a great idea to get into business. I didn't really know what business I wanted, but I liked people. A friend of mine at school had found a couple of record stores called Disco Duck that weren't running very well, and essentially, we thought that would be a great business to get into. We bought both of the stores, closed one, combined the stock and opened our very first store in Pakenham in country Victoria.

BK: Did you like records or did you just like business?

BB: To be truthful, I'd have to say my lifelong ambition since I was about twelve was to be in business. So, first and foremost it was business. At the time, records were really just the vehicle to achieve that.

BK: I know you went on to get more stores, how did that happen?

BB: Well, first, I've got to tell you the truth. That first store in Pakenham was a disaster, financially. It didn't work. It lost money from day one. Both my partner and I thought we were going to work in the store but we had to go back to work. I went back to piecework, which was basically doing any job I could find – unloading semi-trailers of hay, bunching carrots, etc. Then we found the cheapest person we thought we could trust to put in the store. Her name was Debbie Dolan. She was sixteen and my partner's next-door neighbour, so we knew her.

Really, that was the start of my journey. I just started learning. That was before mobile phones. I was in a rural environment so I'd have to find a phone at lunchtime. I'd ring up and say, 'How are you going? What's going on?' We'd go down in the evenings and do the bookwork, the ordering, run the business side of it. We really learned a lot, even though we were losing money.

To this day, I still think it was the best lesson that I ever learned. It was really hard to work to fund the store and run the business outside of hours. The hours were crazy, but I was twenty and thought we could do it all – no risk, nothing to lose, what the hell? The worst we could do was keep working until we'd paid off the rent.

I really enjoyed it. I discovered that customer service was something that was very special if you delivered it properly. That's the deal. We worked at making sure we had the right product. We would do anything. I would deliver music in the middle of the night. I would take customer orders. People began to know that they could trust us. Debbie would take the orders and then Jeff or I would deliver them in the evening, which was–

BK: Unheard of?

BB: We didn't know it back then, but it was a pretty special service. We were doing it because we wanted the $12 sale so desperately. I started to understand the right service, the right approach, the ways in which you could really endear yourself to lots of customers. It was a country town, so it was easy. There weren't enough customers, but the ones you had knew you and trusted you.

Then, I did the boldest thing, but it turned out to be very successful. I figured that we were really good at what we did and we'd learned a lot, but it was the location that was wrong – both the town and the location of the store. I saw a music store for sale in Parkmore, Keysborough, which was a proper shopping centre in the suburbs of Dandenong in Victoria. I walked into the store and there, smoking away with his silly cat was a bored retailer. He owned the store but had lost total interest. It was dirty, grungy, smelly and unstocked. The guy had lost the love of what it was about. He'd lost the love of music. He'd lost the love of serving people. He was a classic story of, 'you're interrupting me and I hate you all. The reason I'm failing is because you're all too hard on price. You don't buy enough.'

So we bought that store. It was a big decision. We were losing money like no tomorrow. I needed to keep working to fund the losses on the store we already had and here I was making a decision to buy another one, leave my piecework and work full-time in the record store. But again, I was twenty-one and didn't have a lot to lose. So, that's what we did. That store was turning over $2 000 a week when we bought it, which was terrible. Six months later, we were doing $15 000 a week. I still have that graph somewhere. I graphed it every week.

BK: What did you pay for the store?

BB: I wish I could tell you. I just cannot remember. Whatever we paid, it was a great decision.

BK: I'm wondering how long it took to pay back?

BB: I remember back then I thought, 'If I could make $20 000, life would be wonderful. My own business and $20 000! I remember, once we built that store up, in that year, I made $80 000.

BK: How much was a house worth at that time?

BB: To buy a house back then, thirty-two years ago, about $80 000.

BK: That's a huge achievement, earning enough to buy a house in the town you've grown up in, in a couple of years.

BB: Can you imagine? I'm a country boy. I'm as excited as. But, forget the money for the moment, we achieved that by paying attention to the customers. That's all I've ever done. It's, 'What do they need? What do they want? What are they likely to want? How can I get it? How can I stay in stock?' It was pretty simple in principle. 'How do I start employing a couple of people? How do I get them to pay attention to the customers?'

In those days, it was simple. Look them in the eye, walk up to them, and say, 'Hi!' I had such a ball working in that store. During the day I'd work on my own and, if I needed to go to the toilet, I had such good relationships with customers that they would walk in and I'd say, 'Hey! Nice to see you again. Would you mind the store while I dash off to the toilet?' I think about the things that I did back then, it was–

BK: Crazy.

BB: But it was great fun. That's the sort of rapport I had. I was working very hard, but it didn't feel like work. As a matter of fact, from then on, it's never really been work, to be honest. It's never really been work for me. I actually enjoy most of it. So that was the second store.

'I really enjoyed it. I discovered that customer service was something that was very special if you delivered it properly.'

BK: Did it start to pay out some of the problems in the first store or was it supporting it?

BB: It was supporting it. It was a three-year lease that we took on that Pakenham store and the day the lease came around–

BK: Gone?

BB: Gone. It never made a cent. To put it in perspective, back then, 7-inch singles were $1.99. I remember ringing Debbie one night and asking, 'How did we go today?' and she said, 'We're going well.' The total takings for the day were $3.98.

That sticks in my mind thirty-two years later. Can you imagine that call? We were in trouble, we weren't making any money.

But it was true, it was a bad location. It's laughable. Those one or two stores eventually grew to more than three hundred stores. At our peak, we had Sanity, we had HMV in Australia, we had the Virgin stores in Australia and, essentially, more than one in three records were being bought through one of our stores. And even twenty-five years later, we never, ever, had a store in Pakenham. And Pakenham had grown as a town–

BK: So, it had been marked as never to be forgotten!

BB: Well, no, it wasn't, because I wouldn't put one in there. It was just that we were twenty-five years ahead.

BK: There was no market even twenty-five years later?

BB: Yes. Two green guys out of school thought that you'd just open up a store and it would work–

BK: How important is location to retail?

BB: Well, it was my very first, very early lesson – don't put a store in a town that can't support it. I put the store in an arcade, which is even worse. Only about three people walked down it every day. But it did teach us a number of good things. Location is very important.

BK: So you've taken the step from that one store, you get to the next store. Your takings go from $2 000 to $15 000 primarily around service, around interest in the customer.

BB: Back then, it was all about service, paying attention to the customer. We certainly learned a lot more about systems and processes and structures in order to grow, but I've never lost those lessons. It's about the customer – always.

BK: What are the things that you do to know your customer better?

BB: I think there are two parts to that, particularly if we fast-forward to where we are today. One is, you've got to stay close to your customer. Now, I have a huge, deep fear that my life that's become so–

BK: Not average.

BB: Not average. I was born in the country. I've always enjoyed people. I enjoy watching people. Wondering what they're going to do, what they should do, why they do what they do. You've got to stay connected with your customers. Today, I still think it's vitally important. Which is why I think I worry about my life, about moving to a place where I lose touch with what is normal.

We've got to make sure we keep pushing that in the business, making sure that little things are done. All the CEOs of all the brands today are required to go and do store visits on a regular, continuous basis. Part of that is to connect with the customer, to connect with the team, to make sure that we're seeing things where they're happening, customer touch points.

More and more today, though, it is becoming data-driven. You can actually get a lot of indications when you've got hundreds of stores, as we do. There's a lot of data that gives you trends, gives you directions, what's happening here, why that is selling, why that isn't selling. The product teams as well as the operations teams have to pay attention to that. That's important, and they do.

There is also a part of me still today that enjoys creating new businesses. That's just, in a bigger sense, in the same vein as creating new product. I like to create new businesses. You know, what are people going to want, what's happening out there that's not being delivered that people would want? Some people call that entrepreneurship. I just call it – I'm a retailer. At the end of the day, business is mostly about meeting a need. When that need shifts, you've got to shift with it. And that's really what's happened.

'I like to create new businesses. You know, what are people going to want, what's happening out there that's not being delivered that people would want?'

BK: How did you build up from two stores to three hundred?

BB: Well, that is a very good question. I got to the fifth store and I was asking myself the same question. I was one stressed-out twenty-four-year-old. I shouldn't admit that, but I was. I had no formal training in any of this and, all of a sudden, I was trying to figure out how to pay people and how to make sure that I was paying taxes and doing the right thing.

There were a couple of things that I did. I remember the most scary thing involved my good friend, Craig Kimberley, now of Just Group, or Just Jeans back then. He was the first guy to really nail the specialist experience. He had about sixty stores and back then, he was just–

BK: The dude!

BB: He was the king. So I did probably one of the smartest things I've done, as it turns out. I was flat out running my small little group but I went and got a job at Just Jeans on Thursday nights and Saturday mornings. Back then the stores closed at 1 o'clock on a Saturday, outrageous as that is. So I worked as a casual employee in the Just Jeans store in Doncaster. I got the job specifically to figure out how the hell Craig did what he did. How did he cope with all the problems I had. I wanted to know how to motivate the team, how to train them, how to get the culture and the standards. Actually, I probably didn't even know what culture was back then. I didn't know the word 'culture'. I probably felt what it was, though.

I have to say – and I've told Craig this – I was absolutely the number one casual that he's ever had. I sold like there was no tomorrow. And I loved it. I loved it even more because I didn't have the pressure of running my own business. I was there to see how they ran their systems, how they ran their cash registers, how they ran their training.

I even snuck into a store managers' meeting, which frightened the hell out of me. I was a good, honest, country boy and I was sweating. I sat next to someone and I told them, 'I'm from the Wangaratta store,' you know, hoping like hell. I had my eye on the door in case I had to bolt. I felt like a criminal, like I was doing something awful.

But I sat in one of those meetings just to see how the national retail manager ran it and how they communicated. I knew we were onto something. I knew that I was capable and I wanted to grow my business more and more. The opportunity sure was there for me to do that. I did that for three to four months. It took fifteen years to tell Craig Kimberley that I had done this sort of covert–

BK: Covert operation.

BB: Yes. I was shitting myself when I told him. It was eating away at me. I saw him at a function one night and I said, 'I've got to tell you something.'

BK: What did he say when you told him?

BB: He laughed and laughed. By that time, we were starting Bras N Things and we were a success story in our own right. Then he started to tell people, 'I taught Brett Blundy everything he knows and we're great friends.' He's a great guy. We're good friends.

BK: So, you did your apprenticeship in a Just Jeans store. You've got five stores. What happened then?

BB: Even though I wasn't any good at school and essentially failed, I've got a great capacity to want to understand how things work. I'm curious. I've always been curious and it doesn't have to be about retail. It's just, 'Take me to a factory.' I love it. You know, 'How does that work? How does that get made?' I enjoyed that and I've taught myself to take advantage of that.

That is why things like the YPO (Young Presidents' Organization) have been so very helpful in my life. Even today, it's a commitment and a goal of mine to take two weeks off. I go and learn. It can be straight business conferences or the YPO is wonderful for non-business things, but learning just the same. I still do that today because I believe that you never know what you don't know. You've got to keep going forward.

I encourage all my guys. It's a cultural commitment to continuous improvement. I've always been like that. It was part of the Just Jeans thing, thinking, 'How did somebody else do it?' or, 'That's a good idea. We'll put that in place.' So out of that came the training manuals and induction manuals. I started to understand what culture was in terms of excitement and parties and making sure the team were engaged. Fortunately, I was in the record business, so it was pretty easy.

BK: To do a good party.

BB: I started to learn that culture was everything. You needed an excited, motivated, committed team with an attitude that was about 'we will win'. So you look for those people who are competitive, you look for those people who want to move up and I just got on and started to systemise. I started to look for electronic cash registers–

BK: So the latest technology that you could use to get the best systems in your business.

BB: Just Jeans was very good. They committed way back then to the first AS400, which is now obsolete technology. So really, I found good ideas and put them in place. I would communicate to the team and then run around like a madman, ensuring that what we decided to do got done. That really was how I did it.

The other half of my role was to find the next store. I would simply keep putting all the earnings back into the next store. Wonderful, wonderful experiences, bad experiences too. I was this young guy starting to grow.

I'd come up against something I'd never heard of, like credit limits. They'd say, 'We don't trust you,' and I'd say, 'What do you mean, you don't trust me? I'm paying.'

'You know, it's not that you haven't paid your bills, it's just that you're growing too fast.'

I wondered, 'How can I grow too fast?' I started to hit normal commercial things that I didn't understand. So that was my next challenge. But I thought, 'Hang on. We're a good group. We're running well. We're profitable.'

BK: We pay our bills. Do the right thing–

BB: Then the business community and the banking industry were all starting to shackle us. It really was a very frustrating time.

'Don't tell me it can't be done. Tell me how I can do it.'

BK: So how did you get through that in terms of building the credibility of the group and understanding how to negotiate with the banks and others?

BB: Well, I worry about answering this question because I was a bit brash back then. I couldn't understand. I almost didn't take no for an answer. You know, I'd say, 'Don't tell me it can't be done. Tell me how I can do it.' But I would have to tell you that it was partly just being tenacious.

I'll give you a story about the Doncaster store. A music store in the shopping centre had done a runner – they'd just closed up overnight and gone. So I rang up and said, 'I want to take that store.' They said, 'No, we've got it earmarked for somebody else.' So I said, 'No, you don't understand.' This was in the days when in Westfield shopping centres, the centre manager also did the leasing and he lived in the shopping centre. None of that happens now, but that's the way it was back then, thirty-odd years ago.

So I said, 'I'll be there at 7.30 am for half an hour, I've got to be back at Parkmore Keysborough to open the store.' Not thinking that somebody might not want to get up at 7.30 am let alone meet someone at that time I said, 'I'll be there.' I think it was part excitement and enthusiasm, but sure enough, he was there. He tried to tell me again that it wasn't available but I said, 'What? No, I'm taking this store.' And it worked.

BK: That enthusiasm, that level of energy.

BB: Just not taking, 'No', for an answer combined with, 'We're going to do it.' When I look back on that, probably in part I didn't realise that people saw that it was going to be OK. When they met me, they could see the dedication and commitment. I was absolutely focused, deadly.

So we got that Doncaster store and I was working there one night when this cocky little sixteen-year-old came in and said, 'Have you got any jobs?' I said, 'Sure. What are you doing right now?' I remember it just like it was yesterday. I put him behind the counter and said, 'Work here for a couple of hours. Let's see how you go.' That was how we interviewed in those days. There are so many laws and restrictions and things now, but that's such a perfect way.

BK: Like a work test.

BB: Yes. He did a good job so I said, 'You did an excellent job – you've got the gift, Daniel. You're on.' He was sixteen at the time and I could see that he was going to be a great retailer. I could see he was going to be a great leader. So I said, 'What are you going to do?' He said, 'I'm going to go to university.' I asked him why he was going to uni and he said, 'Oh, because my dad says I should.' I said, 'I reckon you'd love to manage a store.' He wasn't even eighteen at that stage.

We've since become great friends of the whole family, but at the time, I said, 'Daniel, would you ask your dad if I could come out and visit you one night?' His dad said yes, so there I was, aged twenty-two or twenty-three, and I've got all of five shops. I said to his father, 'Your boy's got a great career ahead of him, he's going to go places.' We drank some homemade vino and the next day, I rang up Daniel. 'How did I go?' He said, 'We're right. Full-time. When do you want me to start?' He didn't like school, he didn't want to keep going.

Daniel ended up running the entire music group, Sanity, and retired at the ripe old age of thirty-four with several million dollars in the float, like more than several, a real fortune.

I had lunch with Daniel, his mum and his sisters two weekends ago in Victoria. I ended up employing all his sisters. And he married one of our regional managers. But you can't retire at thirty-four so he went back to work at thirty-six. He doesn't work in the group anymore, but he actually retired at age thirty-four. That's the sort of approach I had back then. We laugh about it now because Daniel's father says it's the best decision he ever made. So that gives you a sense of the way in which whatever the issue was, there was a solution.

BK: So, where does your competitive streak come from? The drive? The deadly focus?

BB: To be honest, I don't know the answer to that. You're not the first person to ask me. My father was a hardworking, determined, wonderful, wonderful man. He died five years ago. My mother was really quite ambitious. I think it's a combination of both those things, probably. But it's hard to know. I've got four brothers and sisters.

BK: All different?

BB: We're all different, but what I will tell you is that we grew up in a very loving, close, country family. I think that was very important in giving me the confidence and the self-esteem.

BK: So it was a get-up-early kind of family life in the country?

BB: Oh, my father would be banging pots in the kitchen at bloody 5.30 am. You know, 'You get out of bed, life's for working, let's go.' He was a hardworking guy. He had his own farm. It wasn't a big business. It was himself and his kids as cheap workers – surely the classic story.

There were a mixture of influences, but I had the confidence to do it. But when I said, 'I'm off!' they told me, 'Don't do it.' I mean, I had to defy every bit of advice that was coming at me from people who cared about me. 'You're lunatic!' they said. I look back and think, 'They were pretty right.' I had no formal training. I didn't know a thing about retail. There was just no reason in the world that it should've worked. But here we are today.

_____

'We grew up in a very loving, close, country family. I think that was very important in giving me the confidence and the self-esteem.'

BK: When you reached eight stores, you and your partner went your separate ways. Did he take those stores?

BB: Yes. I had a 50% partner. We did a deal. He bought those stores. That's when I really started. I thought, 'What do I do now? I really love this retail thing.' I was without a doubt keen to keep going. And it really was a desperate need to keep going. So I looked around. Really, it was probably the first time that I thought, 'What's the next thing? What's going to be the next big thing? What's not being catered for at the moment?'

I'll tell you a very quick story. It happened about three months before we parted ways. We had a very fashionable store manager at the time and one night, she's down there filing and her top's gone, just like that. This is back in the day when bra straps weren't to be seen. Now, of course, they're fashion statements. But I looked down and she has a bra on with a strap that's busted. It's come apart like spaghetti. And she's got this full-size nappy pin holding it together.

At the end of the night, I said to her, 'What's with that safety pin?' And she said, 'Oh, nobody ever sees it.' And she was a fashionable girl. That was the moment that really focused me on lingerie. I thought, that's going to change. Bras back then were basic beige and boring. That's what they were. I just thought, 'They are going to be colourful. Fabrics are going to change. Women are going to care about their lingerie the same way as they care about their shoes or handbags.'

Then, three months later, I found myself looking for the next business opportunity. So I went and decided that it was lingerie. I thought that would be worth looking into. Essentially, that's what I started. I bought a franchise store of The Bra Shop in Victoria. I asked my sister and my girlfriend at the time to work it, because back then it was entirely taboo for a guy to be in a store like that, so I couldn't work the store. Then we started slowly to see if I could stay ahead of the trend of what lingerie was going to do. That wasn't easy because everything was branded. A rep came in to see you and you placed an order. It was very slow and cumbersome, but it was the way it was.

━━━━━

'I just thought, "Women are going to care about their lingerie the same way as they care about their shoes or handbags."'

This is a true story. I figured we needed to sell G-strings. I was so nervous. Back then, you only bought G-strings if you were either a stripper, a dealer or a hooker or something. I remember ringing up my mother and saying, 'Can you take me into one of these stores? Will you come with me?' I'm a country boy. I couldn't go into a store like that on my own and I owned a lingerie store! Anyway, she went with me and it was hilarious. When I think about how the world has changed …

I thought girls would really like G-strings, but I couldn't get anyone to make them. Leotards were big, then and I was manufacturing the G-string leotards that the girls seemed to wear, but that was with the leggings. The bit that was cut

out in the bum was wastage. So I said to the guy, 'You're just throwing that out. If I gave you a pattern, would you make me a G-string out of this stretch lycra?'

He made up fifteen of them. I'm not exaggerating, he made me up fifteen and I took them into the Chirnside store to see how they would go. I knew they were going to be good, because back then the fashion was tight and pant lines were not a good look. I knew that that would also appeal from other angles as well, you know, looking good for boyfriends and so on. So I rang up at the end of the day and said, 'How did we go with those G-strings?' and they said, 'Sold out.'

BK: Cool.

BB: Gone. I was like, 'What do you mean, sold out?' I expected a couple to be sold but they all went in the day. It didn't take long to figure that's what our customers want. So we started manufacturing our own. That was very hard to do as I had one store, then I had another and then I had three. It probably took us five or seven years before the mainstream brands brought out a matching G-string and matching briefs. So I'm counting it as a long part of the story, but it gives you a sense of being aware of what's going to happen and trying to anticipate that. Also, you're going to break down barriers of what exists.

BK: When you had those three stores, were they all franchise group stores?

BB: They were. Then what happened was, Bryan Luca was his name, he had about twenty stores. He said, 'Brett, you're annoying me. You're worrying me. You're too ambitious.' I was starting to get a bit boisterous about what we ought to be doing. So he said, 'I've got four stores in New South Wales called Bras N Things and they're not going too well.' He said, 'Would you go up there and have a look? If you want them, you can have them.'

So I saw them and thought, 'These stores are fantastic but they're not being run well enough. We can do a better job.' I said, 'Right, we'll take them.' He said, 'You take my four. I'll take your three. I'll do it on one condition. You never come back to Victoria.' And that was the deal.

Now, Brett, absolute truth, we didn't sign a contract. We didn't even think about the leases associated with it and we didn't stocktake, nothing. I loaded up the truck and moved to Sydney. We swapped the stores, all done, not a problem. The first thing I knew of a problem was when AMP rang me up at Macquarie, which was one of the stores we took and said, 'We've noticed that cheques are coming from somewhere else. You can't do that.' They'd twigged to the fact that it was a new owner.

Centre management called me in to discuss the fact that I hadn't signed the lease – this was six months later. I was happy to sign the lease but they said, 'We don't know who you are. We don't trust you. You've got no credit history.' All that stuff. So I told him about Sanity and blah, blah, blah. He lectured me about the length of the lease and said, 'Do you know that it's not just seventy grand a year, it's five years.' I smiled at him and thought, 'Of course, I know that, you idiot.' But I didn't say that, of course. He was trying to stomp his ground. I listened, of course, but to cut a long story short, all that finished and we left Victoria alone. We then started in South Australia then Queensland.

BK: You've done the whole country at this point but you haven't touched Victoria. What happened with Victoria? How many stores did you have before you went back to Bryan in Victoria?

BB: We would have had about fifty or sixty stores when Bryan rang me up, we would speak from time to time. We even continued to buy some things together, so there was a healthy relationship. He said, 'Brett, I don't know what you're doing or how you're doing it, but everyone's talking about you. You're clearly successful. You're doing something right. I've got six stores. Would you like to buy them?' And I said, 'Sure.'

So we worked out a deal on those six stores. He had about twenty or twenty-four stores at the time, I can't remember exactly. It doesn't matter. So I said, 'Bryan, there's only one problem. I promised you I'd never come back, but I'm going to come back and I don't want to have just six stores.' Then he said, 'I'll cut you another deal. You can go to any centre that we're not in.'

I thought I would get up to a dozen stores or something, that was OK. So we did that, we started to open a few more stores in Victoria. A year later, he said, 'I've got another six for you.' So I bought them. And then, a year later, he's got another. And so over time, essentially, we bought all the stores from Bryan. I can tell you again, we never did a contract.

BK: But you did sign the leases this time?

BB: We did learn a few things. By then, I had a bit of a structure so we wrote to people. It didn't matter then, because by that time I had the credibility. The landlords were all in favour of us taking over. There weren't any issues. So, that was essentially the Bras N Things story. Tracking back from that, somewhere in-between all that, was Jeff, who took control of the music stores–

BK: Eight at that time?

BB: About eight, but they got into trouble. I remember this number because it was a great number. When I sold that business it was valued at a million dollars. So, I got essentially $600 000 because I had 60% at that time. Then, three years later, we bought it back from the bank.

'I learned that if you're not involved in the business, it's not good. In specialty retail, you've got to have great standards and discipline, great controls.'

BK: How much did you pay?

BB: I shouldn't say, but it wasn't anywhere near what I got for it, because it was essentially a bit broken. That was another very important lesson for me. There were a number of lessons.

BK: What were the lessons out of that? Don't have partners?

BB: That was a really important lesson. No partners makes life easier, in my view. I've got to qualify that because I've got partners right now, but each partner has to bring something different. In any event, even with partners, there can only be one boss. So, that's a hard and fast rule for me. One captain of one ship.

I learned that if you're not involved in the business, it's not good. In specialty retail, you've got to have great standards and discipline, great controls. Every store has to behave in the same way. You can't call yourself a group if every store is ranging something differently or serving customers in a different way or has a different process.

BK: What the brand promise is, ultimately.

BB: Brand promise is gone. What people know from one store to the other is gone. Systems and processes, the back end of the engine in terms of data integrity, payment of bills, processing–

BK: And then, dropping your costs through scale, you get none of the benefit.

BB: None of that benefit. In specialist retail, you have to ensure the brand promise because there are so many people, far and wide. We've got stores from as far away as Siberia (Russia) all the way down to Burnie in Tasmania. It's about empowerment through standards and disciplines and a culture. So, all of that has to be the same.

That means, if we're going to set up a new event, and it's going to happen at 3 o'clock on Tuesday, it has to happen in all stores, at the same time, delivering the same message. Otherwise, you can't control hundreds or thousands of stores. Retailing is a fabulous business when it all works. It's disaster when it doesn't.

You learn most lessons from mistakes. I was fortunate to watch this mistake happening so I didn't have to pay for the lesson. I had instinctively already figured out that systems and processes are about being very disciplined but letting people operate within that discipline in their own way so they can contribute and make a difference. That was a very important lesson. The other one was not to take on too much debt, because that was also part of the failing.

BK: So taking on debt to buy you out?

BB: Yes.

BK: Roughly how many Bras N Things stores did you have when you got the eight back?

BB: I probably only had about thirty or forty at that stage.

BK: So now you've got two businesses to run?

BB: Two businesses and I had moved to Sydney.

BK: How did you make that happen? Was it through your mate, Daniel?

BB: Yes. He was still working in music. It was called Jets.

BK: And he became the guy who ran the eight stores?

BB: Exactly. I grabbed hold of Daniel, who I had always seen as a talent and said, 'Why is this great business that I left now broke?' And he knew exactly the reason why. He said, 'Well, all the things that you had, they changed.' And I said, 'So, how much money have you got?' He said, '$23 000.' I said, 'You whack the $23 000 in. We'll go buy this.' I can't remember what percentage that equated to, but when we floated, he had about 3%. I think he might have had 18% before that?

BK: About 18% when it started?

BB: When we started, that $23 000.

BK: And then, what was the float value, roughly?

BB: A hundred million.

BK: What year was that?

BB: 1997. And we did this in about 1992. So, terrific run. Essentially, we kept it in Melbourne, I was Sydney. Daniel and I spent almost every day of our lives talking to each other on the phone, sometimes ten times a day.

BK: What have been the greatest challenges for you? Most people have identified finding and keeping good people?

BB: Sure it is.

BK: So, you know Daniel is the right guy. He's ambitious. He's got the right character. You give him an opportunity to buy in and you know that he fundamentally respects you and agrees on those foundational principles that you think would make it successful. Even though you're not there, you can ticktack in and it's as good as being there.

BB: It's as good as being there. We had a terrific relationship. He absolutely honoured the principles and the culture in the way that I understood it – customer first and the need to create energy through our culture, standards and disciplines. That was very important. The second thing was we liked each other. I have always had the privilege, as an owner, of working with people that I like.

We had a good relationship. He was the sort of guy that when he was stuck on a decision, he'd pick up the phone and say, 'What do you think we should do here?' And we'd talk about it. Then he'd go off and make the decision. Now, I'm always very involved and I certainly was back then. So, it wasn't that I wasn't playing the director role. We would talk regularly and I'd be a part of that. But fundamentally, I was putting most of my effort into Bras N Things.

BK: And before you got out of that business, he'd done about fifteen years with you?

BB: Yes, probably at least fifteen because he started when he was sixteen, remember? Other great leaders came out of that era also – Greg Milne, Shane Fallscheer and my sister, Tracey Blundy.

BK: How do you find them?

BB: We focused on succession planning. It wasn't even something that I thought was some great business idea. When you're growing retail fast or growing any business fast, you've always got a demand for people so it's forcing you to think about it. It's forcing you to watch people. It's forcing you to give people a go.

Back then, I was young I didn't have a problem with making someone who was twenty-one a regional manager if they had the right attitude. I think, in lots of ways, we've lost a bit of that as we've all got older. The organisation's got older. I've got older. The leadership's got older. We forget that twenty-one-year-olds can do the job. Not all of them, but some of them. We shouldn't look at someone and say, 'You're too green.' If I had done that twenty-five years ago, we wouldn't have many of the senior leaders we do at the moment. I'm a huge fan of youth and energy. And retail is not difficult. It's just demanding.

BK: That's a really good line.

BB: It's true. As a result of that, you're looking for people that have good attitude, that can commit and work hard.

─────────

'I'm a huge fan of youth and energy. And retail is not difficult. It's just demanding.'

BK: And work through the obstacles?

BB: And you can have a stellar career at an early age in retail. We're always behind. Having said all that, we haven't got enough people. And as we go around the world, it's the same thing, trying to find quality executives. Because now, it's not just, 'Oh, we might send you to Western Australia if you're keen.' Now, we might send them to Russia or China or South Africa or Brazil and that's another obstacle. So it takes an even more unique person. So, again, if you're keen and ready, you've got a head start.

BK: Tell me the story of diva. I find it interesting that here you are, a bloke from country Victoria who goes into bras at twenty-odd, and then you get into diva.

BB: It's a fast fashion girls' jewellery. Well, girls are great shoppers. That's the key.

BK: How many diva stores are there globally now?

BB: About seven hundred.

BK: And how many countries are you in?

BB: Twenty-two.

BK: How did you get started in this business?

BB: OK. I've probably touched on a couple of things related to what was driving me in regards to Bras N Things but along the way, I've missed so much in the story. Brett, at one stage, we had a hundred and ten Sanity stores in the UK. So I was having the joy of flying over to the UK every month and spending a week there. While I was over there, I noticed this spectacular jewellery, costume jewellery. I looked at it and thought, 'This is £3. Just look at this stuff.'

It was just mulling around in my mind as, 'That's the next thing'. I wanted to deliver quality stuff that women were going to wear once at $9.95. Or you could wear a different pair of earrings every day to work. It was fast fashion, disposable fashion. And vertical was very important to me.

Bras N Things had started to shift aggressively into vertical, which means we weren't buying brands anymore. We were going direct to the factories, designing, creating our own stuff, and bringing it in. Essentially removing the middleman, making everything faster and more dynamic. Customers loved it. This was going around my head when I was doing store visits as I do every Thursday night. I was walking down to a Sanity store in the Imperial Arcade in Sydney when I saw a store called diva. And that was it. Someone was doing exactly what was in my head.

I loved the look of the store and the product that was in it. I rarely talked to Vanessa, my wife, about business, but I went home that night and said, 'I've just seen this great store that's exactly what I was thinking we ought to do. diva, in the Imperial Arcade.' And she said, 'That's my boss.' She was working for '3', as in '3' Technologies, phones. She was in charge of the rollout. Anyway, she said, 'I've been meaning to talk to you about that. They want me to come and be a part of it. Not just as an employee, but as a part of it.' I thought, 'That's interesting, what are they planning on doing?'

To cut a long story short, we had dinner with Mark and Colette Hayman. They were going to franchise the concept when I suggested I'd fund it, help them with the funding and the strategy. That was the start of diva. So I ended up with a third. Vanessa ended up with three and a third percent.

Vanessa and Colette got on and started rolling stores out. Colette took care of the product, Vanessa ran operations. It was a fantastic success. And a few years on, Mark and Colette came to me and said, 'We're done. Do you want to buy it?' I said, 'Sure,' and that's what happened. So I bought it all and then we pushed it around the world.

There are two things that are very important to diva and now Lovisa. Two years ago, we created Lovisa as sort of a more *Sex and the City* version of diva, which is more appealing to a different stage of life. But diva has always appealed to me because it's global – and I believe retail is going to be more and more global – and because we're totally in charge of the entire supply chain.

BK: So you design the products, manufacture the products and ship them directly into your stores globally?

BB: We do it by air, so it's very fast. It's a very global business because we don't have to worry too much about localised needs. The more global the world becomes, fashion just becomes more and more the same. Essentially, that is why diva and Lovisa are global-growth businesses whereas my other businesses are still predominantly Australian. We're very proud of diva. We're very proud of Lovisa. We're proud of all the brands.

BK: Now, tell me, you've said you wanted to have a national business for no particular reason. Is this what happened with diva? Did you say, 'Wouldn't it be great to have a global business?' I guess what I'm getting at is, was it driven not just by economics, but more by a challenge?

BB: There's no question. Sometimes it's hard to say this without it sounding sort of cute or arrogant, but sometimes you wonder, 'Wouldn't it be good if we could do that?' Absolutely, that comes from a drive to want to do more and be better – continuous improvement. It comes from a sense of, 'Let's break the mould. Let's do things that haven't been done before.'

There are two parts. One is that it's just a part of my nature, probably. But two is it's also proven to be successful because you've always got to be breaking the mould. You've always got to be moving forward.

BK: These are not businesses that you can just sit down and say, 'That's done. We'll just let the cash start rolling in.'

BB: I'm not sure there's any business you can do that to. So I think it's a business necessity, at least it is for growth, if you want to continue to become more dynamic. But you've got to push yourself to improve. You've got to make some mistakes to learn from them, but hopefully not too many. So I think there's a nice combination of it being a sensible thing to do from a strategic point of view. It's also important to do something that keeps you fresh and current and moving forward.'

BK: And good to retain your best people by challenging them.

BB: I think that's the nature of our organisation. I'm not sure that that would be true for everybody, but there's no question that if you're a leader in BB Retail Capital, you know that there are no easy days. You've got to keep going. Not everybody likes that culture because it is continuous improvement. If something can be done better, then it's going to be done better. It's not, 'Oh, it's OK,' or, 'Our result is good.' It really is about whatever we're doing now, we're going to do better next year. And that can be a bit relentless to some. I don't see it that way.

'You've got to push yourself to improve … It's important to do something that keeps you fresh and current and moving forward.'

BK: Also, do you find that you attract people that are attracted to that mindset, to those values?

BB: I think cultures are a wonderful thing because when you step into a culture, culture helps you define whether you're going to like it or not. And not everybody has to like it. That's the important thing. It shouldn't be forced. But it is one that says we will look after our customers no matter what. We will continuously improve, no matter what. Our cost of doing business will go down every year, no matter what. They also happen to be very sensible and appropriate business philosophies, too.

BK: Yes. How much of that is conscious in terms of you sitting down and thinking that through and writing it down? How much of that is from the cut and thrust of day-to-day working out, that it's just necessary to get your costs under control and keep them going down in order to stay competitive?

BB: Easy answer, Brett, and there are two parts to it. In the early days, it was just a necessity. The best thing I ever did was come up with a back-of-the -envelope, napkin-type solution, but there was thinking going on. Now, there is no question with the group the size that it is, that I and others think about it, we launch projects, we have a university every year to bring two hundred and fifty executives from around the world in and we launch programs that are designed to continuously foster that thinking. So, there's no doubt, as we've got bigger, it's become purposeful. It's been thought about. But in the early days, it was just, 'Hang on. How do we do that better?'

BK: Tell me about your training. How much training do you do, is there an induction? Has there been a big dollar commitment to your annual university?

BB: I'm certain that we overspend in terms of how others would do this but again, there are two parts. It's very important now, but I've always wanted to learn and I just expect everybody else should, too. It was a bit of a shock to me that people don't always want to. So I force my guys to read books. But there is no question that it's important.

You asked me about our weaknesses at the moment, and we are not good enough at training all our team. Retail is a high-churn industry so we've constantly got to be teaching and training on both the cultural stuff as well as how to do the job. And we don't do it well enough. We've just introduced some new software last year that I am hoping will make a real difference. It's called World Manager and I love it. I think it's a game changer for retail because it allows us to track and be more interactive with our training in a systemised way. Essentially, that's what it does.

BK: Doing more, more consistent and controlled.

BB: Yes, however change is difficult for organisations and we've got eight thousand people. Humans like to get into a rhythm. Rhythm is very important for business. But when it comes to change, you've actually got to get the team out of their rhythm. So, it's hard.

BK: What's the role of planning? Does it involve retirement?

BB: There's always a plan. But I have to tell you, I'm not one of those guys who plans more than five years ahead. I'll have a view of where we're going but I won't have a hard and fast plan that goes beyond five years, because I have never been able to see a plan that's set that far ahead. Certainly, for the businesses that we operate, I'd prefer to have a view of where we're going and then be flexible, probably a bit of that entrepreneurialism that allows for, 'Hang on …'

BK: Some flexibility.

BB: But in broad sense will I ever retire? Actually I don't think so. I like what I do. I still work six and seven days a week, which is a bit unnecessary these days. I'm probably slowing down somewhat but I still call myself a retailer. Our homemaker property is a very big business now and separate and standalone and Darren Holland runs that. We've just moved into beef, so we've got beef, and we've got fifty thousand head of cattle up in the Northern Territory.

BK: What's it called?

BB: The station is called Beetaloo. It's 2.6 million acres [1 million hectares] so it's very big. And that is absolutely what it's about now. If I had a broad sense of, you know, ten years from now, then we'll have a lot more beef and we'll be good at beef. And the reason beef–

BK: Do you get support? You grow it and sell it?

BB: I absolutely believe in the export market because I'm an absolute believer in Asia.

BK: A lot of people to feed up there.

BB: The world is progressing. It's going to need more and more food. Beef is going to be an important part of the growing middle class in all the South-East Asian countries. Protein is very important. And so, I like it. Maybe it's a little bit of that country boy in me coming back again.

There really are three main areas, but from time to time, good investments come to me. BridgeClimb is a classic example of somebody bringing an idea that just appealed to me. As it turned out, it only appealed to Paul Cave and Brett Blundy and nobody else!

BK: Except a few million people who have now done it!

BB: And that was an eleven-year journey.

BK: To get it approved.

BB: Exactly. So from time to time, those things come along. We've got other investments, but that's essentially the group. We'll get bigger at retail. We'll get bigger at retail property. We'll get bigger at beef. What's after that, I don't know. We'll see where that goes.

BK: What role does money now play?

BB: That's a great question, Brett.

BK: What is it? What's it for? How much do you need? How much do you want? People write you up on rich lists and that sort of thing, but what does it actually mean to you?

BB: I think when you go back to the early days, when I started at twenty. I thought twenty grand would be great. Twenty grand, wouldn't that be wonderful? And then I thought, 'What if we could have an Australia-wide chain? Wouldn't that be great?' Now, we've got five and two global chains.

In the early days, of course, money was nice. It's nice having a nice place to live and a car and holidays, having some of those luxuries. It certainly was a driver for me and I assume a driver for a lot of people.

But you get to a stage where, of course – that's why it's such a great question – because I do what I do because I enjoy it, the challenges of it, taking the risks, and so on. And as it turns out, it wasn't for the money. I'd probably do it anyway. Then it gets to a stage where, of course, I'm very grateful for where I've gone, past the money. If I had any sense, I'd listen to some people, I'd retire and I'd be fine. That's a wonderful feeling.

What I think the biggest thing it does for you, that I really enjoy, is it gives me freedom. And that's what to me, the wealth that's been created through this journey is all about. I've got the freedom. So, I can actually choose whether I want to work or not. I can choose to be the boss. I can choose what I invest in. That's a great feeling, too. That's very important to me.

BK: So, choose who you work with, what you work on, when you work?

BB: All those things. Now, that's not to say that I don't have days where I think, 'Oh crikey, that was bloody hard.' Or if you have to fire somebody that that's still a shit thing to do. But in the main, it's about freedom to be able to determine all those things. That's the greatest gift I think I've got out of that.

Then, in terms of, 'Why keep going?', it's a bit like if something should be done better, then we're going to do it better. I don't know if the other guys gave you this answer or not, but that's what seems to matter to me.

*'I'll have a view of where we're going but I won't have a hard
and fast plan that goes beyond five years, because I have never
been able to see a plan that's set that far ahead.'*

BK: What's come out clearly from my interviews has been that people got into something because they loved it. And the more they did it, the better they got at it, the more great feedback they got, they got great experiences, they met better people, blah blah blah. So, they just keep doing it. And then, when you say to them, 'Well, would you ever stop doing that?' it's like, 'Well, that's actually who I am. That's what I like. That's just who I am more than what I like to do.' And so they say, 'I could never stop being myself.'

BB: I think, to some degree, everything you've just said there is exactly the way it is. You just keep pushing yourself. You're doing something new and that newness is actually pretty cool, too.

BK: And you're hanging around young people who are energetic and want to kick goals.

BB: You see the enthusiasm of those guys. There's a whole host of things, but there's so much joy in watching some of the guys that I've seen. Peter Bond is a classic example. He started working for us and now he runs Russia. He's got equity in the Russian territory because I said to him, 'Get off to Russia and we'll see whether we can make it in Russia.' That was five and a half years ago. Now we've got two hundred and fifty stores in Russia.

BK: Let me ask you about that. How do you incentivise this group of people – straight cash bonuses, equity, what's your view?

BB: What I've discovered is that they're very individual, especially at the level that you're talking about. Everyone's driven differently. Some people will share the risk with you and therefore would share the reward while others just want the salary and they'll still do a good job. In Peter's case, Russia's not the most desirable place for an Aussie to necessarily want to live and he took his wife, Michelle, and now he's got two children born in Russia. You've got to take that into consideration.

BK: So you just have a conversation with people about what their thing is?

BB: These are very personal considerations. I often say, what do you really want

– not what you dream you want. When you ask the question, 'What do you want to be?' sometimes, people will tell me things like, 'I want your job.' Then, when I press them, I ask, 'What do you want my job for?' and they say, 'Because I want to be rich.' Then I say, 'Well, that's not really the reason.'

BK: You can be rich through lots of things.

BB: Exactly. So, it's intensely personal to try and find out what the real motivation, the commitment and the real drivers are. In Peter's case, he was looking to be involved, he wanted to be an owner, he wanted opportunity. He's a fabulous talent and was willing and able to stand on his own in Russia.

BK: No Russian language?

BB: That's right. And to me, that deserves everything and more than he has earned. It's also been the fact that it's a journey for him as it has been for diva and BBRC. But in a part sense, whatever Peter has, which is terrific, it's probably not enough because he's done everything that we would have hoped and more. Then, other people have different drivers. I am a big fan of giving the leadership equity in the business, skin in the game. That's a hallmark.

'I'm a big fan of giving the leadership equity in the business, skin in the game. That's a hallmark.'

BK: Letting them buy in.

BB: Buy in. That's a hallmark of all the CEOs. So, real skin in the game that they have bought into. And usually it's compelling, but they've still got to commit, and they all do that to varying degrees. That's partly because we're a private company so we don't have share options and things like that. Things aren't as freely available. But it's also the way that I like to operate. It also takes quite some time for me. It's not just about being here for six months and you'll get that. I've really got to know that intimately. It's easy to be great for twelve months. It's much harder to–

BK: To sustain that in the long-term. So there's no retirement. What I was going to ask you about next is, you've got your wife, some children?

BB: Sam and Mia, yes, four and two.

BK: Throughout the interviews, one of the big themes has been, what impact does a business, particularly one the size and scale of yours, have on your family life and how do you deal with it?

BB: I'm yet to face those questions, Brett, because they are only young and I'm just starting to experience that. I do find that I have to set time aside. But again, freedom allows me to do that. Take last weekend. We've got a possum that's pooing on our steps so my four-year-old said, 'Why don't we build a possum trap?' I thought it would take one Sunday, but we're only halfway through.

But those are the things that I'm going to have to start to think about. I had quite a lot of fun building the possum trap that I never thought I would. We went down to Bunnings and figured it out and the damn possum trap's cost me $600. We could have bought it on eBay and it would have worked better, but we'll end up catching the possum then we'll let it go somewhere else – and Sam and I are enjoying the journey. I've got the freedom to be able to do this. So, on the one hand, I'm very lucky to have had my business success early.

BK: And the kids later.

BB: I haven't had to compromise and I don't think that I'll have to do that. But you might have to come back in a few years and ask me that question again.

BK: Tell me about the people that have really influenced you in your career. You mentioned Craig Kimberley.

BB: Craig Kimberley, yes.

BK: Who were the others who have really inspired you?

BB: Without knowing it, Craig Kimberley influenced me. I am an absolute Sam Walton of Walmart tragic. As I told you, I was a great learner, and I've been to Bentonville, Arkansas, on several occasions. I was fortunate enough in 2006 to spend three full days with every leader of Walmart. Back then, when Lee Scott was the CEO, I had the great fortune to meet Sam Walton. I also spent three hours with the man himself when he came out to Australia, just by pure chance.

The reason that that's influenced me so much is because Sam Walton built, in my view, the greatest company in the world. It's certainly the most successful retailer. And even though we're in a different sector of the market, the principles are the same.

I've been a great student of Walmart ever since it was only in five states or something. But he was already on his way. And he just made sense. So for three hours, I was riveted. I was a kid of twenty-six and I just went and put so many of those things into the business. So, he, without a doubt, has been a major influence in many of the ways in which we operate. That's when I really understood culture. I instinctively knew what was going on but that word culture hadn't come into my vocabulary back then.

I am a fan of Jack Welch in his sort of candid, direct continuous improvement, 'Be number one' approach.

BK: Yes, bottom 10% of managers leaving every year.

BB: Just in the way to keep it disciplined and focused. That would probably cover the guys that have influenced the business to some degree.

BK: I get that. Now, let me finish by asking you for a motto, a quote, or thought that best summarises your approach to life or business.

BB: I would have to tell you that there are two. I think I probably mentioned one of them, but it's always about the customer. I've mentioned this one already too, but I truly believe that in the continuous learning, continuous improvement is that if something can be done better–

BK: Do it better.

BB: It should be. I say that quite often. The one that I have for the family is that we're a 'yes' family. It's just that one day, it's going to get me into trouble.

BK: What's a 'yes' family?

BB: 'Yes' means 'Yes, can do,' in the sense of no whingeing. Remember, I've got a four-year-old and a two-year-old. 'Could you bring the plate to the table?' 'Yes.' So I think 'yes' is the answer. Everything ought to be 'yes' before it's 'no'.

BK: It can be done.

BB: It can be done.

———

'… I truly believe in continuous learning, continuous improvement. If something can be done better, do it better.'

Bill Bridges

Real Estate Agent – Ballard Property

―――――

'I've learned a lot of lessons by watching other people stop work. It's not a nice sight and while ever you can keep your brain functioning, if you want to work, I think you should work …
In fairness to yourself.'

A prestige property real estate agent in Sydney for over fifty-five years, the legendary Bill Bridges may be in his eighties but he has an undiminished appetite for the next deal and the one after it – be it for tens of millions or just millions of dollars. An ex-jockey who grew up in Cabramatta, some of his self-confessed rough edges are still apparent, but they don't seem to stop him from making those record transactions!

www.ballardproperty.com.au

Interview

BRETT KELLY: It is truly great to be with Bill Bridges, a long-time Sydney real estate agent, today. Bill, where did you grow up?

BILL BRIDGES: I was born in Liverpool, in the western suburbs of Sydney, and I did my schooling at Cabramatta Public School. I think there were only two Asian families in Cabramatta when I was there. They were racehorse trainers. I used to ride track work for them. One was called Billy Bushan and the other bloke was called Jack King.

BK: So, you grew up with horses?

BB: Well, I was an apprentice jockey at Warwick Farm when I was very, very young – sixty-odd years ago – for a bloke called Norman Turnbull. He taught me a lot. He was a scallywag, of course, as they all were in those days. Fortunately for me, I liked food better than I liked riding horses. The two don't work well together, so instead, I spent quite a few years around the racetrack with jockey friends of mine, riding track work and, as always, I was the guy that found the punters for the jockeys.

They weren't supposed to bet, but they all bet. It was like asking a rabbit not to eat lettuce, asking a jockey not to bet. Some bet very heavily. But in those days the prize money was very small, of course. We would race for £10 or whatever it was – it was pounds in those days – and of course they used to hold the horses and wait until they got to the right race and the right price. In those days, you would bet SP. There were only a couple of jockeys who knew which horses could win – a lot of jockeys could ride horses, but they didn't know if they could win.

BK: You did OK?

BB: We were very successful.

BK: And then, after horses?

BB: After horses I became a contract cleaner. But before that, I worked for an SP bookmaker, which was a bit of an ongoing thing. Another great experience, but then I became a contract cleaner.

BK: And was it your business, or were you working for somebody?

BB: I was working with another guy. I was cleaning the Post Office at Balmain and this fellow came up to me, Max van Lubeck. He was a property dealer and a wheeler-dealer in a big way. He called me down from the ladder and said, 'Would you clean a house for me?' So I said, 'Yeah, that would be fine. Where is it?' and he said, 'It's in Balmain, Stephen Street.' I said, 'Oh, yeah? What am I cleaning it for?' and he said, 'I want to sell it.'

So I went and looked at the house and I said, 'How much do you want for this?' I knew nothing about selling houses, of course. He said £3 000, I think it was, and I said, 'Oh yeah. What do I do if someone comes in?' He said, 'Just take their name.' So a bloke came in and we got nagging and he said, 'I want to buy it.' So Max came back and I said, 'I've sold that – will you take three?' He said, 'Yes.' And then he said, 'I've got about another twenty houses. Would you like to clean them?'

Anyway, the story is, I sold thirty-two houses in six weeks for Mr van Lubeck and he thought I could walk on water. But he was a great teacher. And I was a bit of a wild bloke – coming out of stables, all sorts of things, but I was very streetwise and I knew a bit about people. I was not frightened by people and because of the background that I'd had, I went on from there. But I had a bit of a problem getting my real estate licence because I'd had SP betting charges made against me. I had to go to court for my real estate licence and they challenged me, but I had a good barrister called Horrie Miller. The crown prosecutor flew at me. He said, 'You're being entrusted with trust funds,' and 'blah, blah, blah …'

In those days, it was a much simpler situation – now you have to do exams and all. So I got a bit sick of this fellow questioning me about my illegal activities because we all went off in turns, you see … The sergeant from Wollongong Police Station would phone up and say, 'Well, I've got to come and pinch someone, the neighbours are complaining,' and we'd all go off in turn. That was the way it all worked those days.

So, he said, 'Well, what was your job?' and I said, 'I was a clerk there and taking money,' and he said, 'What else did you do?' And I thought, I'll fix this bloke up. So I said, 'Well, every Sunday at the end of the month, I had to take the brown paper bag up to Sergeant Russell at the police station.' This was a lie and I was bluffing, but it worked (of course, this is exactly what went on). I had the licence in three minutes. The bloke didn't want to hear any more about it. He said, 'I grant the licence.'

BK: How old were you when you got your first licence?

BB: I'd have been in my twenties, I think. But I've been in the business for fifty-five years last January [2012].

BK: So, you were licensed and you were working for this gentleman?

BB: I was working for Max.

BK: And essentially, any projects he developed, you were selling?

BB: Yes. He used to buy lots of rows of houses – rent-controlled houses. And of course, we raided Paddington. We used to buy streets of houses for £2 000 and £3 000 each.

BK: OK–

BB: And the same houses today now bring in $1.3 million each. I was the guy that started Paddington, me and two other blokes. But I had to get the tenants out. We got rid of all the rent-controlled tenants which the government loved, because they were all Labor voters. The Liberal government didn't like them …

BK: And then you renovated the properties?

BB: We'd renovate the properties – paint them or whatever – and then resell them. A lot of them were sold back to the tenants. Some of the older tenants have recently died. I saw one of the old ladies the other day. She bought a house for £3 500. I used to finance them. I'd buy them for £3 000 and sell them for £4 000. We'd get them a first mortgage of £3 000 and we'd carry a second mortgage of £1 000, which was a lot of money in those days, but they all paid. No-one ever went bad. And then, of course, as time went on, if they were paying the mortgage, we would sell the mortgage and discount them. It was all manipulating finance. You know, in actual fact, it's going on today because banks are not lending money to people.

'And I was a bit of a wild bloke … but I was very streetwise and I knew a bit about people. I was not frightened by people and because of the background that I'd had, I went on from there.'

BK: Tell me the story about Paddington. It's a well-known area today, but at the time, it was very modest sort of housing–

BB: Yeah. Streets and streets of them. I'd have to look it up, but I think in the 1960s and seventies, there were 37 000 rent-controlled properties in New South Wales alone, mainly in the city areas like Glebe, Paddington and Surry Hills.

BK: OK. So, when you move forward to today, you look at an area like Millers Point, where there's public housing – does that look like Paddington thirty years ago?

BB: Not really. Those areas – Annandale and Leichhardt – are all coming good because of their proximity to the city. People want to live close to the city, but they can't all afford to, so it's going very well.

Actually, we put a house up for auction the other day in Stanmore. It was terribly rundown but it sold for $800 000 – that was $300 000 over the reserve. Now, I don't sell those lesser houses, I let the kids here sell them …

BK: OK, so, you're moving on, you've got your own agency. Was that part of a franchise group or you owned it yourself?

BB: No, he [Max van Lubeck] got me my licence and I worked for him for a long time. He was a fantastic bloke and he took control of me because, as I said, I was a bit wild. I had a bit of a short fuse in those days, and you know, he used to have to pull me into line on the odd occasion, but he was a great bloke.

He liked to drink, which was his downfall, and he liked women, which I won't hold against him, but he was a great bloke and he knew a lot about me. And of course, I knew a bit about him, but he learned plenty from me as well. Because, you know, I was a bit of a rough-cut diamond.

BK: But he was a good man toward you, essentially. Was he much older than you?

BB: Yes. He was an ex-prisoner of war. He was in the air force when he was captured by the Germans. Terrific bloke. Then we parted ways. He fell on a few hard times. One of the main fellows that he was doing business with was a bloke called Alan Blum. He went to jail for embezzlement and the whole thing fell apart. And then I went to work with a bloke called George Cooper, a rails bookmaker in Oxford Street.

BK: As a bookie's clerk?

BB: No, no more bookies. He had a real estate agency as well. Good bloke, too. He's dead now.

BK: And you ran his agency?

BB: I worked with his agency. We worked in the Darlinghurst area. Then I broke into the big diamond side and sold the dearest house in Sydney, to Sir Raymond and Lady Burrell.

BK: Which house was that?

BB: That was Rosemont House. Formerly owned by Lady Lloyd Jones. That was my first break-through. It was a record at the time of £2 800 000.

BK: In what year was that, roughly, 1960s or seventies?

BB: That was twenty-four years ago, actually twenty-five years ago.

BK: So, 1985.

BB: That's right.

BK: How did you come to find that listing?

BB: Well, I was creeping up the ladder, selling dearer houses. And I was becoming pretty good at it, very consistent and then starting in the Paddington area. I sold to all sorts of different people in Paddington, like lots of people and lots of money, and lots of very social women came to work for me and said, 'Oh, give this to Billy, give this to Billy. He'll sell this and he'll sell that.'

BK: What is the art of selling a very expensive house? Where do you look?

BB: Well, to sell real estate, there are three or four things you need. The most important thing is to have energy. And you must have a fantastic memory. And you must know your values. You see, if I go along to someone, or someone calls me up wanting to sell a house, I can tell them what it is worth – if it's 20 million or 30 million or 50 million – because I have sold so many of them. The only way to get to know what a property is worth is by having sold them. You know, people

would say, 'I've had three agents look at this, but we want your opinion.' So I say, what have they sold? I produce a brochure when I go there, like this. Another sale, another record, and a photograph …

BK: This is fantastic.

BB: Yeah. That's the dearest house sold on the waterfront in Sydney, which I sold.

BK: Which house was that?

BB: That is number 25 Coolong Road, Vaucluse. And this is the one I just sold to Jamie Packer. I've sold Jamie the five houses he owns. I sold him the one he lived in in Campbell Parade. I sold him the one he lived in with Kate Fischer. I sold him this one, as well as the one he lives in on the corner of Campbell Parade which I sold to his sister, Gretel, her house for David Archer. I sold him five houses and this one is a record for a rural property in New South Wales.

BK: Oran Park House–

BB: Yeah. It belonged to Ashley Dawson-Damer. I sold that for $19 million for 150 acres.

BK: And who bought it?

BB: A mob called Valard.

BK: Fantastic. Wolseley Road, Point Piper – $45 million.

BB: Yeah. I've sold that three times and I've got a lot of money.

BK: That's on the market.

BB: Yeah. I've got that. So, I sold that to Harry Barrett, the bookmaker, when he won $12 million off Kerry [Packer].

'It's a no bullshit organisation. I mean, I don't bullshit people.'

BK: Is that right?

BB: Yeah. Actually, that's going back quite a few years. I sold that to him and then Kerry won $14 million back off him and he had to sell it again. I sold it to a bloke who's in there at the moment for $28 million.

BK: What do you think it's worth?

BB: Fifty … Well, he wants to sell it in two parcels. It's unencumbered. He doesn't owe any money on it.

BK: So, when you've had a track record like that–

BB: It's a no bullshit organisation. I mean, I don't bullshit people. Some fellow recommended me to someone. He said to the bloke, 'My wife doesn't like Bridges too much. She thinks he is a little bit wild.' He said, 'Do you want an elocution lesson or do you want to sell your house?' So, you know, the more money they've got, the rougher I treat them. Otherwise they get control of you. They say, 'Another agent said he can get another $3 million more than you said,' and I say, 'Well, you give it to him. I can't get you that.' They come back.

BK: So for this sort of property, you put a listing up on the internet. But in practical terms, where does the buyer come from … out of the networks that you've built up over time?

BB: You never know. When he bought that he came in and said, 'I'm Deke Misken' (Altona). He had a herring tin on one foot, galoshes on the other – wouldn't have thought he had two bob.

BK: Well, I googled him. And I thought, he's got a bit of money, this bloke. He's sold all these magazines to Murdoch. *Dolly* and others. And I said, 'You want to raise a bit of finance on this?' He said, 'No, I'll pay cash for it.'

It's still unencumbered. He is the worst owner you can have because he doesn't have to sell. So I said, 'What are you going to do with the money? It's unencumbered.' He said. 'I haven't thought about that.' I said, 'Well, why don't you leave some in on a first mortgage, at a very competitive rate?' You can't borrow money from banks. You may as well say I'm selling a finance package as well as a house. I've just sold one of those for another bloke for five million. I said, 'You don't want the money at your age. Why don't you carry three million for the bloke. It's foolproof, isn't it? He's putting in $2 million. And he said, 'Yeah, OK.'

BK: He gets his 7%, which is pretty hard to get anywhere else.

BB: In this instance, he's getting 8%, but he will carry the balance of 4%, but we're going to load the interest to the purchase price. So, he doesn't pay tax on the interest. This is all about knowing what the next move is. There's a key to every sale. You've got to think where is it going or why isn't it sold, what are they doing wrong and how can I rectifiy it.

BK: So, really looking for a solution to this problem.

BB: That's right.

BK: I have to ask, how old are you now?

BB: 83.

BK: OK. So, you've got fifty-four years' experience. You've been cutting deals and financing property for fifty-plus years. So it's not a surprise with the level of innovation that you've used that people are coming to you for this sort of thing. What makes a great property, what do you think are the things that make people want to own these properties?

BB: Well, it's mainly the wives.

BK: They get excited about them?

BB: The wives get the husbands to spend the money. It's a social thing with a lot of them. Some it's not, but, you know, they just want to be there because it's the best. It's very hard to resist that one. But the one over there is not so good. I've got an offer on that at $28 million. He should be taking it.

BK: Big, old property, isn't it?

BB: Yes.

BK: Alright.

BB: [Pointing] Stokes lives there, and John Howard's brother, Stan, lives there. Mackell Park lives there, and there's Lindesay House up here.

BK: Right.

BB: So they're the only houses in the street. You've got to know your streets and you've got to know your values. And you've got to know why, you've got to be straight with people. People don't want to be made fools of – they don't want to go to the Cosmopolitan or anywhere out with their friends and think they've paid too much money. I drive them around and show them why they're paying $20 million. So, when their friends are saying, 'Oh, you paid too much,' they can say, 'Come and I'll show you what he sold for $20 million.' So, I'm covering all the paths, and I'm sweeping the paths behind me as I go along.

BK: And you know these streets like the back of your hand.

BB: Every blade of grass. And there's a story to every one.

'I mean, the right people have always held property. paper goes out, shares go out. But bricks and mortar go on forever.'

BK: So tell me, you see these properties fluctuating in value, but in your experience, what do you think is the key to good investing in property?

BB: Well, I guess the capital gain you get. That's not there at the moment but it will come again or there'll be no BHP and the Queen's made a mistake. I mean, the right people have always held property. Paper goes out, shares go out. But bricks and mortar go on forever. People have got to have somewhere to live–

BK: Absolutely. And they're not making more of these beautiful old houses.

BB: No. There's very few of them. And some places, I'm horrified. I go in and they say, 'Look what I've done,' and it's enough to give you a migraine. It's awful, you know. But I love selling that sort of house and I love selling country houses. The National Trust houses.

   I've sold Bronte House four times – the lease of it – Matt Handbury lives there now. I sold it to Carol Muller. I sold it to Leo Schofield. I sold it to Peter Symes. I've sold Glen Rock three times, the wonderful old national Hume House [Cooma Cottage, aka Hamilton Hume's House, a National Trust Historic House]. Minimbah House, I've sold that, and I'm just now signing up another four or five beautiful houses. And then I get called – I've just sold one at Berry. So, I get called everywhere.

BK: So, are you selling property all over Sydney?

BB: Yeah. A lot of other agents from the country phone me up and the vendors want a city agent as well. I'm one of the few blokes that they do ... That's the old SCEGGS School that I'm selling.

BK: Right.

BB: The reason people get me there is because I know all the people with the money. And the money is in the city. No-one from the country is going to buy that. I've got to nag someone into buying it from here.

BK: So, tell me. I love your comment about energy. A lot of people think of real estate or other professional jobs as not very physically intense, but it has been my observation that it takes a huge amount of energy to do this sort of work.

BB: Yes.

BK: To make a phone call. To take a phone call and go and see the property, trace it down.

BB: And you can't take your eye off the ball. These people are smart. I mean, you're playing first grade when you put the jacket on here. They're on the ball.

BK: So who are the smart ones? Who, across fifty years, are the smartest people that you've dealt with?

BB: Oh, mate, I've had them all. There are lots of people that are terribly clever.

BK: So give us an example of something that you've seen done in property that you think is innovative or different. Obviously buying a whole street of rent-controlled houses is different. But since then, what have you seen that you've thought, that's smart–

BB: Well, I have seen some things that I didn't think were so clever.

BK: I was going to ask you that. Maybe you can start with them?

BB: Yes, well, when they sold Paradis Sur Mer. I wasn't the agent. A friend of mine was the agent and I used to have a go at him. You know, I'd say, 'How are you going here? They're thick on the ground here, I've got a buyer at $15 million.' I was having a shot, you know, and he'd say, 'They're thick on the ground here at $20 million,' and this was the old Radford place where Susan Renouf lived, you know, and the guy that bought it so cheaply did some things I told him not to and then he got annoyed with me and gave it to someone else. That was alright, the other bloke was a good salesman. So anyway, that ended up selling for $12 million, there was only one buyer on the night, there were the agents, the bank, and one Chinese fellow and I thought, 'You're going to own this tonight'. So I said, 'What happened to the thick on the ground at twenty?' Plenty of those stories, you know …

BK: You see a lot of that?

BB: Yeah.

BK: What's something smart you've seen, or something very clever?

BB: Obviously, the place Mark Bouris bought at Watson's Bay was a very clever move. He ended up nicking that–

BK: It's a lovely spot, isn't it?

BB: Yeah, a lot of space. Beautiful.

'I walk down the street and know everyone, from the paper boy to whatever, and it's "G'day Bill!" – no one calls me Mr Bridges. I like being liked and I don't mind those who dislike me. I couldn't care less and you know, I'm not here for any other reason than to make money, that's the bottom line with me ...'

BK: Beautiful and closer to the city than it was. So, in conclusion, when you sit there and you look at your time spent in real estate, what is it that you think of? You know, you're eighty-plus years old, you're still working, is it the passion – you obviously love it? What do you think it is that makes the difference?

BB: Well, you wouldn't do it unless you loved it. And I obviously like it and I love the challenge of it. And I've learned a lot of lessons from watching other people stop work. It's not a nice sight and while you can keep your brain functioning, if you want to work, I think you should work. In fairness to yourself and to everyone else around you or you become like the blokes that retire and drink too much. I'm not knocking a drink, I love a drink, but you know you've got to ...

BK: ... to do something.

BB: You know, I keep fit to work. I get enjoyment out of work and I meet some great people. And, you know, I walk down the street and know everyone from the paperboy to whoever, and it's, 'G'day, Bill!' – no-one calls me Mr Bridges. I like being liked and I don't mind those who dislike me. I couldn't care less. I'm not here for any other reason than to make money, that's the bottom line with me ... as long as I don't hurt anybody. That's the important thing.

BK: And tell me, how do you find working in an environment with younger people–

BB: I love young people around me. And the old birds with purple hair–

BK: Keep you moving?

BB: I want young people around me ... they keep me young. My youngest daughter is nineteen and my next one is twenty-one. Their sister is sixty and my adopted son is sixty-two. Because I was married when I was twenty and then there is Noeli, he is fifty-eight and from my previous marriage ... then my second wife and I have the two girls that have just finished school up here at

Ascham, not Cabramatta Public … they're both at uni. And I've got twenty-two grandchildren and six great-grandchildren.

BK: Alright!

BB: You'd think I was a Catholic, but I'm not … most of my friends are.

BK: OK (laughs). So now, tell me, there are obviously benefits to an Ascham education, but if you look at your path, there are obviously benefits from Cabramatta Public as well–

BB: The only thing they don't have in school today and should have is a very, very strict class on being streetwise. My daughters are pretty streetwise because they've got me as a father and of course I'm at them all the time; you can't buy that.

BK: That's true.

BB: You know, I see young blokes like solicitors and accountants and doctors who wouldn't know shit from clay – they're not streetwise. There are some pretty clever people out there in the street, they're not quite so well-educated, but they know how to get your money and cause trouble as well. So I think one of the best things you can have in life is to be street smart – and racing is great for that.

BK: The gentleman I interviewed yesterday is a super successful guy and he has stories that are very similar to yours. He said, 'Brett, I failed high school, went to a sort of country school in Melbourne, but there is a trend of people who have done well that don't seem to be necessarily academic initially, but very much driven to do something'–

BB: That's right. You find out how to get money.

BK: Get moving.

BB: As young blokes gambling, I used to say to my mate, this better arrive, we've got to settle. And he wouldn't mind knocking a few over to get there either, you know. He knew that the onus was on him. And because we had to deliver, we had to pay or find the money.

Most of the time we didn't need to, but there were times when we did, because if you're betting, you would say to a bloke, we want £100 on this horse and so he asks you to put in your own £100 with it. To prove it's trying and so you've got £200 on it.

BK: OK.

BB: So, then we had to find the first hundred or whatever it was.

BK: Yeah. To get to the next.

BB: So, that's how you got paid. It wasn't always easy. Money wasn't easy in those days but we used to get up to a lot of tricks. They used to dope horses in those days and do all sorts of things like that, but all of that is gone now. And they've got movie cameras. They're still at it, but it's not as necessary as it used to be. The prize money is good now. If I had a good horse today it'd be trying all the time, because the prize money's good – and rightly so, too. But it's all changed – circumstances have changed and needs change.

BK: Let me ask you two final questions, if I can. Firstly, do you have a motto or quotable thought that best summarises your approach to life?

BB: Free bowels, comfortable shoes, and empty balls (laughs).

BK: Classic! And final question – and this is a rude one. When somebody comes with a $20 million property and says I want you to sell this, you see so many real estate agents hoping to wrap it, dropping commission rates and whatever to sell the property, how do they remunerate an agent at your level for that type of sale?

BB: There is no dropping in commission. As I said to somebody the other day, a millionaire is asking you to drop your commission …

BK: That is always fun.

BB: You know, I said no way. I said I am a bit like the girl in the bar in Bangkok and they said, 'What's that?' I said, 'She lies very still for $50.' They can interpret that any way they like. I don't care what they say.

A motto or thought that best summarises your approach
to life? – *'Free bowels, comfortable shoes, and empty balls!'*

BK: So, what is the commission rate on a $20 million house sale in this market?

BB: It should be 2% plus GST.

BK: Plus advertising?

BB: You've got to get the advertising. But I sell many of them without an ad because I know who buys them. But if a bloke comes along and I know he's going bad – because I've been a knockabout, I'm the sort of bloke you can do a deal with – I'd say, 'You pay me when you're travelling alright', or 'When you get a bit of cash, pay me. Tell me how I'm eventually going to get it.' It doesn't have to be 2%, I'll work on 1% if you've been a good fellow to me … But if they're millionaires, I want them to pay me.

BK: Thank you.

Mike Cannon-Brookes

Software Developer – Atlassian

'Open company, no bullshit.'

Atlassian, a provider of collaboration software for product development, started in 2002. Joint CEO and co-founder Mike Cannon-Brookes met his business partner, Scott Farquhar, while they were both students at the University of New South Wales. Originally started to avoid having to find regular jobs, the company now has offices in Sydney, San Francisco, Amsterdam and Tokyo, employs over five hundred people, has over twenty-five thousand customers around the world and achieved a revenue of $59 million in 2011. Mike Cannon-Brookes and Scott Farquhar were ranked No.1 in the 2012 *BRW Young Rich* list, with a shared fortune of $480 million.

www.atlassian.com

Interview

BRETT KELLY: Mike, can you tell us the story of Atlassian? How did you get started and why?

MIKE CANNON-BROOKES: Scott Farquhar and I founded the business in 2002, ten years ago. The honest truth is, when we started we didn't want to get a real job. We didn't really know what we were doing but we knew we wanted to create something. We had a hunch about how the internet would change software distribution for enterprises. Back then, everything was on CD and, you know, different. We thought we could distribute enterprise software through the internet and that we could do it very cheaply and scale it globally. So we worked pretty hard for a year to find products that would fit those theories. Zoom forward ten years later and we now have a burgeoning business full of products that prove that those hunches were correct.

BK: What was your background, what did you study?

MC-B: Scott and I met at university. We both had Co-op scholarships at the University of New South Wales in Business Information Technology (BIT) – half computer, half finance.

BK: So, you had a hunch. Did you want to prove out the model or did you have a particular passion for a particular industry or were you just looking for some software that you could distribute?

MC-B: We had a couple of tools that we tried making and one took off way better than the others. So we built a business around that tool. It predominantly helps other software or product teams run projects more effectively. It's a project management tool in the abstract sense and it's now used by not only software teams, but also all sorts of business teams and business people doing various project tasks. That tool, called Jira, is still our biggest product. We now have eight, nine, ten other products around that complete a set of tools. And ostensibly, if you look at all the products, what the business does today on a holistic level is solve the collaboration problem involved in software.

BK: Now, tell me about this collaboration problem – what is it?

MC-B: The first thing you have to understand is that there is a big trend at the moment – software is changing the world, software is leading the world. Basically, software is becoming a strategic advantage for every single business out there. So if you look at banks, if you look at car companies, if you look at any traditional business, software and technology is rapidly becoming a true differentiator, a competitive advantage. The tricky part about that is it means that for most of these businesses, you want to own and control your strategic advantage. So, they're 'in-housing' a lot of the technology. But a lot of our customers, like Nike and Ford and other big companies aren't necessarily technology companies.

BK: So they're not software companies?

MC-B: No.

BK: They are big traditional companies and software is a competitive advantage. Do they need to own it?

MC-B: That's correct. Ford is a classic example that's been used a lot in the last ten years and even more in the last five years. Cars have stopped competing on engines and wheels and what they look like, and have started competing more on the technology inside the car. They won't tell you that, though. What they will tell you is that it has a better navigation system, better entertainment system, it plugs into your phone. They talk about the way it unlocks and locks itself, the braking and safety systems, fuel efficiencies – and they are all run off software. So a Ford car has thirty or forty computers inside it. There are tens of millions of lines of code running the car. So when you go and look at the car ads and the differences at your car show, it's really all about the software.

So this change has happened and is still happening. It has meant that software really stopped being something done in the basement by a bunch of guys and started to be something that the board cares about, the CEO cares about. And if you look at businesses, it's changing.

Nike is another good example. They make iPhone applications now and they have shoes with chips in them and they make FuelBands for your wrists that sync up to web services online. It's all part of the Nike story. It's no longer just buying a pair of running shoes, it's how the whole thing fits into a package. Then, you go and look at other brands – how much more affinity do you have for Nike than Puma that doesn't do anything technical. Well, they're going to catch up soon. After all, they're going to be in trouble if they don't. So, as that change is occurring, basically you have more and more people involved in the software process, and not just developers anymore but–

BK: Marketers.

MC-B: Developers, the marketing department, customer service, they all have to be involved because if your Nike shoes break down, what are you going to do? It's not a sizing problem anymore. It's a technical problem. They don't have a customer support department like Apple does, so they need to work that out. So all these different groups are getting involved, and what our tools really do is solve the collaboration problem around building a piece of software in a company so that all those folks can get involved and hopefully get the best successful outcome.

BK: The workforce today is highly distributed. People within these massive global companies building software are not in one room anymore. Your tools enable these businesses to draw the best people from wherever they are.

MC-B: Yes. You definitely have distributed teams – teams in different buildings, companies, countries, even. Often, there are different companies across different countries as well. You may bring in outside agencies to get some marketing help but you need to use in-house customer service, or whatever it is. So a distributed set of skills is also part of the challenge. We have some products that are highly technical and other products that have absolutely zero technical impact at all. They're still involved in the software creation process but where you have a marketing team involved that are not technical.

BK: So your technology needs to be highly user-friendly?

MC-B: Yes, especially if they're at the more business-oriented end.

BK: Tell me about the language. How much is that an issue for you? Is it all in English?

MC-B: No. We have thirty or forty different languages now. It's a lot. So, it's very distributed. Our ten-step projects tend to run in one language and, to be honest, we don't do any translation in the middle, but the software itself, yes, it supports many different languages.

BK: So what's the vision for the business? Why does the business matter? And what's its future?

MC-B: Well, my vision for the business revolves largely around solving the collaboration problem involved in software. It's far from solved. It's still a painful process, creating software. We're trying to make it easier for everybody going forward. You know, we believe it's only going to get more important for businesses to gain advantage doing this, to reduce the time it takes to ship software projects, to improve the input everyone has and hopefully have a better outcome overall.

That's a long-term project for us.

BK: So this is something you're passionate about in the long-term?

MC-B: Yes. It's changing a lot of things. It's giving us better products. It's giving us more dynamic products. You only have to look at telephones. We've crammed a hundred times as much software in the telephone now as we did five years ago. The iPhone was launched in 2007. Five years ago what you could do by basically turning a computer into a phone, not the other way around, totally blew people away. And now telephones, apps, the massive amount of code running in these things has totally changed the way we use the telephone and communicate with people. That's the sort of trend that is only going to continue through technical gadgets and even more so through the software and hardware interfaces that are going to start to creep into all sorts of devices that we use on a daily basis.

'My vision for the business revolves largely around solving the collaboration problem involved with software.'

BK: What are the possibilities that excite you most?

MC-B: Just the blending of all these things. I mean, if you think about your phone miniaturising, all the capabilities your phone has miniaturising …

If we go back to the Nike example, is it really that far-fetched to think that shoes could have a computer in them one day? You imagine, you go for a run, and you run into your house. The shoes know where you've been, they've got the GPS – it's no longer in your phone, it's in your shoe. They've got a little computer that says how many steps you've taken and as soon as you cross into your own home, the Wi-Fi network uploads it to the web. You don't have to do anything. You can start to see the possibilities of putting computers into things. Now, you can get an effective computer that can run code for ten bucks. That will just keep coming down and down and then it will be in everything.

BK: And the miniaturisation of it all as well.

MC-B: Yes. That's more of a far-out phenomenon, what they call the 'internet of things', but it's only a matter of time before all things are connected to the internet. Every door in your household, for example, suddenly gets somehow connected to an internet. So if someone presses your doorbell, it rings your phone and you check who it is. 'Oh, it's my sister, sweet.' You let her in by pressing

a button on your phone. You could even open a door in another country and let them in. Your house says, 'Hey, I'm too hot at the moment.'

BK: Sends you a message.

MC-B: Sends you a message. Automatically turns on the air conditioning. It will let you know. The smartness of things is going to be exciting. It's already exciting. It's amazing. If you think about *Dick Tracy* or any of the sci-fi shows. Even *Star Trek* has a communicator thing that could do anything, look up any information. They're basically on your phone now. You can be anywhere in the world and go to Wikipedia or the web and find information or solve a debate. 'Hang on, let me just look that up. Oh, here's the history of this person or what they've done.' It's phenomenal what we can do now.

BK: The only thing we're missing is flying cars–

MC-B: Right. Communication, information access, images, even just photos. The traditional idea of taking photos and printing them and mailing them to someone or putting them in an album is almost obsolete. Nowadays, we take tons of shots of my son with the iPhone and it gets streamed straight up to the web. We were on the beach the other day and took an iPhone photo. It had gone up to our private group we have in the family and my father-in-law in Michigan had commented on it before we got back to the car. You see, he's almost in the experience. It's like it's a phenomenal change. Every person that carries a camera is able to share photos with the world every single moment of the day.

BK: Then there are the price points, the cost has become so manageable.

MC-B: Yes. I heard a stat the other day that the cost of digital cameras, like their componentry, the little thing that's inside the phone, has come down a hundred-fold in the last five years because of the gajillion iPhones and Android phones and everything else.

BK: Who would be the biggest seller of cameras in the world?

MC-B: Apple or Samsung would be my guess. Their componentry costs are coming down so fast you could put cameras in your shoe. You could put them anywhere!

'… one of the other strategic advantages of every business nowadays is that it has to be attracting (really great) people.'

BK: Your company is growing. How many people do you employ now?

MC-B: We have a little over five hundred staff at the moment in six locations around the world.

BK: Is it challenging, managing them?

MC-B: Yes. We have a distributed company. We have a distributed management team, both of which are quite challenging. Roughly half the company is in Sydney, roughly a quarter of the company in San Francisco and then we have four other offices that are about an eighth or sixteenth each. So even just the two big offices are separated by the Pacific Ocean – two hundred and sixty in Sydney, one hundred and forty in San Francisco. Those two big offices are very separated – five or six hours' time difference, fourteen hours for an air flight. It's hard for us to get people to collaborate effectively over that distance.

BK: Let me ask you about the challenge of attracting really great people.

MC-B: I think it's one of the other strategic advantages of every business nowadays. It has to be attracting people. We spend a lot of time recruiting. We've grown the company very, very fast, if you think about it.

BK: Are you in a competitive space for talent?

MC-B: We're in a highly competitive space for talent. Software developers are gold, solid gold for every business. That's one of the flipsides to this sort of software becoming strategic. If you think about the number of software developers we have now, in five years' time, is demand going to outstrip supply? Absolutely. It's already outstripping supply and it's going to get worse every week, every month. So, we spend a lot of time on talent acquisition. We also spend a lot of time marketing the company to talent, explaining to people what their job will be like, what their day will be like, what the company is like, a lot of time on benefits and, you know, 'why work here' programs, a lot of time on the hiring and recruitment pipeline. We're hiring about three to four people a week.

'… we play a lot of game theory in the business with how we run things. I'm a big game theory fan.'

BK: There's a very cool program on your website about recruitment and working with recruitment agencies. Who came up with that and how effective has it been?

MC-B: We get into trouble here. I mean, we play a lot of game theory in the business with how we run things. I'm a big game theory fan. If you can structure things correctly you can get interesting and accelerated outcomes. We haven't had a lot of luck with recruiters in our business, to be honest, and they've cost us a lot of time. They all want to sit down and spend time understanding the business before they can do an effective job. Then, after every unsuccessful candidate, they want to spend more time. What they're really doing is honing their own sales process with your time to make money for themselves, which doesn't necessarily work for us because they don't have an outsized return.

So what we've done is flipped it around a little bit and said, 'If you're a recruiter, we're going to have standard terms that we put out. You're more than welcome to take them or not. You can totally make your own choice. Then, if you accept them, we have a rule that you can give us up to four candidates and if we don't hire one of those four candidates, you can work for other people. So it changes the game for them because they know we have a very large hiring pool. We're going to hire hundreds of developers over the next few years. If they want to get in on that action, fine. We want to make sure that they're working hard in sending us the best candidates so we have a big carrot for them.

BK: Do you pay more?

MC-B: No. We usually pay less than average. I don't know what the exact recruitment fee is but we're doing huge volume.

BK: So if someone's good, they can do plenty of business with you.

MC-B: They can, but they don't tend to. To be honest, I think less than 5% of our hires come through recruiters. It's not a very successful channel for us.

BK: So where are you finding your best people?

MC-B: Mostly organically. The organic channel works the best. We heavily promote the business that way too.

BK: Is that working well internally, that 'Refer a friend, get an air ticket' idea?

MC-B: Yes. We have all sorts of different promotions to try to get people in. Some of them work and some of them don't. We've had quite a lot written up about us giving new starters and their partner two nights in a hotel locally to say thanks for coming on board. They can take a break, decompress from their old job and take a couple of days out. It's amazing when people walk in. They start with a very positive impression of the business.

Because we're not working with recruiters, we're saving twenty to twenty-five grand, thirty grand, forty grand depending on who you're hiring for a software developer. We can put that money to much better use in making the candidates that do come on board happier and in other innovative ways such as using social media to promote the business for recruitment purposes. Ultimately, it's about making the guys that come on board happy, providing valuable jobs for them that they enjoy and doing all the things that help people stay in with you. We've got a very good retention rate. That then becomes your social network to hire other people.

BK: Will the business go public at some point?

MC-B: That's a potential outcome for us, sure, in the future.

BK: Is it a goal?

MC-B: I don't know if it's a goal. I think if it's the thing that makes the most sense for the business at the time, then we will do that. I mean, we're of the size now that it's a possibility. It's not a question of, 'We need to be this much bigger to make that happen.' It's a question of when the business is ready for it. There are a lot of good things that come with going public. It's playing in the big league.

It means you have to be excellent in everything you do. If you appreciate the capitalist process, the fact that there are so many rules and regulations on public companies is a good thing because it means that they have to be very well administered businesses, right? So the shareholders don't get screwed, which is want you want. At the same time, some of those rules and regulations obviously inhibit some of the growth possibilities of those businesses. So it's about the right timing – when it makes sense for the business. Sure, it's a possibility.

BK: A lot of young people who are interested in building technology companies would say, 'I know that you did a private equity raising, but how have you funded the business over the last ten years?'

MC-B: We're very unusual. We always say, don't copy us as a model. Well, copy us if you can, but don't use it as a case study on how every business should run. We were bootstrapped for eight years – we didn't raise any money for the first eight years. We were profitable, growing very, very fast and heavily invested the profits of the business back in growth every year. So there were eight years with no fund raising, then we raised $60 million from a tier one US venture capital investor, Accel Partners.

BK: How much of the company did they buy at that price?

MC-B: A pretty small piece.

BK: Was that public?

MC-B: No. It's like a very small piece of the business.

BK: Now, when you say you were bootstrapping it, does that mean you were on a subsistence-type wage? What sort of money were you guys pulling out just to live on?

MC-B: That's the old chestnut. Profitable from day one clearly means on day two you weren't paying yourself anything. We didn't pay ourselves for probably six or nine months, as in zero salary. Then, from nine months to about two years, we paid ourselves very, very little, a couple of hundred dollars a week sort of thing. After that we paid ourselves a pretty modest salary for a very long period of time.

BK: What was it?

MC-B: Around forty, fifty grand, something like that. It's an interesting thing, right, because at some point, you can pay yourself more. I mean, we were being paid a modest salary for a far longer period than was necessary for the business.

BK: You get into the habit.

MC-B: Well, you get into the habit and your financial outcome is more dependent on the growth of the business than the salary that you're pulling out. So, if you don't necessarily need it, then why not? You think, 'Well, if I put it in the bank, that's not going to help me. I'd rather invest it in the business.' So we took that long view for a long period of time. The only thing that changed it was our CFO complaining that everything should be commercially accurate, market rates etc. It was a CFO-driven change and even now, our CFO is still arguing that it's not at market rates–

BK: When the private equity guys came in, was it a long process? A difficult process? What was it that you thought that you had to have prepared most in order to make that as successful as it was?

MC-B: Good question. A few things. We spent a lot of time with the private equity guys before that. So, for the first three years of the business, no-one cared. Then, from about year four to about year eight, there was a five-year period where we didn't want to raise any capital. We didn't need to at that point. We probably weren't growing so why would we bother? But the smart thing we did was we were very honest with them. We'd always say, 'Hey, we're not going to raise any capital, so there's really no point meeting.' And they'd always say, 'Ah, but we'd love to catch up anyway, just to have a coffee.' So we tried to always schedule lunches or breakfast so it didn't take any time out of my day.

Then we created a spreadsheet that our PA maintained of all the firms we'd met with, basically if we liked them or not on a personal level. Then, around 2010, we were about eight years into the business and we were really thinking, 'What do we want to do here? Do we want to sell the business? Do we want to recommit for another eight years?' Both of us got married around that time so we took a little time off. I had a three-month break. We both went travelling with our wives and just reconsidered life a little bit. We decided that we had a lot more to achieve in the business. We wanted to recommit and therefore looked at the next eight-year goal, going public and a whole bunch of other things. We thought we probably needed a partner to help us do that. There were a lot of big challenges to get over. Also, there's a thing in software that a hundred million is the ceiling that a lot of businesses struggle to break. They come out with a good product, a good service and can kind of scope it at twenty million, thirty million, forty million, so to fifty and a hundred million it starts to flatten out. They go like twenty, forty, sixty, eighty, eighty, eighty, eighty, and then there's a big problem. We wanted to hit through the hundred and keep going. That was a big thing for us.

So, we looked around and we brought on these guys. When we ran the process, it was very simple. Again, we employed our game theory hats, talked to five firms, told them we were only talking to five firms, told them we were going to pick one, shared exactly the same information with all of them, controlled the process, told them exactly when we were going to be in the States, what pitches we were willing to do, gave them a bunch of time that they're free to do whatever they wanted, a couple of hours. Anyone that asked a question, we shared the answer so there was totally equal information.

We were very clear on what we wanted. We said we wanted a partner. We said how much of the business we wanted to sell. We said that it was clear that we were going to be in control. At the time, we controlled 100% of the business between the two of us. So, you're buying a very small piece. You either like what we've done, understand the fact that we're in control and want to ride with us as a partner or not. So, we were very clear on what we wanted in the timing and how clean we wanted to be. Some of them turned up. We gave them all one shot. It was a one-bid process. We didn't want to run a whole process. We told them there were five criteria that we would rank all the bids on in terms of how much we liked the firm, how much they had helped us out or we felt they could help us out all the way through valuation and obviously the financial metrics–

BK: So what were those five things? How much you liked them? How much you felt they could help you?

MC-B: Personal connection was a big one for us so we tried to meet as many people from the firm. We looked at it as a hiring decision. We were hiring a partner. Were they going to help us out for five years or were they going to help us out for six months, that sort of thing. We got references from all the firms on entrepreneurs they had worked with, were currently working with and had worked with in the past, even the people who had left. We wanted good and bad references. Some didn't really provide bad references or just provided some sort of bullshit answer. References, financials obviously, a valuation of how much money they wanted to put in. That was an interesting one because if we could've sold 1% for a small amount of money, we would've done that. But obviously, we realised that they have to make a return, so there was like a weird dancing game.

BK: The offer had to be big enough to bother?

MC-B: Had to be big enough to bother, right. So, the sixty million – they all wanted to put in a hundred in change and we wanted to put in twenty. So we were driving it in opposite directions. We were also trying to think of what the other metrics were, firm reputation and all that sort of stuff. Branding advantage, that's a big thing. There was a fifth criteria that I forget. We were pretty open with them about how we were going to judge it up front, and the fact that they got one bid only–

BK: Not a Dutch auction–

MC-B: No, we tried to run a clean and ethical process where we just shared all the information and told them how it was going to run.

BK: So what's the motto, quote or thought that really appeals to you about life or business?

MC-B: We have a very strong values-driven company. Our number-one value that's up on the wall over there in the next room is, 'Open company, no bullshit'. We've always espoused all our values very strongly. Building companies is a hard thing to do. It's even harder to do it in a values-driven way. Everyone claims that they do that, but for most people it's bullshit. Our value basically says, 'Hey, look, we're going to be as open as we can.'

Again, open doesn't equal transparency in everything. It's not like everyone's salary is published on a wall, it's just saying, where possible, the default is going to be openness. We're going to share. 'Hey, things are going well, things are not going so well.' You know, those sorts of things. And the no-BS thing is kind of interesting. It's basically saying, 'We're going to treat you guys like adults and not BS you around.' And sometimes, that's painful, right. I had to write on the firm update why we had let people go recently and my philosophy on letting people go. That's a hard thing to read, right?

*'I don't think there are bad people. There are good people
in the wrong places. They're in the wrong job for their skills.'*

BK: What's your philosophy on firing people?

MC-B: Oh, it's a long diatribe. I don't think there are any bad people. There are good people in the wrong places. They're in the wrong job for their skills, or it's the wrong time. It talked about how growth companies are really hard because they outgrow people but the benefit is that they create opportunities all the time. Any crack that opens up as the company grows is filled with another person who takes advantage and grows their own little piece. That's a big benefit. But at the same time, it means certain jobs can grow very, very fast and people just can't scale that fast. It usually means they're the wrong person and then they get fired and it's like, 'Hang on, I was a superstar three years ago and now I'm getting fired. How do I deal with this?'

It's one of the unspoken, hard things about growth companies that that happens. Certain roles are really hard to scale. Finance is a good one – the finances of a $1 million company compared to a $10 million company, compared to a $100 million company, as compared to a publicly listed, billion-dollar company. They're utterly different things. And if that happens in a five- to ten-year timeframe, one person just cannot scale through all those things when it comes to the financials.

BK: And you can't always accommodate them as part of the resulting team.

MC-B: Right.

BK: They're the CFO now and their expertise is about a $10 million company and it's just not going to move to the next level.

MC-B: Exactly. We value people very much and we have these values, but we make no excuses for expecting high performance. We have a lot of rewards for working here, it's a great place to work, but those rewards are built on the backs of all the people that have worked really hard to make this a high-performing place. And if you're not high-performing and then you take rewards, there are probably other places that you should be working. The job that they're doing is not a fit for them anymore.

But it can often be really hard because you can't be transparent about people being let go. Like, 'I had that opportunity, now I'm moving on' – you don't know if they were doing it for themselves or if they were let go. And it's up to them. Often they don't want to tell you and that's totally fine. But, you know, sometimes you can tell. Someone says, 'Hey, I'm leaving tomorrow.' OK, that was unexpected. Something probably happened there. But at the same time, there's this weird stigma that gets attached to people. You thought they were doing a really good job, but you don't have the context. Obviously, the manager of their team doesn't think they were doing a good job so they let them go. You can be like, 'But I worked with that guy three months ago. He was great.' Maybe in the thing he worked on with you he was great. You just don't have the right context. So, that can cause a lot of tension. You've got to trust that the people who do have the context, their team, their manager, the manager's manager, is making the right decision on the part of the company. That can be really hard.

Also, just because they're no longer your colleague, it doesn't mean they're not your friend, like they're diseased or something. That's not the way we run. We've had people leave and come back. We're old enough that people have gone through cycles. And we have a good alumni network, even people who've been let go. We have a really good track record, something I'm proud of. People come back three years later, or a year or two years later and say, 'Hey, thanks for doing that.' Like, it's a weird thing because they end up in a better, happier place but they may not have realised at the time that they're in an unhappy place and then they land somewhere.

For example, someone who's managing a team that's struggling as the team gets bigger. Then they go back to a much smaller company. They go back to a twenty-person startup where they're managing four people and they're so much happier in what they're doing. They feel like they're achieving something and perhaps the lessons they've learned and the things they did wrongly, when they grow that team from five to twenty, they'll be much more adept in handling that twenty-person team in three years' time than they are now. Then they realise that that journey has been a positive thing for them, it's been a growth thing for them, whereas at the time, there's a rejection and a hurt immediately.

And you know, you have to do all these things in a very balanced and humane and heartfelt, compassionate kind of way. It's a tough process for everybody to go through. It's tough on the manager doing it.

BK: One of the things that I've found in the organisaton that I run is that it is very wearing on the leadership. Those conversations are very emotional if they're done in a humane way. Often, no matter how much the boss appears to care, the person on the other end probably doesn't realise that it is emotionally wearing for all concerned.

MC-B: For any manager we have who knows they have to let someone go on a Wednesday, Tuesday night is a terrible night. They don't sleep well. They're humane people. They realise they're doing the right thing for the business, for the team, for the individuals. And there's always that great quote that I like – 'they're firing the person who's not doing his job today so they won't have to fire everybody tomorrow.' If the company goes down the tubes, nobody has a job. People stay up nights, they sweat about it, they feel terrible. It's a really, really hard thing to do and it never gets any easier.

I think the more times you do it, the more you start to be proactive about upfront performance conversations because you realise how painful it is down the end when you get to that point, especially if you haven't had them. If you go to someone and say, 'Hey, we've got to let you go' and they say, 'But six months ago you told me I was doing a good job.' You're like, yeah. I just punted on a hard conversation six months ago, and it's now even harder.

So, you know, we also have this rule that nobody being let go should be surprised. We've failed as a company, as a management organisation if they're surprised at all about that decision. There should be plenty of warning signs. There should be plenty of conversations before it gets to that point. There will be people surprised, we're not perfect, but there should be no surprises.

BK: Excellent, Mike. I really want to thank you for your time.

Mark Carnegie

Investor – M H Carnegie & Co

'… You've got to be passionate about whatever you're doing, and you've got to be prepared to do stuff that other people won't do.'

Mark Carnegie's track record in the corporate advisory arena is legendary – he has been involved in a range of Australian and international deals valued at billions of dollars. With diverse international experience as an entrepreneur and investor, he co-founded Carnegie Wylie which was acquired by New York's Lazard. Now he is using his powers for good in the areas of social policy and philanthropy.

www.mhcarnegie.com

Interview

BRETT KELLY: Mark, I'd like to start at the beginning. Where did you grow up?

MARK CARNEGIE: I grew up in Melbourne. Then, when I was six, we moved to Connecticut, just outside New York, in America. Dad was working for McKinsey there. We came back when I was eight years old and we stayed in Melbourne. I studied at the University of Melbourne and then overseas. I worked on Wall Street and went back to London for a while and came back to Sydney when I was twenty-eight.

BK: Twenty-eight. And what were you doing then?

MC: I was consulting for a west coast private equity firm, Hellman and Friedman. I was trying to help them make an investment in Fairfax.

BK: Was that your first small deal in Australia?

MC: It was my first deal back in Australia. There were plenty of people involved.

BK: So is that when there was a Packer bid on and–

MC: That's right. Packer, Black and Hellman and Friedman were one group.

BK: Where did your interest in finance and business come from?

MC: You know, I wanted to be Jacques Cousteau. I wanted to be a marine biologist. I could see that I was never going to be a particularly high-quality research scientist so I went and did a law degree in England where I would never have got in had I not been able to row as well. Then I worked summer jobs in finance while I was there. It was the fashionable thing to do. And I went and worked in Wall Street for Jim Wolfensohn who was a high profile Australian investment banker.

BK: Would you describe business or finance as a particular passion or something you just fell into?

MC: I have always enjoyed venture capital. Business is a constant war between the people who have to defend the hand – the big businesses – and the attacker hand. Some guy's got an idea about how he is going to change the world to make a bigger business. I have always naturally gravitated towards people who are applying the attacker hand.

BK: Where does that natural inclination come from? Is it quintessentially Australian to back the underdog?

MC: I don't know. I mean, they're two good questions in the area of accounting and finance. I never took a formal finance or accounting degree, but it was one of those things, I found most stuff at university and academically really a struggle. By contrast, I could just understand accounting. It was relatively straightforward how it worked and was put together. So that helped – and when you have a predisposition to something, it is easier because you work harder at it.

BK: One of the things I keep hearing is that, over time, people find something that they are naturally talented at or passionate about and they put more effort into it because they feel more competent.

MC: It's the Gladwell 10 000 hours point.

BK: The guy that puts in more effort normally wins the war.

MC: Exactly.

BK: Did you have any plans for your career path?

MC: It's an interesting question. Eisenhower said, 'In preparing for battle, I have always found that plans are useless, but planning is indispensable.'

BK: Then no grand plan for your life? Just to do a great job at what you're doing?

MC: I would say, you need a broad view. You need to be doing the opposite of what the investment banks and big financial services businesses are doing. You need to fulfill an unmet need; you need to do it in a different way, stuff like that. So you've got a broad understanding of it, which is being where other people aren't, but after that, I tend not to try and get too committed. Then I've taken it in stages. I wanted to be successful and I wanted to make Carnegie Wylie successful.

BK: So let's talk about that. You essentially started an advisory business?

MC: No, we were trying to be an investment business. The deal is, the basis on which X will give you money is so unattractive that Wyles and I thought, we will do it better. We will make more money, a lot more money, from being advisors than we would from being investors.

BK: OK. So you're in the market. At the beginning it was dominated by full-service investment banks where you had to be everything to everyone and do the whole transaction, but you came out as an independent advisory group.

MC: That's right. That was the key thing. There was a huge sector of growth in private equity and we wanted to capture that wave. I had done it with Hellman and Friedman for a long time. By contrast, at that stage, the all-singing, all-dancing investment bank looked like it was going to sweep all before it. Then what happened was the dot-com boom, alternative assets, venture capital was on the nose and people didn't want to give us money. By contrast, in advisory circles, everybody said, 'God, you need an independent advisor.' So because the model changed from hiring a big investment bank to hiring a big investment bank plus an independent advisor, you had this big industry shift.

BK: So the big investment banks started to compete with their clients. How early did you see that, what was the difference that you saw?

MC: Our whole thing was that we were prepared to actually fight for our client. Most people just really don't like conflict.

BK: So would you characterise yourself as aggressive or direct?

MC: I think other people have characterised me that way.

BK: I noticed in the article on Banjo, the advertising group that you and John Singleton invested in, that John comes across in the media as somebody who has always been prepared to take a different angle and to go hard for what he believes in. I have never met him, but that was a critical piece.

MC: Absolutely. I mean you've got to be passionate about whatever you're doing. You've got to be prepared to do stuff that other people won't do. One of my favourite lines of all time is Jimmy Goldsmith's great line that if you see a bandwagon rolling, it's too late to get on. But that's what people want to do. When they say, this is the year to become a management consultant, it's the best time not to be.

BK: So you've got Banjo and One Big Switch. What would you not want to be doing in the world right now?

MC: I wouldn't like to be a mainstream retailer at the moment.

BK: So online?

MC: I think we've got the highest service costs in retail. We've got the highest occupancy costs and the internet is free distribution. I don't think that sounds like a good game.

BK: So where would you want to be?

MC: I think, in the end, even though we look like we're on the cyclical downturn for China, I think the emerging markets are going to increasingly have a larger and larger share of Australian GDP. So what you need to do is find something that's derivative on the secular growth of the emerging markets.

BK: OK, so where do you think those places are right now? What excites you?

MC: I'm not so much a person who will fund and invest in secular themes on the bull side. By contrast, what I'm interested in and trying to do is find places where, as a result of this capital drought and the European banks disappearing, there are things being sold really, really cheap. It's the same reason as getting into venture. Venture had an appalling performance, post the dot-com bubble, so I said, 'Let's get into venture.'

BK: Yes. So with that venture fund, where do you–

MC: Well, we've got prostate cancer diagnostics. We've got One Big Switch. We've got a water treatment business – it's just what deals were looking good.

BK: In a sense, buying assets below replacement cost–

MC: No. I mean the venture things are far more, you know. Could you have a big market? Do you have a sustainable, competitive advantage? How long's your path to revenues? How long is your path to profitability? The other stuff which we're doing at the moment – pubs, marinas, those things – that's all about replacement cost and buying cheap.

BK: Can I ask you how old are you now?

MC: Fifty.

BK: OK, so what's the plan from here? You know, the broad strategic direction.

MC: So the way it works at the moment is I try and do three things: I want to be commercially successful, I want to do a whole lot of philanthropic stuff and I want to speak out on issues of public policy.

'I try and do three things: I want to be commercially successful, I want to do a whole lot of philanthropy stuff, and I want to speak out on issues of public policy.'

BK: Tell me about the public policy issues–

MC: The one that I'm on the record about is the argument that rich people should pay more tax.

BK: In what sense?

MC: If you look where the tax burden lies in Australia, the people who are doing well out of Australia's economic prosperity should pay a greater share of the tax burden.

BK: Through a super profits type of tax?

MC: No. My argument is basically that there should be no negative gearing. Roll back the Henry land tax.

BK: Estate tax?

MC: Yes.

BK: So you would be a fan of estate taxes rolling back capital gains tax (CGT) versus income differential?

MC: Well, no. This CGT thing is ... what Henry says is that we want to reduce the tax on interest income.

BK: Yes.

MC: Increase the CGT and basically we'll still make a concession for interest on savings, but equalise between interest income and dividend income and those sorts of things.

BK: And capital gains?

MC: It would mean that capital gains tax goes up, but not the same as income.

BK: OK. What about incentives to invest? Do you believe in having a tax system that is designed with incentives to invest in particular things or do you think governments should stay out of it?

MC: No. I believe clustering rarely works. I think it's regional. I think huge amounts of economic development are regional competitions. I think with that, without Australia finding areas to compete against Singapore, Hong Kong and stuff like that, we're going to be largely irrelevant. I think Singapore's industry policy is really, really effective.

BK: So, after we've equalised some of those other areas there should be–

MC: Two different things, right? Think about individuals. At the moment, a demographic tsunami is going to hit us. As older people retire, what they call the dependency ratio goes up. We have huge amounts of good fortune at the moment. I'm saying the rich people who are really fortunate at the moment should pay more tax and put that into a savings account or a sovereign wealth fund so that when things are tougher in twenty years' time, as they inevitably will be, we've got–

BK: So the continuation of Costello's first intergenerational report goes on – it's probably a decade old now.

MC: But they've done two or three subsequently.

BK: That's right, they have been continually updated but it's interesting, you heard about Henry, but there's not really been much focus on that intergenerational report–

MC: I think the Business Council did a really good job before the Tax Summit when they said that the numbers are far worse because they have misjudged how much damage comes as a result of the state governments. The expense line looks like this and the revenue line looks like that.

Also, it's this thing that the voters are old and the workers are young. The voters are going to say they'd like higher and higher real expenditure on healthcare. How is it going to get funded? The answer is to fund it while you are working. That's my argument.

BK: And that's why tax rates can only go–

MC: Fifty percent is an absolutely top rate for income tax, top rate. I think it's all to do with these messed-up incentives and other stuff.

BK: So you are in favour of a progressive tax system?

MC: Yes. I thought about all that flat tax stuff but I just don't think it works. I'm hugely supportive of Bruce Bonyhady and what he has done with the National Disability Insurance. And divorce. I believe divorce is a disease, so we are funding a whole lot of stuff to say divorce is a disease, the mental health cost is huge. It's a hidden cost to society and we need to be having a more focused look at it.

BK: A harder look?

MC: At how to deal with it.

BK: So you would call divorce a disease?

MC: We are saying, mental health is so many things, it is not like schizophrenia, no. Here is a middle class thing that happens to a third of middle class families that has huge, huge costs, right? Nobody investigates that. How do we do that?

BK: OK, so how are you doing that?

MC: Through the Menzies School of Health Research in Darwin. We're using them.

BK: You're funding some research they are doing?

MC: We've got to see what we come up with.

BK: What is your interest in disability?

MC: I have an interest in early intervention and the National Disability Insurance Scheme (NDIS). My youngest child was deaf. We had a whole lot of stuff that we

had to do to help her. That was fine because Tanya and I had the resources to do it, but there are a whole lot of people who go through the same thing and don't.

Bruce Bonyhady has come up with a National Disability Insurance Scheme. They got the first round of funding this year. That's doing well and I'm really, really supportive of what he is trying to do. In contrast, there are people who say the full effect, which would add six billion dollars a year to the budget is too much. My argument is, that's failed accounting. This is an investment, not an expense. Down the track, early intervention saves money and improves lives.

BK: So for the child with a hearing issue, early intervention changes everything. It takes them from being dependent at eighteen to being a contributor.

MC: Exactly.

BK: Interesting. So why venture capital? I've read a bit about how they raised a lot of funds for the internet boom. Those funds essentially killed the venture industry in Australia. How big is the fund that you have?

MC: It's small. Twenty million from us and twenty million from the government, so forty million, but the thing that's clear is you don't need huge amounts of money in the new world–

BK: What is an effective or average size of an investment for you guys?

MC: I don't know. Accel, which is the most successful venture firm in the world at the moment, is willing to do things as small as a hundred thousand bucks if they have to because everyone is realising that it's a smaller and smaller number of investments in the portfolio that make all the money. The history was always a third of your investments were going to be responsible for your entire outcome. Now, it's like 3%. That's a tiny percentage doing this stratospheric ...

BK: It's a lot more small investments.

MC: And the big ones can pay out at a hundred times of what you invest.

BK: So, how big is your team in that business?

MC: About half a dozen do both the normal investment plus the private equity, because it all sits together.

BK: What's your criteria in the venture space? When you look at a business to invest in, what are you looking for? Where do you start?

MC: The quality of the guy, right? And then, is the market big enough? Can you put the risk upfront? Therefore, you know whether you've got something really good. How is it going to be sustainable? That is, how are you going to create a competitive advantage?

BK: Any view towards the exit or do you guys prefer to buy and hold?

MC: Basically, we buy things to sell, so we're not like Warren Buffett, but you can find ways out if you've got a sustainable business model, there will always be someone who wants to buy it off you.

BK: That's very Buffett – if it's a great business he likes to keep it. Tell me, what are you looking at when you look at that person you're going to invest in?

MC: It's really, really diverse. There's the way they think about the world. Are they trustworthy? Are they willing to learn from their mistakes or take counsel, take a difference of view –

BK: What distressed assets are you looking at? What do you like about pubs?

MC: No-one is ever going to have a drink on the internet. I like that. My kids buy their shoes, their clothes on the internet, but they ain't drinking on the internet.

BK: When you look at them, how do you price them?

MC: Well, I halve what they were before—

BK: Any sense of a model of earnings or is it a real estate play as well?

MC: You can borrow at five and you can buy them at twelve. Before, you could buy at five and borrow at twelve. I like the former, not the latter.

BK: I read that the plan with that portfolio is to group them together and then list it?

MC: List it or sell it, I just don't know. Returns at the moment are just so good for what we do. We've got a happy operator, we make a whole lot of money. I mean, how good is that?

BK: Hold them forever if—

MC: We'll wait and see.

BK: Marinas?

MC: They're basically the same as the pubs, which is 60% off some of them.

'I've got no interest in doing big deals. There are just too many people doing it. I'm interested in doing small deals …'

BK: OK. What else are you looking at?

MC: I'll look at anything. I just wait for the phone to ring. I was looking at a pain management business recently. My whole thing at the moment is because of the way the intermediations work, there are a whole lot of people who expect to get paid $500 000 a year as investment bankers. They need to do big deals. I've got no interest in doing big deals. There are just too many people doing it. I'm interested in doing small deals because—

BK: There's no-one there.

MC: Exactly. I always go where the money ain't! It's not contrary, it's just what I've always said about capital. It's a commodity, right? Being in my business, you are the high-cost provider of a commodity. That's a shit business, right? You don't want to be the high-cost provider.

BK: So you're running here, basically, one man at his desk and, you know, six men at a desk.

MC: It's twenty men at a desk but the whole thing is you need to manufacture something out of a commodity. So you need to manufacture a solution. For a guy's problem, if all you are is a low bid on a capital availability–

BK: Bad business to be in.

MC: Whereas if somebody's got a problem and you can find some way to fix it, fantastic.

BK: How important is your knowledge versus your ability to deal with people versus the people that you know?

MC: I think they're all together. It's one of those things, everyone knows everyone in this town. If you know them and know their strengths and weaknesses and how they can fit together to provide a solution–

BK: That helps. So when you look forward, or look at where you've been, what are the things that you've got really wrong or that you've learned a lot from?

MC: Mate, you'd be here for hours.

BK: So the biggest thing you've learned? Biggest mistake?

MC: I've always said you can only lose your money once. So I have never regarded my failed investments as a huge problem. Provided you've got a diversified portfolio, you only lose your money once. So your mistakes are selling your winners too early and doubling down on your–

BK: Not selling your losers earlier?

MC: Yes. Peter Lynch describes that as watering your weeds and cutting your flowers. Ultimately, that's where the problem is. There's a thing called confirmation bias in bad investments and you've just got to be ruthless about the fact that routinely you stuff up.

BK: How important do you think self-discipline is? A willingness to be objective?

MC: You are buggered as an investor, a genuine investor, over time if you are not able to be objective. You are gone.

BK: Do you have any advice to young people seeking to build a career?

MC: It's great, that John Paul Getty line, isn't it? 'Work hard. Work hard. Rise early. Strike oil.'

BK: It's a good one. But is it also about finding something you really love?

MC: Absolutely.

BK: You can't just keep going to the point of being very, very successful if you don't have the passion to just keep going.

MC: But I think it's about drive. The other description I have for the young kids is, you need some grit in the oyster if you're going to try and make a pearl.

BK: Tell me, how old are your kids?

MC: Eighteen, sixteen and fourteen.

BK: What do you say to your kids?

MC: I just say, you know, work it out. I don't care whether you're feeding refugees at Darfur or working at Lone Pine Capital. Just make sure you're working. Make sure you're engaged and make sure you do what you love.

'Just make sure you're working. Make sure you're engaged and make sure you do what you love.'

BK: You talk about the divorce disease. For business owners with really intense careers and businesses they're building, how do you keep a marriage and family on track? I don't think there's a silver bullet–

MC: Well, I'm divorced so that's the reason why I'm big on the divorce thing – I know the cost of it. It's a really, really big challenge. It really is. It's stressful. Building a business is stressful. It takes a lot of work. I did a ton of business in Asia. It's just really hard.

BK: So what is it? Is it because you're not there, you're not engaged? You're more engaged in business and you don't spend enough time with your kids when you're there.

MC: I'm sure you've heard it a hundred times from all sorts of people. You've got choices and you don't spend enough time with the kids when they're young. You know, I tried to overcome that subsequently.

BK: So when you look back, what would you change if you could change anything?

MC: Let me think about that, I'm trying to work it out. I mean, I wouldn't have travelled as much as I did to Asia. I would have tried to find a different way to do that.

BK: Is there a motto, a quote or a thought that best summarises your approach to life?

MC: I used to have one about persistence, but the one I have now is the Puggy Pearson quote – there are only three things you need to know about poker. The 60/40 end of a proposition, money management and know yourself. It was used by some of the big investors and there's never been a better quote about investing. So, that's my quote.

Nicola Cerrone

Master Jeweller – Cerrone

'I still sit down with special people who want to get something really special made, and that is the beauty about this business. It is the creative side, to make something which wasn't there yesterday.'

Nicola Cerrone, one of Australia's most successful and awarded jewellers arrived in Australia as a twelve-year-old from Italy. After finishing an apprenticeship as a jeweller, he started his own enterprise from a small terrace house in Leichhardt over forty years ago. His passion and talent have seen Cerrone expand to include three elegant boutiques in Sydney and a client base that extends throughout Australia and the world.

www.cerrone.com.au

Interview

NICOLA CERRONE: I want to tell you this story because it is important that you understand more than just me. See, I looked at every business in the world and they were all disappointing. When people are disappointed, they are upset. It's not a good feeling. In the long term, we all lose. You achieve a lot more with sweetness. When people are happy, they have a lot of drive. But if you disappoint them, they don't want to do anything anymore.

If you look at southern Europe at the moment – Greece, Spain, Italy – they are struggling because their entrepreneurial spirit has been squashed. I am lucky because I can do things here, I can do things overseas and I enjoy it. Anyway, my daughter said, 'Dad, why don't you go to China, employ people who already know the job, bring them here, and after six months, send them back.' So I said, 'Dominique, that's not solving the problem.'

Because now, for instance, we've got a thousand stones to be set every week. And if there are only three or four guys doing the job, they can ask you for whatever they want. But if you've got twenty guys, the competition becomes better and the manufacturing becomes better and more competitive. So I said, 'Dominique, I'm going to ring up the headmaster at TAFE and I am going to say, send me half a dozen of the best kids you've got.'

And that's exactly what I did. I employed them. After about six or seven months, out of six kids, one or two started coming in late and not taking the job seriously. So I decided to talk to them in a group and explain things to them. I said, 'You remember a couple of months ago, we had Ian Thorpe here. We reminded them that for him to be a world champion it required sacrifice, sweat, tears and pain. For him to lift his game, there was pain throughout his whole body because he had to do better than anybody else. He had to be the best in the world.' And I said, 'What you are doing is exactly the same.'

Just because you are employed by me, it doesn't automatically mean you are going to become a diamond setter or a jeweller. You've got to practise, practise, practise. The same way I had to do it. When I was learning on the job, my friends used to go out chasing women and drinking and …

BRETT KELLY: Carrying on.

NC: But I used to work until one or two in the morning. I was practising.

BK: So let me go back to the beginning. Where were you born and where did you grow up?

NC: I was born in Italy, on the east coast. Around about 250 kilometres from Bari, in Lanciano.

BK: And how old were you when you came to Australia?

NC: I was twelve years of age. I grew up in Sydney, here in Leichhardt.

BK: And then when did you start your apprenticeship as a jeweller?

NC: I think I was about eighteen. I had already worked in a fruit shop and sold newspapers. What happened was, when I got to Australia, my father found me a job on the second day after I arrived. I did everything to help my parents. My father was the only one working so I tried to help them give my sisters and myself an education, that sort of thing. I used to go to school in the morning, work in a shop and then at night, I used to close up the shop, clean up and then do whatever homework I needed to do. But I wasn't really a good student.

'I've got to do things that I really want to do and not what my father wants me to do, not what everybody is telling me I should be doing.'

BK: Most of the people I've interviewed have said that studying didn't interest them, that they needed to find something that interested them.

NC: It's the interest; it's the passion.

BK: How did you become a jeweller?

NC: After a couple of years I thought, I've got to start doing something serious here. I've got to do something that I really want to do – not what my father wants me to do; not what everybody is telling me that I should be doing. So my father and I started to look for a trade for me. Because back in Italy, we were country people, it was all about the 'contadini', working in the fields. It was a cultural thing. But instead of working in the fields, you do much better learning a trade. It was a step up in life, you know what I mean?

So I started going to interviews with hairdressers, dressmakers, all sorts of things. All sorts of trades. Then, my father met a guy that he used to do gardening for, a jeweller who was looking for an apprentice. I went for an interview and was accepted. He gave me the opportunity to learn the trade, the basics. So then I stayed at Dee Why around the surf club there. I met a lot of Aussie guys and beautiful women. And I started to enjoy life, what Australia was all about.

And then the passion came – the passion that I not only had to repair jewellery, but that I had to make it.

BK: Make it from scratch.

NC: Design it and create it. That became my instinct. I was with him for a couple of years until a German Swiss, William Fisher, one of the great jewellers, was looking for an apprentice. So I went for an interview with him and I became his apprentice. He took me under his wing. I was the only student he ever taught. And to me, he is still one of the best jewellers in the world.

BK: So how long did he train you for?

NC: I was with him for about four years, until I was about twenty-three, when he said, 'I can't teach you any more. The only thing I can advise you to do is to travel the world.' And that is exactly what I did. I went to Asia, Europe, America, South America and then I came back to Australia and started my own business in Leichhardt in 1972.

BK: So today you have a great business, a great profile, people know what you do, but tell me, when you started the business, did you just open your doors and hope for the best? Who were your first customers? Did you just try to sell to your family and friends? How did you promote the business?

NC: Well, you know, Brett, I look back and I say that was very clever what I did, but in those days, I did it because I wanted to do it, without realising it. I did it because gold was so pricey. My material is very expensive. It's unreachable. Some of the things that we have to work with. I mean, a million dollars is nothing in my business, that is one ring. So, I used to borrow my friends' jewellery, repair it, fix it, polish it and give it back to them because I was practising. And these people were impressed. No charge. I just wanted to have it in my hands.

BK: And then they would come back and buy other pieces.

NC: And that's how it all started. Then, when they needed a chain for their christening or something, they used to come and buy it from me. And that's the trust. In this business, it was all about trust. Today, it's all on the internet. Press a button and it tells you what the gold price is. In those days, no one knew what the gold price was. In those days, the jeweller was like the priest.

'I used to borrow my friends' jewellery, repair it, fix it, polish it and give it back to them beacause I was practising. And these people were impressed. No charge. I just wanted to have it in my hands.'

BK: They wouldn't leave their ring with just anybody.

NC: They wouldn't trust just anybody. The priest and jeweller had the same ethics.

BK: So here, around here you–

NC: I've got on with virtually everybody – the Italians, the Australians. You know the next-door neighbour and their friends.

BK: So no big marketing budget?

NC: No, absolutely not.

BK: Just doing a great job, one person at a time. So then the business grows and grows over thirty-plus years.

NC: I want to say one little thing that is very important. In those days, there was nothing getting made in Australia. Everything was from England, Italy, France, Germany – everything was imported. So I started manufacturing here.

For instance, everything that was made in Italy, was made straight. So I made it a little bit crooked and people were excited because it was not the same as what they were used to. I used to make it with flair! That's what gave me the edge very quickly. I came back to Australia and had a little workshop downstairs here. I ran a little bench and after about a week or two, I employed a guy to start doing polishing. I used to work nearly eighteen hours a day.

BK: A day?

NC: Seven days a week. It was really full-on because people just felt comfortable. Then, we started to see the opportunities and I started to sell my collection to shops in places like Double Bay and Kings Cross. I used to go in with one of my collections, for instance, twenty rings that I'd made, and they would buy them all!

BK: So you started wholesaling from an early stage.

NC: Wholesaling has helped me a lot. Then one day, I started to employ people, teach them, guide them, you know, because there were no jewellers in those days.

BK: So where does the drive come from to build this type of business?

NC: I think it's instinct. It's part of being an Italian and being a young boy who immigrated to Australia for a better life. To build your castle. There were the right ingredients at the right time. There were opportunities and you were rewarded – you worked hard; you made money. Today, you work hard, you pay more tax.

BK: Was there a particular driving idea or person in your early careeer?

NC: I think what made me fall in love with this was when you make a business, and then you make the customer very happy. You know, they'll give you a hug, they'll give you a kiss. That was a great response. That gave me great power. And it's a very emotional thing because you give a piece of jewellery when there's an anniversary or a birthday. Then they invite you to their weddings and you become a part of their family. Very rewarding.

BK: This is a side of business that people so often miss – a lot of people think business is just about making money.

NC: No!

BK: But, in fact, you meet so many people and you're a part of their lives.

NC: I never really look at money. I never look at money because I used to do things for nothing. You know what I mean? I'm not possessive over money. I don't care about the money. That is secondary. Of course, you need money to live, to do what you need to do, to buy materials, to get ahead and all that. But towards my customers, it was never their money. Just to do a great job. To be part of their lives. I'm always saying to people that if you've got a business, you look after people. You become a part of their lives and you meet their kids and their family and that's all great and you make money anyway.

BK: That seems to be a mindset that separates people who do well from others.

NC: You know, a lot of people come into our business. They think there is a lot of money to be made but they only last four or five years and then they go. They're not interested in the people. If you just follow the money, well then you're lost. It's a dead end.

BK: So now you look at your business and it seems so natural, but where did your confidence come from? Did it grow over time?

NC: I have talked about the old times with my mother, because my father has passed away. I spend time with her constantly; she reminds me about my

childhood. You know when someone is going to be successful. It's like that even with nature, you know which trees are going to give you great fruit. And I think that people are exactly the same.

I mean, on my mother's side, they are very entrepreneurial people. On my father's side, they were working in the fields, but they worked very, very hard. I think I bring all these different influences together. My mother reminds me that when my father used to say, 'Come and work with me in the fields and we'll work together' I used to say to him, 'No, I want to have my own paddock.' I wanted to prove to my father that I could do better than him. You see, that's the instinct.

BK: So you have the drive.

NC: You have to have drive. I also think it's because my father left my mother with me and my three sisters to work in Australia.

BK: How long was it before you came out?

NC: That was about three years, so we were by ourselves from when I was about nine to twelve.

BK: And your sisters are younger than you?

NC: They are all younger. I really was the figurehead. My father made me responsible for looking after my family.

BK: So, what does a typical day look like for you? Do you get up early?

NC: I get up at about six-thirty in the morning. I do my exercises on my treadmill. I have a good breakfast together with my wife and we talk about our family or whatever. I do not mix family and business. When I get home, I don't talk about it. I stop. And when we are at work, we don't talk about family.

BK: Has your wife always worked in the business?

NC: There were times when she didn't, she raised our two kids, but now the four of us are all working together.

BK: How is that going, working together?

NC: Look, we all have different fields and we all have different areas. My daughters are very passionate about what they do. One is involved in human resources and one is involved in operations.

BK: And what does your wife do?

NC: My wife does her own range of jewellery. Semi-precious jewellery.

BK: Often in businesses, husbands and wives–

NC: Becomes a problem. I think the difference is that my wife knows that I'm the captain. I do ask her advice, but at the end of the day, I make the final decision. She's got her own business; she does the design and puts all the colours together. She enjoys what she is doing.

BK: One of the common themes I find among successful people is that they never intend to retire. Do you have a thirty-year plan or do you just keep doing what you're doing?

NC: I think the thing I enjoy about this business is that you can always do it a little bit better and you can always do it a lot more precisely than what you are doing. I think the enjoyment is in the precision. It is not the quantity, it is not the money, it is the precision. And that's what excites me.

BK: Do you see yourself retiring?

NC: I'm enjoying my business much more now that my family is all here. My kids, my wife are here. So that way, I can have a little bit of an easier time.

BK: You can work as hard as you want.

NC: And enjoy my real hobbies like the farm, the country, the animals.

BK: Your family was on a farm, and now you've got a farm in Bowral. Is that what you love doing when you're not at work?

NC: That's what I do. I grow my own vegetables. I supply all the locals, all my friends with vegetables.

BK: And if somebody wants a special piece, do you still make jewellery?

NC: Oh, my word. I still sit down with people who really want to get something special made. And that is the beauty of this business, the creative side. To make something that wasn't there yesterday from your imagination and because customers want to have something really different.

BK: Let me ask you, what do you think are the most critical issues facing Australian businesses?

NC: Well, at this particular time, I think the problem is that they have destroyed all the energy of a businessman. It's just not exciting to be a businessman.

BK: Do you think there is a need for people who are in business to be good examples and inspirational to young people?

NC: This is one of the things that I keep saying. I mean, this is a wonderful country. But why do we keep promoting people who break world sporting records? It's great for our young people to achieve, but I think there should be an equal opportunity for people who do other things, like great musicians or great business people or even great doctors, great scientists.

BK: How many people do you employ here?

NC: We've got over fifty.

BK: You make a difference to their family.

NC: We do. Some of my staff have been with me for thirty years. Most of my staff have been here a long time.

BK: So, they're passionate about the business, about what you do.

NC: They're connected with me because they know. There is a history; they know the energy of the business; they know the will of the business.

BK: They've been through the struggles and the good times.

NC: They live with the same integrity.

BK: How do business cycles affect a business like this?

NC: In my business, the Christmas period is very busy and there are certain months when we are quiet, but because we are creative people, this gives us an opportunity to restructure ourselves, redesign ourselves, reinvent ourselves and that's a great thing. Because if you are flat out all the time, you've got no idea where you're going. No time to think. So, there's nothing wrong with that.

BK: So, who has really inspired you? Obviously, your mum and your dad in different ways?

NC: Yes. But I think my master, William Fisher, was the one who really inspired me. He made me understand that you should never cover your mistakes. Fix it. Don't try to cover up. Isn't that good? Melt it down and start again.

BK: Most people can't do that with their work.

NC: That's true. You know, I think it's probably a good thing. It's a good feeling to start again, because it is not perfect.

'The thing I enjoy about this business is that you can always do it a little bit better, and you can always do it a lot more precisely than what you are doing … And that's what excites me.'

BK: Now, let me ask you about the GFC (global financial crisis). What impact did it have on your business?

NC: Well, I mean globally, it was a problem. In my business, I would have to say it wasn't as bad as I would have imagined it.

BK: You just kept working harder?

NC: I just kept working harder. The thing is, I can't make mistakes today, it costs a lot, so we run our business a lot more precisely.

BK: Does this ethos of improving things go right across the business in terms of how you try to do your purchasing or your HR or your marketing?

NC: Absolutely.

BK: It brings about improvements?

NC: Absolutely.

BK: I can tell from sitting here that you care about what you do. How demanding are you of yourself?

NC: I am a lot more precise now than I was before. And I'm a lot more tolerant. You know, I think about things more now, whereas years ago, I used to react immediately, which was a big mistake. You're not thinking properly when you're angry; no-one can change anything when someone is angry.

BK: No, it's very destructive.

NC: It's very negative. I can control my emotions much more than what I used to which makes me much more comfortable.

BK: But you don't seem to have lost any of your drive?

NC: No, because, you know, I still love beautiful things. Beauty is in my nature. It's in my genes.

BK: Is it an Italian thing?

NC: (Sighs.) I don't know, but beauty, I think, can come from anybody. You've got to appreciate beauty.

BK: So, how much are you into design, architecture, fashion and beauty?

NC: Well, I'm involved in this constantly. I mean, with my business, I let a lot of young people influence me. I'm very open-minded. I don't have this ego that says, 'I'm the designer.' The idea of Cerrone is that we work together. I make the final decision, but I need everybody to put in. Because today, it's a very competitive world.

BK: And you do more as a team–

NC: Than what you do on your own.

BK: So is that why you've adopted the 'Cerrone' brand rather than 'Nicola Cerrone, Master Jeweller'?

NC: Absolutely. I get my staff involved. I get my wife involved, my kids. We all know we are responsible. I am a responsible human being. I think it's the foundation.

───────

'The idea of Cerrone is that we work together.
I make the final decision, but I need everybody to put in.
Because today, it's a very competitive world.'

BK: So, you were nine years old when your father left for Australia, leaving you and your family in Italy for three years. You basically had to look after your mum and three younger sisters. Today, this concept of accountability and responsibility continues.

NC: It's thinking about your customer, what your customer is spending. It's a responsibility.

BK: You're in a business where people are often trying to induce you to buy things that are in their interest, not yours. For example, a couple come in and they're going to buy an engagement ring. Do you get them to buy the most expensive ring?

NC: Never, no. The way I work is I want them to be comfortable and happy. I don't try to make them spend more than what they want to. At the end of the day, an unhappy customer, or unsatisfied customer, is of no benefit to anyone. Just to give you an idea, say they've got a budget of $10 000. You might be a great salesman, and sell them a ring for $20 000, but what happens in the long-term? You lose a customer, and that could be worth not just $10 000, it could be worth $100 000 in the long-term.

BK: So you've always had a long-term mindset?

NC: Always long-term. Because often, the first transaction takes a lot of time. One of the interesting things I have seen with jewellery is, for instance, my mate – I think they've been married fifty years now – has often updated the diamond in his wife's ring. And he's always gone to the same jeweller. That's a long-term relationship rather than a transaction.

BK: Absolutely.

NC: That's exactly the same thing that we do. You know, someone comes in and starts with an idea of say fifty points (0.50 ct). Then they're successful, and two years later, they come back to buy a carat (1.00 ct). It's so important not to make your customer do something that they don't want to do, or push them into something they don't want to buy.

BK: OK, now tell me about debt in the business. How much debt have you run in the business over time? Because during the GFC, many big businesses that you would have thought would have done better, had real problems because of over-gearing.

NC: That's right. The way I've done it is that before I went to the bank and borrowed money, I bought a house. So what happened then is that the bank started to feel comfortable. Then I said, OK, I'll open a business. You've got your house, worth for instance, $10 000. You can borrow another $2 000 for your business, you know?

So, what happens then is you increase your business, your turnover becomes bigger, then you can buy another house. And that's how I was able to go to the bank and borrow money. Buying properties against my business. Not because I like properties, but if I didn't have any properties, my bank wouldn't even look at me. I have the bricks and mortar.

BK: A business is a 24/7 commitment. How many times have you been genuinely worried about what the future looks like?

NC: Never.

BK: Just unwavering confidence?

NC: Look, there are times where you over-extend or there are times when I've bought some big stones and I've thought, when am I going to sell this? But somehow, down the line, there is always a customer who will come in and buy it because it's unique. It's like a painting. A very unique piece; unique diamonds.

BK: It takes some guts to do that.

NC: I'm a little bit risky.

BK: You've done some serious pieces of work.

NC: Yeah. I've done it, because I think when you're enjoying what you're doing, you don't think about the risk. You are happy doing it, you're comfortable doing it, but you're not worried about the risk. But I know my barriers. You know there's a limit and you stop.

BK: But it seems that you've never gone off into other strange directions. You've really stuck to buying property and building your jewellery business.

NC: I've done quite a few little silly things. I mean, I opened up a store in Canberra and one in Melbourne. That was a silly mistake.

BK: Why did you do that?

NC: Because I was young and, you know, business was good.

BK: Where are your stores now, in the city?

NC: Always around Sydney – Castlereagh Street and Martin Place. I think that's the best thing I have done.

BK: Where are you at now?

NC: We are focusing on our corporate and wholesale divisions. I also have my own overseas customers, clients who I am in constant contact with.

BK: What do you do for them?

NC: Custom-made pieces. I'll go to them or they'll come to me. They contact me when they are looking for a specific thing.

BK: Then you'll go and source that?

NC: I'll make them the piece and I also do private exhibitions, private functions. Private exhibitions are the best.

BK: Where do you take your best work?

NC: I've been to Cairo, Lebanon, Jeddah, Riyadh. I take all Australian products because I am very proud of my country and of what we have here – the opals, the pearls, the diamonds.

BK: You've bought some of Argyle's rare pieces?

NC: Absolutely. I have used some in the most expensive pieces of jewellery sold to the Australian consumer. I've sold a diamond for nearly $1.5 million.

BK: For one stone?

NC: One stone in a ring.

BK: Beautiful.

NC: You know, there are things that you can be proud of because they're unique.

BK: Have you ever sold a piece to someone that you just can't believe they bought it from you?

NC: Yes, sometimes you make these pieces out of the blue, you know. One day you're bored or something and you start making things. And then you say, 'Who am I going to sell this to?'

I think I've got to say that one of my favourite moments in my career was when Celine Dion's husband rang me. He wanted to buy the best piece of jewellery in my shop because it was Celine's fortieth birthday. That was one of the most beautiful things, because it absolutely came from nowhere. I didn't know where this connection came from. He wanted to buy a piece of jewellery that was close to my heart. It is a beautiful bracelet. Celine connects with music in the same way that I am connected to jewellery.

One of the other special moments was when I made the chalice for Pope Benedict, when he was here for World Youth Day 2008. And, you know, the Pope held it and blessed everybody at the last Mass in Randwick with it. Half a million people. Beautiful. And they took the chalice back to the Vatican. Amazing. But the beautiful thing was that we had to design it from scratch and it was a very Australian piece with diamonds. These are special things, really. It brought joy, not only to me but to my family, as we were sponsored by the Catholic Church to come to Australia; they paid for my fare.

'The customer is number one, but what you really shouldn't forget is your responsibility to who you are; you should not forget your roots. You should not forget what it is that you are capable of doing or can afford or manage.'

BK: Now, tell me about tax. What's your view of tax? I hear a lot that payroll tax annoys people. The more people you employ, the more tax you pay.

NC: Absolutely. The payroll and the group tax.

BK: Do you think taxes are too high?

NC: Look, I think the GST was a great thing because it brought us to an equal level with everybody else; it made us competitive. Today, I am happy to be able to have tourists walk into my shop – I can compete with countries like Hong Kong, Tokyo, Europe and America now. A lot of people, a lot of the sales and a lot of the businesses are selling up because so many people are buying things offshore. It was worthwhile. Imagine paying 30%. It's not competitive.

BK: So what do you think are two or three things that you should definitely not forget if you want to succeed in business?

NC: Well, the customer is number one, but what you really shouldn't forget is your responsibility to who you are; you should not forget your roots. You should not forget what it is that you are capable of doing or can afford or manage.

BK: So your own capacity?

NC: Capacity. It is really important that whatever you do in life, you can still hang on.

BK: You've got to keep testing yourself.

NC: You must over-extend, because if you don't over-extend, you will just stay where you are.

BK: So obviously, you need drive and determination and confidence? What is the thing that keeps you balanced? How important is listening to your wife? Because I sense that you and your wife have worked very effectively in the business together.

NC: It is very important. You need your wife's opinion. My mother and father never really said to me, 'You must do this. You must do that. You must not do that.' My mother and father always gave me a free rope. Even if I made a mistake.

BK: But that feeling that you guys are a team, I guess.

NC: Of course, you've got to have a feeling of unity. That someone, even if you make a mistake, will back you up. That's the goal.

BK: So how hands-on are you in the business now, like, if you go down into that workshop–

NC: I know every detail. But I don't need to know, it's all organised. I have a report every day of all the customers that come into my store. I know what they came in for and who looked after them.

BK: Very interesting. Now, tell me about your people. How do you attract good people and how do you keep them happy?

NC: You need the instinct to know if these people follow the same dream as you.

BK: Instinct and practice, I guess. You get it wrong, but–

NC: It doesn't matter, we all get it wrong. I mean, some of my staff have made some big mistakes. They want to resign and I say, 'No, you are not going to resign, you are going to stay here and fix it.' It's the easy way, to resign if you make a mistake.

BK: But, you know, often bosses will fire someone for a mistake.

NC: No, no. Fix it.

BK: Good. Now, everyone I have talked to who has built a serious business knows that there is an impact on their family life, particularly during the early stages when they are working as you said, seven days a week, eighteen hours a day. When did you get married?

NC: I got married when I was twenty-three.

BK: So your wife has been with you the whole journey?

NC: The whole time. Almost forty years.

BK: So when she had your first daughter, you were working very hard.

NC: Very hard, but you know, she had her own interest in the family, looking after the children, taking them to school, giving them a good education and being part of the home. But when we came home, we were home.

BK: How often were you home?

NC: Well, we used to have breakfast and dinner together, and after dinner, I'd go back to work.

BK: You lived in the same premises that you worked in. Have you ever felt that you didn't have enough time for your kids?

NC: No. I made the time when I needed to make the time and when I had to make the time.

BK: Now, if you ask your children or your wife, would they say they had enough of your time?

NC: My children have never said to me that I was never there. Because there was always someone there – my mum or my father or someone. But the difference is, with a lot of people, when I go to their home, it's always about business. That's the biggest mistake they make and they will never be able to fix it because they are talking about the same thing all the time and they can't see the problem.

BK: So you need an interest other than the business.

NC: You need an interest; you need a break.

BK: So what are your interests other than the business? We've talked about your farm, but before that?

NC: I used to go home and we'd talk about family life, you know, what we were going to do. Where we were going to go for a holiday, a trip as a family, those sorts of things.

BK: So you always had holidays?

NC: Not really. But we used to have a break or have somewhere or go to. I see a lot of family at work. You need a little bit of a break.

BK: So leave that at work. It's very good advice.

NC: You know, sometimes my daughter brings her kids to work, but it's not the place for them – they can come in, walk around, but this is not their place. Let's be realistic and logical. You've got to keep these things separate. That's the only way things will work.

BK: You have had a very rich life. What are the great joys of building and owning a business? If you had to write an ad, if you had to write the promotion copy for why you should build a business, what would you say?

NC: I think it's because you become a responsible human being and that's a good feeling in your life. To be proud and responsible and have ethics in life. That is very important. You've got to have those things. You get to know yourself, who you are and what you have contributed to life.

BK: So you look out and you see all the people that you have served now for forty-plus years.

NC: For me, that gives me a great joy. I have customers that are third generation who'll come in and buy jewellery from me. You know, the grandmother got her engagement ring from me. To me, that is a great thing when people see you in the street and say, 'Oh, you remember this ring?' You know, they are just walking with a walking stick. That's a great joy that money can't buy.

On why you should start a business: *'I think it's because you become a responsible human being and that's a good feeling in your life. To be proud and responsible and have ethics in life.'*

BK: And if you could make your dream piece of jewellery, what would it be?

NC: I think it's in the moment, you know. In the moment, you're not really thinking about it. I mean, you're thinking about what you're going to make, but a lot of the time what happens with me when I sit down is that I'm just in the moment. You find what works for each unique stone, that's the challenge

The thing is that in my mind sometimes what happens is that I am really bored. I am thinking things are not so happy. But really, there are better things to do in life than just be miserable. You know what I mean? Like, the diamond bra, you know? It made me healthier. It made me stronger. It made me open-minded. It made me laugh. And that's what you need, a reason for doing what you're doing. It is not about money; it's creative. You are trying to show people what your mind is thinking. But I do it for myself; I am not doing it for anybody else.

BK: It must be a great joy when people love what you do.

NC: Of course. That's what I love the most about my business.

Lorna Jane Clarkson

Activewear Designer – Lorna Jane

'My professional and personal goals are pretty much the same: I want to continue to inspire and encourage women all over the world to live a more active life.'

Lorna Jane Clarkson is an icon of the Australian fashion design industry. Having revolutionised the women's activewear category over 20 years ago, she has gone on to create a multi-million dollar enterprise as founder and Chief Creative Officer of Lorna Jane. From working part-time as an aerobics instructor while making her own fitness gear, to opening over 130 stores throughout Australia and the United States, Lorna inspires women across the world to embrace her Move, Nourish, Believe philosophy everyday.

www.lornajane.com
www.movenourishbelieve.com

Interview

BRETT KELLY: Was there a particular driving idea, person or event that really had the most significant impact on your life?

LORNA JANE: Whilst I believe my life has been a series of events that led me to be the person I am today, there is one single cognitive pop that has significantly shaped the last two decades of my life.

In 1989, when I first sat on my living room floor, unpicked an old swimsuit to cut a newspaper pattern for an aerobic leotard, the concept of activewear was non-existent. The concept derived from a personal desire for active attire that was feminine, fun and functional. It is this sole thought and the chain of events which quickly followed that has truly shaped me. I am thankful that there were women out there who shared this need and that to this day, women see a need for activewear that makes them feel alive.

One event in particular, was the daring decision to quit my day job and make activewear full-time. It took courage to give up the security of my full-time job, but in the pursuit of personal passion I held close the belief that I would make it work no matter what. I've always been driven to do my absolute best in any circumstance, no matter the challenge.

BK: It seems so natural now that you would own your own business. When you started, was your intention to develop your own business?

LJ: In the beginning I never really though beyond the fact that I wanted to spend more time doing what I loved to do. I had been teaching aerobics part-time and I loved it, so by supplementing that with making and selling activewear, I effectively got to spend more time at the gym. It was only as the popularity for my designs grew that I realised there was potential to expand and meet the growing demand for fashionable fitness wear.

In the early days I had no intention of opening my own stores, but listening to my customers describing their experiences in traditional sports stores made it pretty clear to me that this is what had to happen. And then I guess demand just took over from there, one store led to five, which led to twelve, and before we knew it we were a national Australian retailer specialising in women's activewear.

Do I wake up some days wondering how it all happened? Absolutely! Would I change a thing? Absolutely not! Are my dreams for Lorna Jane bigger and better? You bet!

BK: Was it love at first sight with the fashion and fitness industry?

LJ: For as long as I can remember I've been interested in fashion. I was crocheting bikinis at school when I was 16, customising my clothing from 18 onwards and spending my weekends at 21 designing and making my own clothes. That combined with my love of health and fitness has been the driving force in my life. So I guess you could say that I have managed to take the two things that I love most, and effectively build a lifestyle out of it.

Do I love what I do? Without a doubt. Did I realise where my love affair with fashion and fitness would take me? Not in a million years!

'In business you need to be adaptable, responsive and constantly looking for ways to do things better and faster. I approach each day with a plan but make sure there is enough flexibility around it to do my best work … because who knows what opportunities will present themselves?'

BK: What does a typical Lorna Jane day look like?

LJ: I guess the first thing that most business owners will tell you is that there is no such thing as a typical day! In business you need to be adaptable, responsive and constantly looking for ways to do things better and faster. I approach each day with a plan but make sure there is enough flexibility around it to do my best work … because who knows what opportunities will present themselves?

I start my day with exercise and then head in to the office. I do a quick thirty minutes catching up on emails and any other digital correspondence then I jump in to meetings, meetings, meetings. There are meetings about everything Lorna Jane but the most important ones for me are design meetings and fittings as well as marketing plans, and campaign imagery and ideas.

As the Creative Director of Lorna Jane there is a lot of detail to attend to and my focus on the product and the look and feel of the brand takes priority over everything. Some days I may get some time at my desk to design, write or work on new concepts, whereas other days it's more meetings and team discussions.

I usually leave the office around 6pm, head home for a relaxing walk with my family or a quiet yoga class before dinner. Because I work with my husband, it is not unusual for us to discuss business over dinner, plan the next day's schedule or celebrate a recent victory.

'Do I love what I do? Without a doubt. Did I realise where my love affair with fashion and fitness would take me? Not in a million years!'

BK: What do you think are the most critical issues facing Australian businesses?

LJ: Businesses in general, whether they be in Australia or any other part of the world, need to be relevant and compete at a global level to be successful at what they do. With the influx of digital communication, things move faster than they ever have before and it is critical that businesses stay ahead of the game and remain relevant.

Lorna Jane sits across multiple categories of fashion, health and fitness, as well as retail, so we must communicate with our customers through all of the channels available and integrate our bricks and mortar offering with our online presence.

Social media has become a vital tool in connecting with our customers, and we have an incredibly engaged audience. This has allowed us to directly spread our brand message, as well as receive instant feedback on new styles and our monthly campaigns from those who matter most – the women wearing our product.

By maximising the potential of your position online, and allowing your business to grow from the traditional bricks and mortar environment, you will significantly expand and understand your audience in today's fast-paced retail world.

BK: Are you competing with someone else, yourself, or is it just an approach to life?

LJ: I am always competing with myself. I think the desire to be better, do things better and conquer new horizons is what drives us forward in life and it is the same for Lorna Jane.

My dream for Lorna Jane is to be constantly evolving so that we meet and exceed our customers' expectations. It is my job and the role of my team to make sure this happens. If you are constantly watching or worrying about what similar businesses are doing then it is my belief that you will never reach YOUR full potential. Over 20 years ago when we started Lorna Jane, the concept of a specialised women's activewear brand was unheard of – and I am still asked at least two or three times a week if I would ever consider starting a menswear line – so we have been forging our own path since 1990.

The culture of our brand and what we represent is the same as the first day we started. We try to improve what we do and how we do things every day. Our message is clear, what we want to achieve is clear, and we don't really think

comparing what we do or competing with other brands is a good use of our time when we have so much to achieve, so far to go and so many women to inspire towards active living.

BK: It is understandable that you have confidence, given your successes in the women's activewear industry. Did you always have that confidence?

LJ: I believe that success builds confidence. Am I more confident today then I was when I started Lorna Jane? I hope so! Have I always had a belief in myself, and my ability to make good decisions? I think I will have to say, yes.

But let's put it into perspective. When I first started Lorna Jane, the decisions I had to make were so much smaller, so I had the confidence to make them. Because I built my business slowly, from a couple of orders a week, to taking a small space in a fitness centre to finally opening my own store, I had the luxury of making good and bad decisions along the way without breaking the bank.

Character as well as confidence is built from the lessons learnt in those early days in business, and over time we learn how to make more good decisions than bad and I believe, become more confident.

BK: Is there anyone that you have looked at, that has really inspired you?

LJ: I am inspired by people who are not afraid to be themselves. The Steve Jobs story is inspiring because with all his idiosyncrasies, Steve remained true to his belief of putting amazing technology into people's lives. I think the success of Lorna Jane is hugely based on the fact that we are an authentic brand with a real story and a real person who lives and breathes the philosophy of the brand. We don't try to be like someone else or another brand. We strive to make amazing activewear and inspire women to move, nourish, and believe in themselves every day.

BK: What impact did the GFC (global financial crisis) have on your business?

LJ: The GFC was a challenging time for all businesses and we certainly had to take stock and look closely at the future plans for our business, but overall I think it provided Lorna Jane with opportunities to grow. We were still a small to medium-size business at the time and our exposure to the slowing of the economy was minimal.

We were just about to embark on a growth strategy so to do this at a time when most businesses were slowing their growth and even closing stores gave us incredible access to retail positions that otherwise would not have been available to us. We stayed true to our core values and continued to offer our customers a brand experience that was relevant but also offered them the fit and quality they could depend on.

BK: What are your views on debt in your business and life?

LJ: My views on debt are the same in business as they are in my personal life … never live beyond your means. It is a simple philosophy but it has served my well.

BK: What is the best client, customer or supplier lesson you have had?

LJ: I am constantly listening and learning from my customers … they are my inspiration and a huge part of the reason why I love what I do.

One of the main reasons that I started opening Lorna Jane concept stores was because I wanted to give my customers a unique experience. I wanted to make sure that when they purchased their Lorna Jane activewear their experience would be as close as possible to meeting me personally – which is what had happened in my first store, as I worked the shop floor everyday.

Interacting with your customers is the best way to learn how to improve and evolve your product and I still love to go into stores and meet the amazing women that love and support our brand.

I have customers who have turned their lives around because they have been inspired by our brand philosophy. Others who have been inspired to follow their passion and start their own business because they have read my story. There are so many customers' stories and experiences, but I guess my lesson is that if you follow your dreams and inspire others to do the same then they will inspire you in return.

BK: What is the worst client, customer or supplier lesson you have had?

LJ: Quite honestly, I am sitting here trying to think of one and nothing comes to mind. I am sure there are days when I read a negative comment on Facebook or a supplier has let me down or a staff member has disappointed me, but I don't hold onto that stuff. And trust me, with a business the size of Lorna Jane things can go wrong every day … you just learn to cope with it and keep moving forward.

I never let the negative things that can happen in life allow me to take my focus off what we are trying to achieve at Lorna Jane. Yes, crappy things happen to all of us, but my motto is kick them aside and keep moving forward.

'I think the success of Lorna Jane is hugely based on the fact that we are an authentic brand with a real story and a real person who lives and breathes the philosophy of the brand. We don't try to be like someone else or another brand. We strive to make amazing activewear and inspire women to move, nourish, and believe in themselves every day.'

BK: Is there one thing that you think that anybody who wants to succeed in business should definitely not forget?

LJ: Never forget why you started the business in the first place. Sometimes the daily grind and the complexities of actually running a business can be overwhelming and all-consuming. You started your business because you had a dream … my advice is never lose sight of that dream and do everything possible to achieve it.

BK: What impact does a business of that size have on your family life?

LJ: I think to successfully run a business there really can be no divide between business life and family life … not in my case anyway.

I am lucky enough to have built a brand with my husband that represents the way that we live our life. So whether we are talking about new concepts for Lorna

Jane or planning a weekend away it is not too much different … we are both just as passionate about work as we are about play.

Running your own business is demanding and it is important that you love what you do so that you don't start resenting the time you need to invest, especially in the early days. As your business grows and you get more staff hopefully you can spend more time outside of your business working on future planning and new concepts.

Both my husband and I are very hands-on in our business, and we love the interaction with our staff and our customers. We still go to the office every day and are quite often the first to arrive and the last to leave. Not all businesses are the same but this works for us, and it is what makes us happy and our business successful.

BK: What are your future plans, what are your personal future plans, what are your goals for Lorna Jane?

LJ: My professional and personal goals are pretty much the same: I want to continue to inspire and encourage women all over the world to live a more active life. We create great activewear but we also champion active living through all of our channels, whether it be through one of our stores, online, or through digital media such as Facebook, Instagram and Twitter; and we encourage our audience to move their bodies every day, nourish from the inside out and believe in themselves.

This is what drives me forward every day – the belief that I really can make a difference to the women that support Lorna Jane by giving them the tools to live their best life through active living.

'I never let the negative things that can happen in life allow me to take my focus off what we are trying to achieve at Lorna Jane. Yes, crappy things happen to all of us, but my motto is kick them aside and keep moving forward.'

BK: What are your passions outside your business?

LJ: My business and personal life are so intimately intertwined it is honestly a little hard to separate them. I work with my husband and we promote our personal philosophy for life – Move Nourish Believe – within our company and to our customers.

This philosophy encompasses so many of my personal passions that I guess

I can only answer this question honestly by first letting you know that I do not differentiate between passions within and outside of my business … my passions are my passions and they are all-inclusive.

I am passionate about being fit and healthy, and anything to do with these two subjects interests me. I love to try a new exercise concept, read about breakthroughs in sports or nutrition and collect healthy recipes absolutely every day. I am a constant reader and my perfect day would most definitely include finding a quiet corner to flip through a chapter or two of my latest captivating novel or inspirational biography.

I love to travel, I love to run, I love spending time with my family and friends, I love collecting and sharing inspirational quotes, I love work, I love the weekends, I love inspiring meetings, I love customer feedback, I love time with my dog, and I love designing activewear. I guess what I am trying to say is I love what I do. I have designed a life that enables me to wake up every day and appreciate the fun, the lesson and the sense of achievement in everything that I do.

'I guess my lesson is that if you follow your dreams and inspire others to do the same, then they will inspire you in return.'

John Cutler

Bespoke Tailor – J H Cutler Pty Ltd

'The best thing about the business is the opportunity to get to know and understand and relate to a whole raft of people you'd never meet otherwise.'

John Cutler is a fourth generation bespoke tailor having been in business in Sydney for more than a hundred and twenty-eight years. The firm has strong links to London's Savile Row and its client list includes a diversity of discerning clientele, locally and internationally. A gentleman and a businessman, the belief that a good bespoke tailor has to have an element of a servant's heart has been integral to his success.

www.cutlerbespoke.com

Interview

BRETT KELLY: So, John, how did you and your family get into the art of tailoring?

JOHN CUTLER: My great, great grandfather, Joseph Handel Cutler, was an engineer from Staffordshire, England. He decided that his business was no longer economically viable and he had heard about a gold rush in Ballarat, Australia. So he packed up his family, his wife and two boys and his wife's sister, and they hopped on a ship in 1861, *The Donald McKay*, and came to Melbourne. They travelled on to Ballarat where he worked with one of the big companies on the goldfields as an engineer. They had a house there and so forth, even a family plot in the old Ballarat cemetery.

He had a son also named Joseph Handel Cutler who came to Australia with him. He was the eldest of two boys and six years of age at the time. Schooling in Ballarat was pretty rough in the 1860s. He followed in his mother's passion – she was a dressmaker; he decided he wanted to become a tailor, and left Ballarat for Sydney. It was a bit unusual, but maybe it had something to do with family. I don't know, maybe to get away from the old man? Do his own thing? So he hopped on a Cobb & Co. coach up to Sydney. He worked for a while and then started his own business in 1884 at 70 King Street. The name of the company was J H Cutler – his name, Joseph Handel Cutler.

BK: And where does the Handel come from? From the composer?

JC: Yes. At school they called me the musical poet: I'm John Handel Lawson Cutler. So I got the Handel as well. But it is John, rather than Joseph. I don't know where it originally came from, but it goes back prior to my great, great grandfather in the family history.

BK: So how old was he when he trained in Sydney to become a tailor?

JC: He was a teenager. In those days, apprenticeships normally started at fourteen, fifteen, sixteen. I don't exactly know how old he was, but I know he died in 1931 and he was seventy-four. So he would have been pretty young when he did an apprenticeship and had the confidence and ability to open his own business. I've actually got some photos looking down King Street taken in 1884 from York Street. There's a man crossing the road with a peg leg and an old cart with the wheel off. It was like a Wild West town.

'I thought university was a waste of time for me …
So I left school at sixteen and worked for two years …'

BK: So then he handed the tradition down to his son and then on to you?

JC: No. His son was Leslie Frederick. His son was Bruce Lawson and I am John Handel Lawson. I'm fourth generation: great grandfather, grandfather and father.

BK: You were saying before that you started in Sydney at fifteen or sixteen?

JC: I was sixteen when I left school. I went to Sydney Grammar School in the first year of the Wyndham Scheme where it went from five years to six years, but you could leave after four if you were doing something like a trade. The sixth year in the Wyndham Scheme was originally for people who were going to university.

BK: And you knew you wanted to be a tailor?

JC: I thought university was a waste of time for me. I was already making the occasional waistcoat for my teachers and was working Saturdays in the shop. So I left school at sixteen and worked for two years – half a day in the shop and half a day in the workroom. Then, when I was eighteen, I sold my motorbike and my drum kit and bought a ticket on the Castel Felice and went to England.

BK: How long did the boat trip take in those days?

JC: Five and a half weeks via the Panama.

BK: How long did you spend in England and what were you doing there?

JC: Three years. I was eighteen when I left and I came back on my twenty-first birthday.

BK: So in England, you worked for Dormeuil, selling fabrics?

JC: Dormeuil Frères. It's a big fabric warehouse, weaver and so forth, selling fabric all around the world to the tailoring trade. I worked through all the departments from export to home trade to patterns to design, and through that I got to know a lot of the tailors in London. I also attended the renowned Tailor and Cutter Academy in Gerrard Street in Soho. I graduated with a diploma in cutting gentlemen's tailor-made garments. And I came back into the family business. I became the head cutter at twenty-three and took over the business when I was twenty-seven.

BK: What did your father do then? Did he stay in the business?

JC: My dad had heart problems and he was happy to retire. He was sixty-two.

BK: OK. So in that situation, did you continue to pay him? Did you have to buy the business or did he just walk out one day and leave you to it?

JC: I was married with a child by then and a small family tailoring business was not big enough. I also have a brother and he was in the business as well and it was not big enough for three families. So it was either a matter of me taking over the business or me leaving the business and setting up on my own.

Luckily, my grandfather had bought 7 Bligh Street in 1932 at the height of the Depression for £3 000, so that was in the family. We occupied that building for fifty years until 1982. My dad had turned the building into a family company. He sold it to form a family company for $80 000, so when we ended up selling when dad retired, we sold the building.

It gave him $80 000 and then it was divided into four. Quarter for mum, quarter for him, quarter for me and quarter for my brother. That gave him enough money to invest and to retire. They also owned their house in Pymble and they sold that and moved to a retirement place.

BK: So you're twenty-seven, you've got a business, a wife and a child?

JC: Yes. My brother was also working with me, but he is a painter, an artist and that's where his heart and love was so I ended up swapping my share of the building for his share of the business. That gave him enough money to go and buy a house and …

BK: Do his painting?

JC: Get himself off the bill. Unfortunately, as happens in life, later on, he had two or three children and his wife left him and she ended up with 80% of the building. He now lives in a retirement village up in the mountains.

BK: Does he still paint?

JC: Yes. He has had a different life. I got the business, which had a decent overdraft and everything, and it was sink or swim! So that's how I started.

BK: So how did you find your first bunch of clients? Obviously, you had some clients from your dad's work?

JC: We'd already been around for a hundred years. Perhaps not quite, but a good number of years.

BK: So you had a good brand, you were well known.

JC: We had a good brand locally. A good reputation. I trained in England so I had that sort of kudos, but really, you sink or swim depending on what you produce.

BK: Absolutely. What's the key to finding a good customer and keeping them? Obviously, your business has retained customers for over a hundred years.

JC: I believe you're only as good as the last suit you made. You can't rely on or dwell on history. It's nice to have, but in the end, the client is coming because they want something of a particular quality and it is of value to them. You have to be able to produce the goods. Tailoring is a very personal business, you know. You get someone in the fitting room without their trousers on – I don't care whether it's the prime minister or the barrow boy. It's pretty much a leveller, and you'll find that in tailoring, in bespoke tailoring, it's a bit like being a doctor. It's a bit like being a father confessor.

People will tell you a lot of things, about their problems, what's going on in the world, you know. It's quite an eye opener so you get to know people on a pretty personal level. All sorts of people. You get to know a lot of public figures on another side, behind their guard. In fact, in a sense, you're creating that guard, the armour that you wear out. My job is to turn dreams into reality. I believe that a good tailor, a good bespoke tailor, has to have an element of a servant's heart. I believe that my job is to fulfill a commission – not to put something up and say here, come and buy this. It's a matter of not pandering to, but fulfilling the desires of my clients. And the only way you can do that is to get into their head. It's psychology. It's a matter of finding out who they are, what they want, why they want it, how they came to be there.

I've just got a natural way of getting on with people. It's pretty easy for me to ascertain where they want to fit in terms of their appearance. Some of them will ask me to design things for them, others will have their own ideas, others don't care. So, if they're happy with me, they'll stay with me.

'My job is to turn dreams into reality. I believe that a good tailor, a good bespoke tailor, has to have an element of a servant's heart.'

BK: What's the oldest client or the longest client, multi-generational client, that you've had?

JC: Three or four generations, city and country.

BK: What's the thing between length of people?

JC: I'm making at the moment, I have been making for about ten years – it's a lovely story actually – for a fellow by the name of Warwick Smith. He was a federal parliamentarian from Hobart, then was number two or three in the Macquarie Bank under Alan Moss. David Clarke was a very good client of mine as was Alan Moss. Anyway, there was an article written in an airline magazine recently, and his mother, in a retirement village, got hold of it and immediately phoned him and said, 'Warwick, you have to go and see this John Cutler,' and he said, 'Why is that, mother?' 'Because your father and your grandfather all had their suits made by Cutlers.' He said, 'Is that right? I have been going to see John Cutler for the past ten years!' So he has actually written one of the testimonials for my up-coming book, and it's a wonderful testimonial. A nice one where he called me an avuncular character, which means I treat my clients as if I was their uncle.

BK: So when you look at the business and you look at the fashion trends and the things that affect you, so much has changed in so many businesses. Why have you been able to maintain and grow your business notwithstanding all of that change over the last hundred years?

JC: When we had our centenary in 1984, I had a big dinner with a lot of clients. I had one-time Justice of the High Court of Australia, Anthony Larkins, as the after-dinner speaker. He had a great sense of humour, a great guy and wore a monocle – a real character. Bruce Stannard, who you may know as the editor of *Australian Business Monthly* magazine, was MC for the night. I asked my father why he thought most family businesses go out in their third generation. He said, 'The first one has the vision and the drive. His son catches a bit of that. The third one, it's a bit remote …'

BK: Privilege.

JC: He sees the money, he blows it. That's the general pattern. So I said, 'How come, Dad, when you think about it, why have we lasted for four generations?' And he said several things. One of them is that each succeeding generation had a genuine passion. And secondly, the retiring generation, on retiring, totally left the business alone. And I remember with my father, the day he retired, he went to the door of the shop, he turned around and he said, 'I will never put my foot inside this door uninvited and I will never discuss business unless you ask me.' They are the words that my father said when he retired.

BK: Very interesting.

JC: And so he said, 'I have enough confidence in you for you to do what is right.'

He said, 'The world is changing from an older generation trying to rule the roost – but their ideas don't change with the community …'

BK: So they end up out of touch?

JC: And they become irrelevant. He said, 'If you want to turn this business into a jean shop or a jean factory and you feel that is the way forward, I would be happy for you to do that. I've done what I can. I'm out of here now. It's all yours.' And then he said, 'Don't ever think that you own this business.' He said, 'This is a family business, you have a long-term lease. The same as I did and my father. And a duty to care for the past.' So there are three good reasons.

BK: So, to the future, do you have a son or any children that would want to come into the business?

JC: I have four children. I have a daughter, Rachel, who is thirty-six. She is married with four boys under twelve, so she has her hands full. She is quite creative. She has made some children's clothes and things and sold them at markets. I have a son, Toby, thirty-two, who is a barista, coffee maker and cook. Another son, Simon, is in hospitality. He is twenty-nine. He actually ran the cellar at Manly Pavilion. He is now working for a beer company called Murray's who are just starting a beer café in Manly. He'll be managing director there at that age, which is fantastic. He never really had a passion for clothing. I have another daughter, Charlotte, who is thirteen and at Blue Mountains Grammar School.

BK: So she could be able …

JC: Maybe the next generation is a girl. I'd be quite open to that. But I don't put any pressure on her. Her mother is a magistrate, law right through her family for generations – her father was a Supreme Court judge, grandfather was a Supreme Court judge – and she's headed that way. Charlotte probably feels a bit pressured about that way or my way. I always just say, 'Sweetheart, do whatever you want to do.' She loves singing, she loves acting. She might end up at NIDA or anything. We'll wait and see. She's a very talented and creative girl.

BK: Yes.

JC: Anyway, what I have done, because I do believe in passing things on, I am imparting as much knowledge as I can to my protégé, Sam Hazelton. He has been with me for three years and he is absorbing the day-to-day activities, what makes the whole thing tick.

BK: Teamwork, yes. Now for you, I guess most of the people I have spoken to that are over fifty that have great businesses, their word on retirement is that they are never going to retire because their business is an extension of their great passion. What are your plans? Could you ever see yourself retiring?

JC: No, even if there was a windfall and I had a lot of money, I would still want to make clothes for my clients and my friends, they're like family. I still have the passion for it and I still want to do it. I might do it in a different way, more leisurely. I wouldn't want to continue doing it with commercial pressures because that would kill you in the end. I mean that's what's really changed, what it takes to run a business these days. You know, with all the compliancing and the employment and all that, it's so, so hard. So I have actually taken steps to divest myself of some of those responsibilities. For example, I've got my foreman in my workroom to start his own business. He now employs the tailors and I commission him or contract him to do the work so I don't have the responsibility. I mean, he is twenty years younger than me and he wants things to go on, so it is actually a very, very great story. He came to me for work experience some twenty-two years ago from Cabramatta High School.

BK: Is he Vietnamese?

JC: He's Chinese Cambodian. He lived through Pol Pot. His whole family lived in Phnom Penh and they were forced out into the killing fields because they became known. Through that whole process, one of his family was killed. He told me a story one day that they were walking down this wooden track in the middle of the night going somewhere, the whole family, single file, and his younger brother stopped to have a piss in the bush. A Khmer Rouge soldier was hiding there and he was going to shoot him and kill him. The father went to him and begged for his son's life. He let him go in the end, you know. Bloody tough life.

In the end, they escaped over the mountains to Vietnam and they settled there. His father had a business there. At a very young age, Leng started working in a factory, in the workroom, on shirts and trousers. He learnt some cutting and a bit of sewing. The father died young and one of the brothers came to Australia and then brought the family. They were refugees.

Leng spent a few years at Cabramatta High to learn English. He came to me for work experience for a week or two. I was really impressed with his attitude. Totally different to young people I'd seen around. On leaving school, he came back and said, 'Hey, remember me?' and I said, 'Yes, would you like a job?' So I put him with my best tailor and he went right through, he became a coat maker a trouser maker. And then he was a foreman, and he now runs his own workroom, runs my workroom, which is in his own name.

BK: So the hardest thing about a business today, you think, is the compliance, the regulation, the laws. What would you change?

JC: In my sort of business, which is a creative business, you've got to have a passion. They think because they have a certain talent, they will be able to make it. But to successfully run a small business like mine, people don't realise that you actually have to be multiskilled. You have got to get on with people. You have to be able to make people feel comfortable and then you've got the book work and all that. You know, if two tailors get together to start a business, one of them is full-time doing things other than sewing.

BK: Just administration and compliance and answering the phone …

JC: Sam and I arrive at 8.30 am and, you know, at 11.30 am or 12.00 pm, we're still sitting at the computer trying to go through emails and ordering and doing stuff.

BK: Other than making a suit.

JC: If you are a small business and you can't afford to employ too many people, the community is such now that with all the legalities and counselling and all that, you have to have experts working with you or you can outsource it, otherwise you'll end up with a lot of shortcomings.

BK: What's the best thing about your business?

JC: The people. The best thing about the business is the opportunity to get to know and understand and relate to a whole raft of people you'd never meet otherwise. It is a leveller and it's right across the board. Some people spend a lot of money on something for a particular occasion, like a wedding, and then there are people at the other end of the socio-economic scale. And everything in between.

BK: How much travel do you do and is that a part of keeping abreast of the changes?

JC: I get to travel overseas a lot. I was in London for three years, then when I came back, I said to myself that I would go overseas to Europe or somewhere at least once every eighteen months. Once a year was pushing it a bit, particularly when I was in my twenties.

BK: Yes. You're busy and you've got kids. So, do you still go over and do buying and look at cloth?

JC: Now, I go more often. I'd like to go a couple of times a year. I go to different places because I have good clients in Vancouver or elsewhere in Canada or in the States. Most of the Asian clients, for example from Indonesia and Japan, come to me, but I also have clients in London.

BK: And do you take formal sittings in London or in the US?

JC: London, mainly. In Savile Row there are actually fabric warehouses that are in a building and they have within their complex, three or four fitting rooms. They're called journeyman tailors from the Midlands or Scotland. But, of course, they have to use their own cloth.

BK: Tell me about your vicuna overcoat. How did this gentleman come to you?

JC: He's a client from Vancouver. He was a brewer who came to Australia. He was employed by Rosemount and he ended up the managing director of Rosemount and Penfolds under Oakley. He used to take the top Rothbury and Penfolds stuff over to America and sell it.

BK: So, what is vicuna?

JC: Vicuna is an animal, like a llama. They live in the Andes, in Peru, mainly very high up and they just take the fur from under the neck, the softest bits. There's actually a whole ceremony, a round-up ceremony, a shearing ceremony with all the local herdsmen.

BK: And where is it woven?

JC: Well, the fleece is bought by the top mills around the world, in England and Italy, by Zegna, Dormeuil etc and they weave it. They also mix it with cashmere or with wool. There is actually a worsted, spun, pure vicuna suiting. But we are talking about three or four thousand dollars …

BK: A metre?

JC: A metre.

BK: So, this coat. This gentleman says this is what he would like. Had he seen the material before?

JC: He didn't know anything about it. He came in and said, 'I want an overcoat. I travel to America a lot for business. I go in the winter and need to keep warm. I need an overcoat.' He said, 'Maybe cashmere.' I said, 'Yes, we could make you a cashmere overcoat, but then we could make you a vicuna overcoat.' And he said, 'What's that?' You see, money was not an issue. I purchased three lengths in 1984 from Dormeuil for our centenary – a camel colour, a navy blue and a black. They had asked, 'What would you like for your centenary?' and I said that I would like the opportunity to buy three overcoat lengths of pure vicuna, because I knew it was difficult to buy at the time. I knew they had some because I used to sell it for them. They had it tucked away in a bank vault in London. They ended up getting it out and selling three lengths at a reasonable price. So, I had that tucked away for my superannuation.

BK: Just looking for an opportunity to make something of it.

JC: Finally, along came my client, and he said, 'Is this the best?' I said, 'Yes, it's the best.' Then he let me come up with designs and things. It was the navy blue one he liked. Then I approached him and said, 'This is something I always wanted to do. I always wanted to make a garment as though machines didn't exist. The way it was done a hundred years ago. How would that be?' He said, 'That would be wonderful, go for it.' No money was ever discussed. Every time he came, he just handed me his credit card and said, 'Just take some more money.' It ended up at $50 000. And he was so impressed with it all in the end that he ordered a second one about a year later, a camel coloured one.

BK: Has he ever told you what it's like to own such a unique garment?

JC: His whole wardrobe is full of my clothes. And he takes great joy in waking up every morning, going to the wardrobe and deciding what he's going to wear that day. You know, he'd have some seven or eight lovely cashmere sports jackets, a dozen suits, shirts, shoes, you know, he's just a convert.

BK: Great client–

JC: Disciple.

'Don't be scared of mistakes. You've got to step out and try things and do things and if they don't work, you know not to do it again.'

BK: When you look back at the history of the work you've done here for so long, what are the best things that have happened that you remember. What are the lessons that you've learned? Often, people tell me that the lessons they have learned are often from the worst things that have happened.

JC: You're right, you learn by your mistakes …

BK: Absolutely. So, if you are talking to Sam or a young guy who is going to go into this type of business, what would you say to them?

JC: Don't be scared of the mistakes. You've got to step out and try things and do things and if they don't work, you know not to do it again. But, it could be in stepping out and doing something that does work …

BK: It changes everything.

JC: But this is your life, for the good, so don't be scared of taking that chance just because it mightn't work. It's probably a bit simplistic …

BK: But it's true, you cannot make tomorrow out of yesterday's answers.

JC: A lot of people have dreams and ideas and never follow them through.

BK: Yes, a sad way to live. Tell me a motto or a quote or a thought that best summarises your approach to life. What have you learned? Or even a recurring theme that inspires you to keep moving?

JC: I'm a very passionate person about what I do. I love cooking, you know. So I think that my bit of advice to someone like Sam is to follow your passions. For a young person who's going into this trade, if they don't start with passion, if that's not the theme …

BK: There is no future. No question. That brings to mind the great Steve Job's quote where they said to him, 'What's the secret of success?' And he said, 'You guys, you've got to be more passionate about it than anyone else because any rational person would give up because it's just so hard.'

JC: So have that passion and believe in what you're doing.

Collette Dinnigan

Fashion Designer – Collette Dinnigan

'*Follow your instinct no matter what anyone says …*'

A passionate, creative force, Collette Dinnigan has run a successful fashion business for several decades. With retail outlets and clients through Australia and overseas, she continues to take on challenge after challenge, most recently the international online environment. Her distinctive identity and reputation is exceptional and highly sought after.

www.collettedinnigan.com.au

Interview

BRETT KELLY: Collette, yours is a great story. How did it start?

COLLETTE DINNIGAN: My childhood was quite nomadic. I was born in South Africa where I lived until I was eight years old. Then I spent the next few years living and sailing on a yacht. We ended up settling in New Zealand when I was about nine and I went to school there.

I think having such a nomadic existence as a child made me impatient as a young adult. I had that Gypsy blood from a very early age, although I wanted to be a vet and ended up studying fashion. Fashion wasn't really my biggest desire, but fashion design was a three-year diploma and that was long enough for me.

I believe, from what I have heard since, that I was the one person in my year that they didn't think would be a fashion designer. There was a process of elimination – exams and practicals every year. The course starts out with twelve students, but ends up with eight or six. It was a very difficult course, very intense and not what people think.

There is a lot of history and a lot of business studies. I was so determined to prove everyone wrong and I did. Then, funnily enough, I was probably one of only two or three people out of everybody in that whole course who went on to make a career out of it.

BK: Was that because you're in a workshop type of work?

CD: Yes, that's what interested me. It is a craft, it is a journey, having an idea. Then there is something that I can touch and it is creative. I was also working on films. But in the nineties, when the government stopped the subsidies for the film industry, it was just a disaster. Everything fell apart and I had to do something, so I set up my own business.

I had actually worked for somebody before but it was always about copying what was overseas and that didn't even figure into my sensibility. It was quite extraordinary. It was not an idea that people saw through from a concept. So, to cut a very long story short, I started my lingerie business.

BK: What did you do first with the lingerie business?

CD: I designed a collection and then I took it to the USA to sell. I got some press but I wasn't very savvy at it, regardless it got a lot of attention. People started ordering from word of mouth and then I opened a store. I was across all aspects of the process, not just retail. I did the draping, the patterns, the cutting. I could sew a garment. I had basic skills in bookkeeping.

I see it now in a lot of students coming through who want to be fashion designers; they are not hands-on. They do not have the craft. They are not trained. I was very practical, but having a business was not something that I wanted necessarily.

'I think having such a nomadic existence as a child made me impatient as a young adult. I had that Gypsy blood from a very early age …'

BK: So, why lingerie?

CD: It's beautiful. Using silk fabrics and vintage laces and mixing both together. There was nothing in the marketplace like it. I approached department stores and different shops in Australia, but they wouldn't buy it as a lot of the care instructions were dry-clean only and they didn't think it would sell. That was seen as its downfall, it is always the same, but you need to do something that no-one else is doing. So if you've got an idea and you believe in it and you're passionate about it, do it. I then opened my own store in William Street, Paddington.

BK: What did your life look like at that point? Often when you start a business, you're cutting these things, you're sorting the fabric, you're building this product from the ground up, you're doing the catalogue, you're shooting it, you're trying to sell it, you're talking to department stores – what else were you doing at that time other than your business?

CD: I was in my twenties and I was working eighty to a hundred hours a week. My friends were having weekends and parties but I had no life outside work. I love my work and it is so frustrating because I employ so many people, and there are so many great positions in this company, but sometimes there is so little initiative, there is not the enthusiasm that I had. For many of the new generation it's about being right. It is so frustrating because I don't know if it is this generation or our workplace or technology, or what's happened, but they don't understand that you do not learn by always being right. You learn by making mistakes and the world becomes a bigger place because it opens you up to other opportunities.

BK: Many people that I've spoken to have said that they've learned much more from their mistakes than from their so-called successes. What is the biggest mistake that you've learned a lot from?

CD: I haven't fixed it yet! I am still trying to find the patience, but being privately owned, not having a board and not being a public company, I am not in a luxury position; there are disadvantages. It's very lonely being on your own in the business. However, when there is a global financial crisis or something occurs that will have impact on the market place, I am able to change the course of direction very quickly.

It frustrates people in here because they don't like change or interruptions or the extra effort to see it through, but that has been the key to the survival of our business. Whereas a lot of other companies either don't see it or aren't able to implement changes quickly enough. I guess that has kept me on my toes. It has made me work very hard because, of course, you're mentoring everyone through it. But I've been very loyal to my staff through all of these different global crises. Economically, it's affected our American market, but I've never let staff go. Sometimes I think that is probably a big mistake too, because ultimately it affects the cashflow of the business.

BK: So the biggest challenge in the business is attracting and developing good people?

CD: Yes. I think the biggest challenge is having a business like mine in Australia. It's all international now because Australia is moving its manufacturing offshore. It's a dying business here.

BK: You do all of your manufacturing here?

CD: The main line, yes. Environmentally and ethically I work as conscientiously as I can, but it is a very costly country to manufacture in. It's not competitive now our dollar is stronger. There are a lot of things against us. I find that to be a country that is the new frontier and relatively young in white settlement brings with it a lot of opportunity. We've got a great backyard to test in but ultimately the market's not here, there's not the population, there isn't the tradition of generations of people who have craftsmanship in my industry.

BK: As you try to grow the business, are you looking at employing people overseas?

CD: It is a very costly process, and it is difficult, especially at the luxury end of the market we're in. What I am doing is that I'm looking more at licensing opportunities and online. A more globalized approach, where there's a third party manufacturing. It's something that I probably would not have done many years ago, but we're still able to deliver a good product at a better price.

So now I have my mainline brand, for which everything is designed and cut and manufactured here. Then I have my Collette by Collette Dinnigan line, which is a lower price point, but younger, more daytime, contemporary. I design all of that here, but it's manufactured mostly in India and China. I spend quite a lot of time travelling to these countries and factories to work with them because I have long relationships with them all. These collections are sold internationally and nationally to the likes of NET-A-PORTER and David Jones.

Then I have my lingerie brand and I've just done a bridal lingerie collection as well, which is up-market and that's also outsourced to another factory but I still design it all here. Then I've got a few other projects that are going with other companies in different areas.

'You need to do something that no-one else is doing.'

BK: Baby clothes?

CD: Yes, I am relaunching Collette Dinnigan Enfant next year in David Jones.

BK: Now, you are selling on NET-A-PORTER, but how big is the online opportunity for your business?

CD: I think it will be huge. On the first of August 2012 we launched our own Australian site on which we're selling all the brands, including swimwear. We launched the swimwear in September, starting with Australia, but we will also be going live to the world. It will be interesting to see what happens because most of the searches and hits we're getting are from international customers. We're doing three live websites. One will be in US dollars from America, one is in UK pounds and the other will be for Asia. So each of them is specific to its market in terms of duties and taxes.

BK: Are you excited by the experience you can give your customer online? Is it a passion for you?

CD: Yes! I've got very different ideas to how other websites are run, so I'm hoping we can deliver it all, but the team is very excited by it. There are a lot backroom things that you need to make sure work properly.

BK: Is all the technology being built for you?

CD: Yes, I've got third parties involved.

BK: You've mentioned the global financial crisis, but talk to me about the cashflow cycle in this type of business and the challenge that presents, particularly in a creative context where you are trying to deliver something beautiful, but the cost of doing different versions of it might be substantial. How do you manage the cashflow of a private company?

CD: Having retail stores is important but the most crucial thing is to have a good product. It must be good quality, value for money and building a brand that people want to buy with excellent customer service. And regardless of everything else, you know, we've had bad weeks and good weeks in retail, but ultimately, what we do is a very good product and requires a lot of attention to detail – it's nurtured through. Our quantities are low in production so it's relatively exclusive for a very good price.

BK: How big is a typical range?

CD: Probably a hundred pieces, but then there are some things that we only make two or three of, for example, the exclusive, beaded, high price ticket numbers for the world. The maximum we ever do would be two hundred of a print dress for the world. And we label everything – one of two hundred and two of two hundred and so on – so everyone knows exactly how many were produced.

BK: Are you making couture for individuals?

CD: Not really. With bridal, we have. And we will sometimes do one-off pieces for very special events, but they are always based on something in the collection.

BK: You have built a strong personal profile that has enhanced your brand. How has that come about?

CD: I don't know. I never set out to have a huge profile. I don't think it is just about every fashion designer being a celebrity. I think maybe ten years ago it was like that, but I think now it's more that people have reached a certain level of recognition in their industry like Neil Perry or Marc Newson. People who do great design and great things: they have longevity and they create and they are recognised. I think that's what's happened.

There is always a lot of intrigue about me being female, too. I guess it's also having a family and running a business and being creative. I'm not in a normal situation where I would have a business partner and I'm just being the creative, which ultimately I would love.

Everything has been very instinctual, but it's been difficult to do both because essentially I am doing two really big full-time jobs.

BK: So tell me about that. You are doing the creative work, you are the head designer and you are running the business. Do they feed off each other? Do you find it a positive experience working on it all together, or do you find it a lot of work?

CD: I find the business side a lot of work now. It would be easier with a smaller team. I find the emailing side of everything so frustrating.

BK: The internal email or external or both?

CD: Both, but mostly internal. For example, I will ask the young ones here, the eighteen- or twenty-six-year-olds if they've spoken to someone and they'll say, yes. So then I'll ask them what they said and they'll say they're waiting to hear back. That's not speaking. You speak. You pick up the phone and get an answer.

'People who do great design and great things: they have longevity and they create and they are recognised.'

BK: I was with a really great guy the other day and he has essentially banned internal email. He says, 'Get up off your stool and talk to someone. If they are not there, then send them an email.' He thinks that the power of the telephone is not appreciated in human interaction.

CD: I just find it so frustrating. That's why I think the business side of it is actually harder for me now than it was years ago. I am constantly triple-checking to get to the bottom of things, even externally on email. People don't think. They don't stop to read it before they send it and it's gone. Whereas if something is verbal, you get the reaction of the person on the other end of the phone. So it's very difficult but what do you do?

BK: So is it age? In our business, I find that it seems to come down to values.

CD: It is not necessarily age, but I find that an older person wouldn't see speaking as an email.

BK: How many people are in the business now?

CD: A hundred.

BK: That's a big business

CD: Yes. I think a lot of businesses, even very good communication businesses like PR and marketing, find the same level of frustration in not being able to get efficient communication, team camaraderie, talking about solutions, problems – they all keep to their own department. Rely on email too much ...

BK: Do you do group meetings?

CD: Yes, we have management meetings once a week and then all departments do meetings in the mornings, but it's difficult. Before it was just a course of business and in the early days it was with a bottle of wine and plates of cheese and everybody would have a drink and they'd chew the fat and talk about everything. You know you'd have to go to your computer and probably put all that code in and that was kind of a chore.

But things have changed. I think it's a balance between backing up and having a backup, but keeping everything in a way that's much more efficient and it's better for the environment without paper. But on the other hand, our business is about touching, feeling, communication, creativity and customer service and loyalties and values. It's upsetting to invest so much time and then if somebody finds it too frustrating and they don't want to put themselves through it they leave and you think, 'How much more time do I invest in training?'

BK: So you would suggest putting an issue out there as something to discuss and not being personally attached to it so that you can work it out? Often we see people aligning themselves so tightly with an idea that they can't cope with any different view. I imagine design is an interesting training for business because, so often, what you would sketch might look very different when you try and make it. Is testing and changing a big part of your design process?

CD: Yes, it's a process of elimination. A lot of it is getting it right, it's attention to detail. I don't think it's a good business model because our salary components are so high. Also, the amount of time we have to spend on such little turnover. For instance, we probably need to make a thousand dresses to be truly profitable. But ten years ago, when the dollar was a lot lower, export value was a lot higher because our production costs were attractive, especially to America. So even though their economy is in terrible shape at the moment, although they are picking up a little, it's still not attractive because our prices are too high regardless.

BK: I guess many Australians don't realise the impact of the dollar. They just think it's great because you can have a more affordable holiday overseas, but for innovative businesses that are trying to export, it is just ridiculous.

CD: It is. It's very hard to survive. There's very little support for an industry like ours from the government, and just look at retail now. I don't know if you have driven up Oxford Street, Paddington, but the shops are empty. There aren't the local businesses and the smaller boutiques. We used to have cobblers, we used to have delicatessens and now it's high street brands and customers can buy them in shopping centres. I think our councils have done a really bad job of not keeping and conserving the retail and arts environment.

BK: You mean making it an attractive place to come?

CD: Yes, especially Paddington, for boutique shoppers. That's where I had my store, in William Street. I was so pro keeping that street as it was but they changed the whole area and it's like you could be walking through a desert now – shop after shop is empty. And even now I think, why not talk to the landlords. Why don't councils give them a break and say: 'If you redo your facade or do this to restore it, we will give you a tax break on it and a subsidy …'?

BK: You're quite right. Why would you go to that street if you can drive and park at a large shopping centre? Especially if the parking is not as easy on a strip, like in Paddington; there has to be a unique and attractive offer. But one of things I have observed in retail is that the luxury brands are doing better than they've ever done before. Globally, they are making bigger profits than I have ever seen. Do you think the world is coming back to quality and uniqueness and a customer experience that it is really something else?

CD: You know I do, I think most definitely, but there is also a lot of people can't afford to buy, either. And the gap is growing and that worries me. There really are a lot of extraordinarily wealthy people and those people aren't as environmentally conscious as you would believe. I don't know about their values either because we have a third world that really needs to be pulled out of poverty, but pushing prices down a bit as a manufacturer does not do that. It doesn't encourage them to get their own ecosystems and their own environments back up and running effectively. They just push down further and further with very little return for so much hard work. It doesn't matter how wealthy or poor people are, everybody wants a bargain.

BK: Have retailers effectively trained their consumers to be that animal?

CD: I don't think department stores have the luxury, as I talked about before, that a small business has where they can change and implement new systems quickly; they are still old school. They haven't moved with the times as quickly as we have. And there hasn't been the customer service you need. I think they need to clear stock and customers are relying on that. They are not shopping elsewhere because they are used to getting everything at 50% off. It is affecting smaller businesses that don't discount so then they are forced to either close or discount. And with our product, when we do limited editions, my thing is it is not so seasonal. It's a beautiful dress and we only made three of them. You know, we are not going to put it on sale after it has been in the store for three months.

BK: Is that a message you can get people to hear?

CD: I think most people do because we have customers that travel from overseas and will walk in and fall in love with it. A lot of it is occasion-wear. It's timeless in one way and it is still seasonal, but obviously at the end of the season we might be left with 5–10% of our stock and we will do a sale, usually to our VIPs first.

BK: So that position that you've taken, do you think there is a future in a return to small production and more exclusive quality?

CD: For our business, definitely. I don't think customers necessarily want to be wearing the same as everyone else. People want more individuality, more privacy, more personality. They don't want mass brands. Luxury now isn't about just an income, it's about quality customer service and can't-buy experiences. That's definitely changing at the customer service level: instead of giving a discount, we will give a gift to someone who is a good customer. They realise it is something very special and that they have been acknowledged for their loyalty to our business.

BK: How good is your database from a technology point of view?

CD: It's as good as the people that use it. That's the thing with all our technology, we have so much opportunity, especially online.

BK: Technology isn't a silver-bullet.

CD: It is actually a lot of how it's set up and the users.

'Luxury now isn't about just an income, it's about quality customer service and can't-buy experiences.'

BK: One of the most topical businesses today is Apple. They've grown to sixty-five thousand employees and they seem to be delivering a level of caring as well as a product that is extraordinary for the size and scale of what they do. What's interesting though is the comment that Johnny Ive, the chief designer, made on the death of Steve Jobs – about his sense of caring. Is this true in your experience? What I am finding is that the most frustrated business owners are the ones who really do care the most.

CD: Yes. I really, really care. I get upset, I get emotional. I get all of those things. It's not, as I read in the press, 'Collette is very difficult to work with' or 'she is a control freak'. As a customer, would you want me to be on some island having a pina colada in a hammock while a team of people run around and I don't touch the product? Would you want me to not be emotional about something that is not done properly? I really care and when we've got an idea and one person lets the team down and can't be wrong, it is so difficult. We all care, and the people that care are passionate and they show it. It is a creative business. I can't say I'm proud of it but I do get upset sometimes. I get annoyed with myself and wonder why I can't remove myself and be objective about the situation? I understand we'll never be 100%, but I don't strive for 90%, I strive for 100% on everything.

BK: But ultimately, these things go out with your name on them. The product is more than just a product, isn't it?

CD: It is. I care and I would not send it out the door if I thought it was inferior.

So, just because it has got my name on it, it is not even an option. If I don't think it is right, it won't go.

––––––––––––

'I don't strive for 90%. I strive for 100% on everything.'

BK: Let me ask you. You mentioned before that you are a woman running this business. For you, in terms of your experience, what's the difference between being a woman and being a man running this business?

CD: Well, I haven't worked in many other businesses so it is difficult to compare in this particular industry, you have a lot of females and a lot of very emotional people, a lot of creative people. If you were working, for example, in a law firm, you'd probably have a majority of males who had all done a similar degree so philosophically they'd all sit around a boardroom table with the same level of communication because they have the same basic tertiary education.

But in this business, you get a lot of women who are anything from sixty-five-year-olds down to eighteen-year-olds – some have experience, some haven't, some have had a tertiary education and some left after secondary school, some of them have a lot of craftsmanship experience and some have none. Running this kind of business, it would be great to have more men involved.

I always admire male friends who are in business. If they have problems and they're annoyed with their comrades at work, they go down to the pub and have a beer with them. They talk about sport and say, 'You're an idiot' and shake hands and they're off. Whereas females tend not to talk about it, they don't rationalise it. It's not an open table, it's not discussed, it's not objective, it's a grudge, it's held, it becomes a terrible kind of cancer that infests everything and when it's all too late they leave. And I find there is a lot of maintenance in that.

BK: Is this the great passion of your life? Could you see yourself doing anything else?

CD: Oh, I can see myself doing lots of things, but whatever I did I would definitely have to be using my hands and being creative. I could never see myself running a business or in a business management role or some kind of production capacity. I can only see myself as an ideas person or a creative person. What I would ultimately love is to have a business where you're just the brains, the creative energy and then everything is outsourced to manufacturers and somebody else takes over.

BK: A little bit like Apple?

CD: Yes.

BK: Did you ever imagine that the business would grow and develop in the way that it has? That it would be so successful?

CD: I can remember in my twenties being very frustrated by the world because I had so many ideas and nobody would buy them or listen to me. I thought I could do everything and I thought it would all happen in a year. And you know, twenty-five years later, I know I can't do anything in such a quick turnaround. So it's a whole pendulum swing to the other side. I feel like I have so much more to learn. I don't feel like I'm empowered with knowledge. Ultimately, and what I didn't expect, was being able to appreciate the simple things in life. It's funny, with all the opportunities I get given now and the private jets I get asked to fly in, the parties I want to go to – they're not the things that float my boat. Family is my priority.

BK: What are the things that most excite you?

CD: Well, my family and my friends. Actually having the time to make decisions. I haven't had time for so long to just do the simple things. For example, I got married a year ago and we haven't even ordered one wedding photo, we haven't even taken them off the memory stick. I find those things quite frustrating.

I like being organised in my home life. My work life is so cluttered and full of paraphernalia and memories and everything so I like home to be quite simple with just laughter and good food. I'm very environmentally conscious, very organic in my approach, not just to food, but the way that things happen in life. Business is pretty structured and there are a lot of formalities, even though it evolves in a creative way in the design room.

I have had so many great opportunities, met so many amazing people along the way, made amazing friends. I would never turn back the clock for that, the growing up process and the travel too, but now I just want simplicity. Especially since I'm having another baby. Last time I was back at work within three to four days and people were coming into the hospital and giving me folders of work to do. I don't want that to happen this time. I actually want to be woken up by a baby and know that I can sleep through until ten or eleven in the morning if I have to.

BK: So tell me about that. You're having a baby and you've had the benefit of all of this experience of life. Does that feel amazing in that it involves the

opportunity to say, 'OK, this is how I want it to be this time. Every time I do something again, I want to learn from last time, I want to do it better'?

CD: Yes. My husband and I feel very blessed because it's something that's kind of the icing on the cake. We didn't know if we'd be able to have children. I hadn't given up, but I felt a bit despondent after quite a few years of trying unsuccessfully. But ultimately, as you grow older, family and children are more important – you probably feel that too – it takes away your selfishness.

BK: There are huge personal development costs, though.

CD: I know, I mean it is hard work. It's not all the joy you might think. We had my husband's birthday in New Zealand on Monday and I took my father who is eighty-four and sometimes very grumpy. We also had my daughter and her friend and another family friend and we're at this beautiful restaurant having dinner and my dad was grumpy and wouldn't talk and I was fighting with my daughter – it was like the eighty-four-year-old and seven-year-old were behaving like three-year-olds and wouldn't eat their lunch!

But that's family, and it's hard, but ultimately it takes away that selfishness, it gives you the best joy and something else to think about. Like if it is really bad weather and it is school breakup time you don't think about your weekend, you think about your child, how are they going to get home, etc? Everything changes …

----

*'As you grow older, family and children are more important
– it takes away your selfishness.'*

BK: It changes your focus entirely, doesn't it?

CD: Yes. It gives you clarity. Unfortunately, my mother died about twenty years ago and she said to me, 'You'll only know what it is like to be a mother when you have your own children. You don't appreciate anything.' I hear that and it resonates with me … you will only appreciate what I do for you when you have your own children. It is such a huge investment.

BK: And what do you want in the future for your business?

CD: I guess a pared-down business development and production environment to a much more creative hub where I can get involved in other projects, not necessarily just fashion. They would all be similar in an artistic sense though, whether it is interior design or fabric design or extensions of things that I am passionate about.

BK: Have you got role models in your industry?

CD: I guess in the early days I looked at people and other fashion businesses but they're all European-based and the reality is now I have taken my focus away from them because you can't keep looking abroad. You have to look in your backyard and get your business solid and sound and structured here otherwise the business models don't apply to Australia when you have a much smaller market.

'My mother said to me, "You'll only know what it is like to be a mother when you have your own children. You don't appreciate anything."'

BK: Is there a smaller depth of talent?

CD: Yes. Everything. Australians and New Zealanders have to be more versatile now that they are relying on a smaller customer base. Their product has to be much more creative whereas you can go to America and it's much more generic, I feel. Online there is nothing special and with recessions and financial downturns, things really sift through and work out what is best. You see it in the restaurants. You see it in everything. Now, essentially, people will pay for good quality but they want value for money and good service.

BK: Do you have a motto or a quote or a thought that summarises your approach to life?

CD: There are lots of things but the most important thing for me is to follow my instinct no matter what anyone says. As I said, in the early days, I was frustrated because I wanted everything done so quickly. I probably told too many people my ideas and listened to too many other people until it confused me. I had too many influences. So I have ended up being quite basic.

The big motto I have in my life is to trust your instinct. I often focus on the quiet achievers who actually don't have much to say but sometimes have the simplest and some of the best ideas. It can actually make a huge difference.

James Erskine

Entrepreneur (Sports / Entertainment)
– Sports & Entertainment Limited

───

'… the thing is just go on, just go and do it. I think it's amazing when you decide that you're going to do something, somehow it happens. It just happens if you decide and you're determined.'

James migrated to Australia from London in 1979 to set up IMG (the International Management Group) in Australasia. In 1997 he started SEL (Sports & Entertainment Limited), extending the variety of services he offered. His rollcall of engagements is an international who's who and includes a plethora of legendary identities – Muhammad Ali, Greg Norman, Tiger Woods, Sir Jackie Stewart, Dame Kiri Te Kanawa, Clive James, Michael Parkinson, Captain Mark Phillips, Zara Phillips, Shane Warne, Andrew Hoy, Matthew Lloyd, Michael Lynagh, Todd Woodbridge and Matt Giteau. James transformed sports marketing and talent management across the region and beyond and has many a fascinating story to tell about the behind-the-scenes deals.

www.sel.com.au

Interview

BRETT KELLY: Most people in business describe managing people as their biggest challenge – attracting talent, developing it, retaining it. You've had an illustrious career managing people but what I think is fascinating about your story is that you've worked with the most talented people you can encounter. I'd love to start at the beginning. How did you become involved in talent management?

JAMES ERSKINE: It was the luckiest day. It was just pure chance. I had been a medical student at London University's Charing Cross Hospital failing with great success. In 1976 The Open Championship was at Royal Birkdale, which is where I am from. It was really hot, and my father, who was involved with the Open, asked me to go and help him with the crowd control. That was when I met Mark McCormack. I always was a mad keen golfer, and a bit of a golf historian – I liked the scores and records and I used to follow Arnold Palmer around when I was a kid of eight. He had won the Open at Royal Birkdale in 1961. I met Arnold again in 1976.

Anyway, it was there that Mark asked me if I were working for him, which three British golfers would I sign up? I said, 'That's easy. Nick Faldo, Sandy Lyle and a guy called Martin Foster.' He looked at me in a strange way – he had this funny way of getting a pen out of his jacket – and he said, 'Would you come and have lunch with me next Tuesday?' I didn't know what I was doing the following Tuesday, I didn't plan that much. I really wanted to go and play golf with my mates at Birkdale. The bottom line was, I met him and we did a funny deal. I eventually said, 'I'll work for you for six months. Don't pay me anything. I will tell you after six months if I want to stay and how much I want.' He said, 'That's a daft idea, I'm not going to do that.' So then he said to me, 'OK, what does a young doctor make?' So he paid me that. £2 200.

To be brutally honest, I had no idea what was involved in the sports management business. McCormack had Palmer, Nicklaus and Player, IMG was relatively small at the time – I think there were under twenty people worldwide.

My first assignment was to go to Jersey to see Tony Jacklin – he wasn't happy. They'd done a stupid deal about his commissions so I basically said, 'Tony, pay us our normal 25% because Jackie Stewart is paying us that, Jean-Claude Killy is paying us that and John Newcombe is paying us that. At the end of the day, if we don't generate enough money for you, I'll just give it back to you when I leave.'

I had not thought this was going to be a long-term career. I was staying in a flat with all these nurses and medical students and when I got home they said a Mark McCormack had been calling from America. I didn't take any notice of it because I couldn't afford to call America. Eventually, he got hold of me and said, 'Where the hell have you been? What happened with Tony Jacklin?' 'He was fine,' I said. 'He is going to pay us our normal 25%.' He said, 'He wants you to manage him worldwide.' So I said, 'Well, he didn't say that to me.' Then Mark said, 'Well, you better come over to our golf meetings in Cleveland, Ohio.' I didn't know where Cleveland, Ohio was. I'd never been to America. I didn't even own a suit at the time, I might have owned a a blazer. So he said, 'You better get a visa.' And off I went.

My father was a great raconteur, but he wasn't a great businessman. My maternal grandfather was a very good businessman, he'd had a substantial family textile business, but I had never wanted to get involved in it, too many rows in family business, but I suddenly realised that maybe I had a bit of business acumen. I sat at this meeting with all these golf executives – because IMG was mainly golf in those days and a bit of tennis. They were talking a different language so I said, 'Guys, I'm just new to this, but if I were a client,' – and I put myself in their position – 'I'd want you guys to make me the money. I mean, I'm playing the golf and I just want you to make the money.' The first question should be, if you're going to change someone's golf clubs, can they play with them because if they cannot play with their clubs, then it's like a doctor with the wrong tools.

So it seemed to be quite simple. As luck had it, we started to represent Wimbledon and we did a tour of Muhammad Ali in 1978. I was just at the right place at the right time. There was no competition, really. I had this briefcase they called 'Jaws' because it looked like an old medical school bag. It had all these contracts in it. The story got exaggerated but I signed up all these Spanish golfers and legend has it, I signed up a Spanish waiter by mistake! I decided that the top Italian golfer would probably make as much money or more money in Italy as maybe the third- or fourth-ranked golfer would in England, so it was that sort of theory, get the top player in each European country.

I met Bernhard Langer. It was funny, he was literally a kid. I was twenty-three and he might have been twenty-one. There was a guy called Jan Brugelman and we were in Frankfurt at a golf club. It was windy and we were on the balcony. Langer had a two iron. It was about 220 yards out into the wind and he said, 'Watch this,' and BANG! it finishes eight feet from the flag. And then, I'm sipping my beer and Jan says, 'Now James, zis is the problem …' And he proceeded to four putt. I signed up Bernhard Langer and history shows he became a superstar and sorted out his putting for the main part.

BK: Great game. You did it?

JE: Do you know, it was a fun business. I've always been a manager, not an agent. I mean, an agent goes and gets the money and does the deal and then buggers off. We basically manage people's careers. I'm not interested in the short-term.

'I was just at the right place at the right time.'

BK: How long did you spend in England and how did you come to Australia?

JE: From 1976 to 1979 I was with IMG in London, eventually running their UK and European golf business. Then, in the middle of 1978, Mark said to me at the TBC championships, 'Would you consider going to Australia?' Well, I'd never even thought about it. I didn't really know, being from a little place like Birkdale with a population of about ten thousand people in the north of England. I didn't know much about Australia at all. I thought, 'Oh my, there would be kangaroos hopping down the high street. I'm going to miss all my mates and London and all that sort of thing. You know, I had a very close relationship with my parents and had a girlfriend there. But anyway I plucked up the courage, I went downunder in 1978.

It was the 150th anniversary of Western Australia. A guy called Laurie Kiernan who owned Channel Nine in Perth (he was an ex-truck driver). His general manager, David Aspinall, who went on to work for Alan Bond and Bell Resources picked me up at the airport. As we were driving down George Street, David shouts to a guy called Warren Boland who is driving us, 'Warren, wind down the window.' There was a Channel 7 News van parked in George Street, 'Get the bazooka out.' So Warren gets a pretend bazooka out and pretends to blow up the Channel 7 truck. I said, 'What, don't you talk to each other here?' and he said, 'No, there's a war. We live next door to each other and were always throwing bricks over the fence.' I thought, 'What have I got myself into here?'

I ran that golf tournament. Peter Jacobsen and Curtis Strange headed a great tournament. Then McCormack said I'd better go and see Kerry Packer. So I saw Kerry and he said, 'A bright young bloke like you ought to come over and open an office.' So Mark had set it all up. Kerry basically said to me, 'We'll give you offices. I know Mark McCormack doesn't like paying for things.' And I said, 'If I have an office in your office, none of the other networks are going to talk to me.' And he said with a broad smile, 'Precisely.'

The other thing that was really interesting was that we'd sold *The Parkinson Show* to the ABC from the UK. The reason we'd got Parkinson was again luck. We had asked him to help us get George Best and Geoff Boycott. Parky said, 'If I do that, you help me.'

BK: So Michael Parkinson introduced you to the other guys?

JE: Yes. In those days, Parkinson was getting next to nothing, like a thousand quid for a show in the UK. It was big money in those days probably for television, but we managed to get him $11 000 a show on the ABC. So Kerry organised for me to have dinner with Sam Chisholm, David Evans and Bruce Gyngell at the San Francisco Grill. The first thing that came out of their mouths was, 'We want Parkinson.'

BK: Right.

JE: So Gyngell said he'd pay us $200 000. I was thinking in my head, thirteen shows times eleven and I said, 'We're almost getting that now at the ABC. It's not worth changing.' So he said, 'Then we'll do twenty-six shows and that's five million a year.' Well, I was trying not to smile. I was thinking, 'It just shows you, if you're not in the country, you've got no idea.' And what I realised then was that at 8.30 pm on a Saturday, everybody was watching Parkinson. I mean, he was getting well over a million viewers. But being in London, we didn't realise how popular Parky was. That was a big lesson.

So eventually there was an auction. Channel Ten, then owned by Murdoch, got Parky, now Parkinson was only paying us 10%. He'd done us a favour. So I picked up the phone to Michael after this and downplayed it. I said, 'Michael, if I could make you at least a million pounds a year to come out to Australia for four or five months, will you pay us our normal commission?' And he said, 'James, if you can make a million quid a year, you can have what you bloody well want!' And we are still managing him today. He has been very much a father figure to me. If I got slightly cocky, he'd get slightly cranky if you're not looking after him in the way he wants, he repeatedly brings me down to earth. We've had a handshake agreement since 1976. Even when he went from making a thousand pounds a show to £250 000 a show he never once said, 'Look James, let's change the commission.'

BK: So let me ask you, when did you come here?

JE: I came in November 1979. John Newcombe was my referee. Suddenly I got my passport back and it said 'permanent resident' – in those days they gave them away. So I came and have lived here permanently since 16 January 1980.

BK: And then you set up the Australian IMG office. How long did you run that for?

JE: A long time. I set up Sydney, we had an office in Christchurch, but moved it to Auckland. Then we went to Asia and had offices in Hong Kong, Singapore and China. I left IMG on 26 June 1997. It was about twenty-one years for most part a very enjoyable twenty-one years. My only job.

BK: Now, let me ask you. Obviously, Mark McCormack is revered as a huge figure in the industry of talent management. What was he like and what's it like working with a person like that?

JE: Well, first of all, he was definitely pioneering. He basically understood the value of sports and sportsmen in the international market. He understood that people got a huge amount of pleasure out of sport and that they lived a lot of their social life through sport even if they weren't necessarily sporty themselves. I think he understood what the fans wanted. He understood what television people wanted, too. So he certainly was a pioneer in those things.

He was quite entrepreneurial, but then at other times, he could be not very entrepreneurial at all. I suggested that we should buy television stations (at a couple of times in history we could have bought both Channel Ten and Channel 7 for very little). He turned around and he said, 'Look James, basically we sell programs to television stations.' And I said, 'Yes, but if we owned the television stations, think what we could do.'

BK: So for a time there, he had the content. Today, obviously, with the internet and the way the media has changed, content is king.

JE: Content is always king but we should have definitely broken into the television market in certain areas of Australia. It would have been pretty easy. There were three commercial networks and it would have been easy to take advantage of that. It was disappointing. I mean, it was just a way that he didn't want to go. But look, he was good. I mean, he wanted to run everything. He was a bit of a control freak in that sense. When I said, 'Look, your three children probably aren't all capable of taking over this business.' Nepotism is great if they're geniuses, but how often does that happen? You know, Jack Nicklaus' sons aren't necessarily going to be the greatest golfers (and they weren't). Same with Gary Player.

So one of the things I said was, 'You've got to spread the spoils. You've got to give people some equity in this business.' I mean, we all got paid quite well, but he didn't see that so I said, 'Look, Mark, my view is if you don't do it, people will leave.' And, of course, they did.

BK: It's hard to retain the best talent. So how did Mark bring you into the business and keep you there? How have you brought great people in your business?

JE: Well, Mark kept me by paying me and it was a great job and fun life. I also had quite a lot of autonomy. I was down here in Australia, he wasn't around the block. So I had a huge advantage not being in London or New York or Cleveland where he was a lot. Now, for a period of time, I wouldn't say I was the golden-haired boy, but certainly, I was one of the guys that he would listen to a lot and get advice from and I got us into the entertainment business. Certainly, he was very pro us doing that.

We were in the model agency business already, and we got into the business of underwriting all sorts of events. I thought we should own events. No-one can take them away from us then because if you represent things we can get fired or paid less. So I thought we should basically do that. Look, Mark was fantastic at all that and the sports world owes him a lot – a genuine pioneer.

'Nepotism is great if they're geniuses, but how often does that happen?'

BK: And then what did you take from the experience you had, obviously working with great talent to attract that talent?

JE: IMG was good because he had good people. There was no sort of cookie-cutting machine to get great people. I mean, I was a failed medical student.

A lot of them were actually lawyers. That was very good training, to be a lawyer. But some of the lawyers weren't very good at selling. There was a whole mixture of people.

BK: What makes a great manager?

JE: I think you have to be personable and you have to love what you are doing. You can't be frightened of the word 'no' because you get a lot of 'no's' – you get a lot of 'no's' because your clients don't want to do a lot of the stuff and you get a lot of 'no's' during downturns, like we're in now. You can knock on twenty doors and everybody says no. So you can't be frightened of or get depressed about things that don't go anywhere. I think if you believe in what you've got, all sorts of things can happen. You know, when we saw Bjorn Borg, we knew he was going to be a great tennis player. As soon as I saw Nick Faldo play golf, I knew he was going be a great golfer. Up here (points to head), he was brilliant. He was the Steve Waugh of golf.

BK: I saw a great profile on Nick Faldo once about just how disciplined and mentally focused he is.

JE: Yes. His management and his tactics around the golf course were probably second to none. Nick Faldo will be in a rocking chair and will sit there and think, 'I won six majors. I've got the most out of my talent.' There will be a lot of people who will sit in rocking chairs and say, 'I could have done better.'

'I think if you believe in what you've got, all sorts of things can happen.'

BK: So of the people that you've managed, what have you learned the most?

JE: Well, first of all, they're all, in varying degrees, selfish. The people who are successful in most sports are all selfish with their time. Most of them, the people that are really great, are not obsessed with the accumulation of money. They realise that they will make a lot of money for a long time if they carry on winning, although they live in a stratosphere where a day of their time is worth two years' work to most people. They don't get bogged down by it.

BK: It makes no difference.

JE: I always remember Nick Faldo being offered US$500 000 to go and play in Japan in the mid 1980s. It was a fortune. I mean, the average salary was £25 000.

And he looked at his diary and it was his daughter Natalie's second birthday. So he said, 'Mate, I can't do this.' So I got the diary and I crossed out the birthday and put a ring around another date. 'This year, Natalie's birthday is here! She's going to be two years old.' I mean, Gill and Nick looked at me as though I was a Martian, but I said, 'Put the money in a trust account for her.' So I did it with humour. But that's what good management should be like.

But to answer your question, successful people are very focused. We manage Michael Clarke and he's unbelievably focused. I'm not saying that these guys don't make mistakes but today, mistakes get magnified.

BK: Because they're under huge scrutiny. Everyone's got a camera. Everyone's got a video.

JE: The days of JFK compared to the days of Obama are completely different. A lot of people today don't realise the pressure that brings.

BK: I knew you'd taken on Shane Warne, but how long have you managed Michael Clarke for?

JE: I started about three weeks before he got his 329 not out.

BK: So let me ask you about that, because with him in particular, there seems to be a real change in the way that he is presenting himself or is being presented. And there are certainly very different results on the field. What influence can you have as a manager? Where does the advice start and stop – good counsel? Is it just commercial advice?

JE: No, very little influence, most is common sense.

BK: Are you doing for them what Parkinson has done for you?

JE: Well I can be quite brutal with what I have to say. One thing, when people are well known and they're successful, in all forms of life, others just think or presume they know a lot about things that they don't actually have a clue about. And part of the reason is, people ask them their opinion. They're not experts at everything but because they're well known, people expect them to give an answer.

With Michael, I met him with Shane Warne a year and a half before I started managing him. He was with Lara Bingle and he said, 'We see ourselves as the Australian Posh and Beck.' And I said, 'Well, you're not and I'd get rid of that idea if I were you because it won't work here.' And there was a sort of silence. Then later on he came to me and said, 'Let's get together.'

I said to him, 'You know, people don't want to see you as this flash kid. It's a huge responsibility being captain of Australia so don't chew gum when you do interviews. And take off your cap. It's common courtesy. And just be honest. Just be yourself.'

BK: Just be yourself.

JE: I said, 'I don't want to change you. Just be yourself. Don't be worried about what you say. If you think that you played like a load of turkeys, tell them that you played like a load of turkeys.'

And then the next thing that happened, he said, 'I don't really want to go out there as one of the top batsmen without a bat contract.' I said, 'You haven't got a bat contract? All you're doing is kidding yourself. Put the McGrath sticker on because it's a great cause and Glenn is a great guy.' Then he got the 329 and we did his own range. Now, was that a strategy? No it wasn't. It was common sense commercially and he scored the runs. He did all the hard work.

BK: But he had enough respect for your experience to listen and get on with it?

JE: I had to persuade him to go out with a plain bat, but Michael learns quickly, you have to when you have the responsibility of being captain. He had to deal with Ponting still there, which he knew was a big advantage with all his experience, Clarke played a blinder. Now for the Ashes.

BK: You can see it on the field.

JE: So he was bright enough to turn it around and take it all on board. I mean, we had a chat about it and I said, 'Listen, I know Ricky. He has made all the mistakes. He's got all the experience. He's a huge asset to you.' No different from Shane Warne, who was a huge asset to all those captains before. You know, you don't think Tubby Taylor wandered over and asked him what the weather was going to be like – he was asking him about what we should do. So, be consultative. I mean, in any form of life. If you are in an office by yourself and bouncing a ball against the wall and you never talk to anybody, it's tough.

BK: Michael's marriage–

JE: I didn't know he was getting married. I had no idea, but the fact that he did it in that way, he did it brilliantly. And then it was agreed to release just three or four pictures to everyone. It was refreshing to have just a family wedding.

BK: So, of the clients that you manage now, obviously, you manage Shane Warne–

JE: I've managed him since 2005.

BK: So what's a good client when you're looking in the market? Do you approach them or do they approach you? And what do you take on and what won't you take on?

JE: Most people, funnily enough, have approached me.

BK: Do you still look after Anthony Warlow?

JE: No, we don't. When I was at IMG and in SEL's early years we did. Anthony is a huge talent and I'm glad he's off to work on Broadway. We tend to get people when they were already stars, they are already well-established.

'So, be consultative. I mean, in any form of life. If you are in an office by yourself and … you never talk to anybody, it's tough.'

BK: And what type of client wouldn't you take? Is it just if you can't do enough for them, or is it personality?

JE: I've turned down a lot of people – people who are madly influenced by their parents or wives or girlfriends or have a reputation for being unbelievably difficult. Life's too short. I'm lucky now, I don't have to deal with people I don't want to work with. At one stage I wanted to retire by the time I was forty-five. I don't know where I got that idea from.

BK: So talk to me about retirement. One of the constant themes I'm hearing from people who do what they love is that they have no interest in retiring.

JE: I think that's right. You basically change the way you work, and you have other people doing a lot of the work, you delegate more and better. You change your routine a bit. My doctor said people die much younger when they retire. Everything is slower. And you see people who retire, some really bright businessmen who retire, suddenly they're taking twenty minutes to make a decision on whether or not to take the car in for a service. I wouldn't want to go like that. Also, I'm lucky because my job's been my hobby.

BK: I've found that a constant theme, that it is more of a hobby, it's what people love doing.

JE: I'm always late because I never look at a clock.

BK: Because you're enjoying it.

JE: I mean, you have shitty days, you have shitty weeks and shitty months. Financially, I've had shitty years. It's not much fun when you go and lose, three or four million dollars on an entertainment event. But on the other hand, you can't win them all.

BK: Have you ever gone public?

JE: No, I've never thought about going public. I would never go public, I've got no interest. What I think you're referring to is that we basically set up the new V8 Supercars and sold it.

'I'm lucky, because my job's been my hobby.'

BK: Yes.

JE: It was in 1997 and the brainchild of Tony Cochrane, who was a 25% partner of SEL (Sports & Entertainment Limited). He worked with me at IMG and came with me to SEL. We set up this deal where instead of taking commissions, we had a 25% stake in the V8 business. And it grew and grew from a small business to a company that was making in excess of thirty million dollars a year. No debt, nothing, just hard work.

Then the teams turned around and said to us, 'Well, we would like to make some money out of this.' A lot of mechanics and drivers had become team owners and year after year they'd ploughed all the money back into the business. They thought if we can get a good price, they could actually make a few million themselves. I didn't want to sell. I don't actually like selling things and it was a great business.

Actually Ross Stone, who is one of the team owners, a lovely guy from New Zealand, said to me, 'James, we've all done bloody well out of this.' He said, 'It's gonna change all of our lives if we sell. You've got all the commercial rights for V8 Supercars. We are only going to be able to sell our future cashflows going forward if you don't come to the party. Would you just quietly consider it because I think we, meaning the teams, have been very loyal as you've been to us and we'd like to make some money.'

And I basically thought about it. And he was 100% right. So I said OK, but on two conditions. One, we're not going to go and sell this thing cheaply, so I put a number on it of $320 million and, secondly, I said they would have to stay in with at least 30% because they were the act.

BK: Basically, no-one is going to want you to not have any hurt money in it, but if I'm out, I'm out.

JE: Because then you can sell to whoever you want. You can get the highest price. And that was basically the deal they agreed to. I didn't think in my wildest dreams it would ever happen. Well, I know nothing about private equity. I don't know anything about the stock market. I've never bought a share in my life. So I just sat well back, thinking they'll probably wheel me in for a couple of presentations.

Actually, they didn't even wheel me in because they thought I'd say, 'You blokes aren't capable of running this show.' So that's what happened, it was bought by Archer and I am still involved with the new television deal and stuff but that was it. The nice thing about it was that it was a success and we all remained friends. Tony then left us and went on to be the executive chairman of the V8 Supercars. I think it's a different life being in a private equity situation. But he is doing what he wants to do and he does it well. There will come a time that he will want to take a back seat.

BK: Yes. Any regrets? What are your biggest regrets in business? What are the biggest mistakes you made? The things you've learned the most from?

JE: It's interesting. I think that I would have liked to have managed Seve Ballesteros. We did quasily, at one stage, and Tom Watson. Again we did in a quasi way. He was a client but left before my time. I'd like to have managed and got to know those two people better. And I would have liked to have managed Torvill and Dean.

BK: Can you tell me about the change from IMG to setting up SEL?

JE: Yeah, I was frightened by it, but I knew it was the right thing to do. I mean, used to have twenty-five phone calls before 10 o'clock and on the first morning, not one person rang. I went to lunch with a friend and said, 'I think this is going to be a disaster, no-one's called me,' and he said, 'Don't be ridiculous.' But it was a funny thing, having all that clout with IMG and then thinking maybe I'm not going to have it now. I think that if I had my time over again, I probably would have tried to set up SEL at the age of thirty-four rather than forty-four. But I was in a comfort zone at IMG. I also liked the –

BK: Collegiality?

JE: Yes, I liked that, but also the security. I mean, some people laugh because I am a risk taker, but I wouldn't go and put all my eggs in one basket. It's limited risk. I'm quite conservative really.

BK: One of the biggest lessons? One of the things that have taught you the most?

JE: I think the biggest lesson I've learned is to listen. And when you do a deal, always let the other person go first because it's amazing the number of times people have offered me more than I might have asked for myself.

▬▬▬▬

'I think that if I had my time over again, I probably would have tried to set up SEL at the age of thirty-four rather than at forty-four.'

BK: Tell me about debt. We're past the global financial crisis. You've mentioned your view on risk. Obviously, we've seen countries and companies and all sorts of people doing interesting things. Explain to me your concept of risk, of not putting all your eggs in the one basket.

JE: Two things. In my era as a kid, you were well-off if you had a fridge. No-one had a dishwasher. Some homes had a colour television and some had two televisions. But this generation – our children are far more into consumerism. They've got all the gadgets. But the first thing that people have got to turn around and do is work out what's important.

I've always got this line that it's far easier to save a dollar than make a dollar in times of recession. So, you have to go back to basics. Pick the low-hanging fruit because everyone is trying to go and do this blockbuster thing. Life is cyclical.

And, I mean, the business that we're in is sport and I've sold a lot of major television sports. I've represented the Olympic games, Wimbledon, Royal and Ancient, and all sorts of people. Sport is always going to be there because it doesn't fluctuate from year to year.

BK: It's very much a constant.

JE: Yes! If you create a new drama series or a new reality TV show you hope and pray everybody is going to watch it. It may work, it may not. The AFL Grand Final might be 3.2 million viewers or it might be 2.8 million, but at the end of the day–

BK: That's a hell of a lot of people.

JE: And it's always going to be in demand. I mean in the history of Australia since I've been here, there has never been a network that's survived that hasn't had a major sporting franchise.

BK: So tell me about innovation and technology. What impact is that having on your life and work?

JE: Well, I'm the wrong person to talk to because I hate all that stuff. I mean if I had my way, I'd have a car that still had the windows that wind down. I literally only got an iPad three months ago because everyone got fed up with giving me hard copies. I like a piece of paper to write on, write down comments you can think about later. I don't like looking at screens. I like being outside. My first meetings are always at Bondi or Watson's Bay, somewhere near the water. I don't text people. I talk to people on the phone.

BK: So, human-to-human interaction.

JE: I can pick up the phone to you and know the sort of mood you're in. I've got a very simple theory: people like doing business with people they like and people they trust. Most of the major deals I've got have all been handshake deals. I've done the Olympic Games on a handshake with Kerry Packer. And Dick Pound, the Chairman of the IOC's TV committee at the time, said, 'James, where is the contract?' I said, 'Don't worry about the contract, it'll get signed. He's already sent me the cheque.' It's better than the contract. That's how it works.

And if anyone dudded me – and I've been dudded – I will never do business with them again. They've had one chance. Why would I want to do it? I don't mind if someone says they've promised to do something but they can't. We've all done it. So I think it's just common courtesy, really.

BK: So what about Kerry Packer?

JE: Look, I liked him. He was just an absolute sports fan. He could be quite bullish in a way sometimes, but when you stood up to him he could also admit when he was wrong.

'I've got a very simple theory: people like doing business with people they like and people they trust. Most of the major deals I've got have all been handshake deals.'

BK: Let me ask you one last question. Which motto or quote or thought best summarises your approach to life.

JE: Just be yourself. Yes, be yourself. I mean, there are so many different ways and life is not an exact science. I've met eccentric people who are charming, I've met billionaires who are charming, and I've met people who never quite make it and they tend to be more of a pain in the arse than those who have really made it. People who really are secure within themselves and secure with their own ability, I think that people really get that.

There are a lot of emotions that are completely wasted. Jealousy is a wasted emotion, envy is a wasted emotion, probably the thing is just go on, just go and do it. I think it's amazing when you decide that you're going to do something, somehow it happens. It just happens if you decide and you're determined – now, the idea should not be flawed in the first place – but once you've decided that it's a good idea, then –

BK: You put effort into it.

JE: Yes. You know, I spoke to David Gallop this morning about his sudden departure from the Australian Rugby League. I think in three months time he will think that it was a complete blessing in disguise – umpteen things will open up for him that he would never have even thought of, whether it's television or radio, books, on boards, whatever it might be.

But there is always a fear factor of what's going to happen when you make a move. It's not necessarily an enjoyable feeling, but it's enjoyable when you plunge in and go and do it!

Matt Moran

Chef / Restaurateur – Aria Restaurant

'I hated school. The school hated me so it was kind of perfect synergy. I dropped out when I was 15. I didn't really know what I wanted to do whether it was motor mechanic, painter, pastry chef at one stage, butcher … I had no real interest in food. I had no real background of food. My parents were not foodies.'

Matt Moran is a well-known Australian chef, restaurateur, media identity and co-owner of a number of successful restaurants including ARIA Sydney. Raised on a farm, he started his career at age fifteen as an apprentice at La Belle Hélène restaurant in Roseville on Sydney's North Shore where he developed and finessed his skills in classical French cooking. Matt and business partner Peter Sullivan launched their first restaurant, The Paddington Inn Bistro, in 1991. The success of this venture has led to a spectacular and surprisingly multifaceted career for a boy from the bush.

www.ariarestaurant.com.au

Interview

BRETT KELLY: Matt, when I first met you, you mentioned that you grew up in Blacktown. Can you tell me how you got into cooking, or cheffing – which is it?

MATT MORAN: The majority of my early life was spent in the country. I was born in Tamworth. We had a sheep farm in the mid-seventies and then we moved to a dairy farm. Typical farmers, you know, rich one year, poor the next.

There were about three properties in the greater family. Unfortunately, the family got very poor and lost … all of it, actually. And then, when I was about nine, we moved to Blacktown. I did my schooling there. I hated school. I dropped out when I was fifteen. I didn't really know what I wanted to do. I had no real interest in food and I had no real background in it, either. My parents weren't foodies.

I have this argument with my son all the time about how lucky he is to eat out at cafés and restaurants. We worked out by the time he was eight he had eaten in four hundred cafés and restaurants! I remember going to my first restaurant when I was about thirteen. It was the Black Stump in Blacktown. So he is well ahead of me at the moment! I suppose the culture has changed a lot since then, too. My nan was not a bad baker, but it was only scones and tarts and rice pudding. Stuff like that. I'd never eaten a lot of good food. Fish, for instance. I had this theory that I hated seafood until I actually started in kitchens. The fact is that I'd never actually eaten it – I'd never even seen it! The extent of my seafood knowledge growing up was limited to a McDonald's Filet-o-Fish.

BK: Or fish fingers?

MM: Man, that was it. So, you know, I wanted to leave school but I wasn't allowed to. I was very young. They actually put me in school when I was four – I was the youngest in my year. I think because I was a little bit difficult as a kid, my parents just wanted me to stay in school. I'd done a little bit of butchery growing up – Dad used to slaughter his own. And then I liked the idea of starting really early and finishing at midday, so I thought maybe I'd like to be a pastry chef. I did a little bit of work experience when I was in school and I compromised and decided that I wanted to be a chef. To be really honest, I would have done anything to get out of school.

BK: And were your parents saying that you had to go and get a job?

MM: I had to get a job. My brother was quite academic and he had a lot of skills, but I was the opposite. I don't think growing up in Blacktown helped me to pursue an education.

BK: Which school was that?

MM: It was Grantham High. It doesn't exist anymore. When I was there, there were about a thousand students. It was always one of the roughest schools in the state. It had such a bad reputation. It went right down to about four hundred students so they changed it and it's now a selective sports school, called Seven Hills Sports High. It does incredibly well in sports. They have the best baseball teams, basketball teams, the best rugby teams or league teams. There are a lot of islanders out there so that's why they're very good at rugby.

Anyway, I started working on weekends in Parramatta, but to be really honest, it was just steak and chips and washing up and stuff. The guy offered me an apprenticeship, which I thought was pretty cool, but it was six months down the track when he had renovated or something. So I just started looking around for another job. I probably went to around twenty to twenty-five interviews all over Sydney. I remember going once to the Harbour Watch or something, down on Pier One. I remember the boss saying that if the first five guys didn't work out, he'd give me a call – I didn't do too well.

And then, I went to this job interview at La Belle Hélène, which is a little French restaurant on the north side, which, little to my knowledge, was one of the best places in Sydney. They had a very good reputation. It was always full, it was always busy. A very classic little French restaurant which was pretty mind-blowing for someone who had never seen that sort of thing before. So I went in and did a trial. I always had a very good work ethic. I suppose it was something Dad had instilled in me, growing up on a farm. So working wasn't an issue.

I remember the first day at the restaurant. I just remember seeing what they were doing on the plate. Little things like fanned strawberries and the way it was decorated. Things I'd never seen before. Instantly, I fell in love. And, my personality is a bit obsessive, so I became obsessed by it. I got the job, left school and started at La Belle. It was pretty full on – fifteen-hour days, six days a week. For a kid that came out of Blacktown and had no discipline, it was bloody good. I wanted that job.

BK: What was the boss like?

MM: Look, he was a very good cook, a brilliant cook. He had lots of energy and lots of passion. Really tough, though. The sous chef was really tough, too. It was a really hard environment, a really, really tough environment. You know, the sous chef used to walk behind you. If you weren't standing properly on two legs, he would actually knee you in the back of the legs so you'd collapse. It was full on.

But I thrived in that environment. I loved it. I absolutely loved it. I spent four and a half years there and ended up being the head. You know, it is that very French, classical training that every cook needs to learn.

BK: Did you go to TAFE while you were working there?

MM: Yes, Ryde TAFE. It's a strange thing. I did really poorly in school, but I absolutely smashed it. Being French-trained at La Belle, which was very classical, and doing French study at college, I pretty much topped every part of it.

BK: It's interesting that so many of the people that we've interviewed really struggled with school because they didn't fit in. And they didn't want to, either–

MM: I fitted in sportswise, I'm not a small guy. I played rugby and all that. I loved that part of it.

BK: But the academic side? People I've spoken to have said that they weren't really engaged in school, but then they go off and find this thing that they love and they have a passion for it.

MM: I enjoyed it. I was probably a bit cocky in those days. I thought, I work in one of the best restaurants in Sydney, I should be the best at this. I felt really good and I was the youngest.

BK: What did your parents say?

MM: Look, you know, cooking back then wasn't really seen as glamorous.

BK: Not like the European tradition.

MM: Not really. But chefs in France are gods. And in Sydney, it was very different back then. There weren't celebrity chefs. Most chefs didn't actually own the restaurants. There were the money guys, the launderers or the crims that opened restaurants. Cooks weren't seen. Cooks were out the back. They never went into the restaurant. They never wrote books.

And to me, that's a big thing now but I did it because I absolutely loved it. It wasn't about the dough and it wasn't about becoming successful. It wasn't about being on TV. It wasn't about writing cookbooks. It was very different to how it is these days.

BK: So you just found your passion as a chef?

MM: Yes.

BK: Often what I've seen is that through that passion, they get great feedback and they do better and better and everything comes from that. So what about the culture of celebrity? Of course, now you're a celebrity chef, but the journey that you're outlining isn't one of a guy that wanted to be a celebrity. It's a guy who wanted to be a great chef.

MM: To be really honest, I was quite shy, too. I could never have got up in front of a crowd and done a bit of public speaking. You know, it just wasn't me. It was a progression. And I'm sort of intense when it comes to what I want to do. I'm kind of directed and ambitious, I suppose. You know, I moved through the ranks very quickly at La Belle, then at nineteen I was poached by The Restaurant Manfredi which was THE restaurant – it was awarded a Three Chef's Hat.

So I went there and I'm a bit compulsive. I love to work. I loved the knowledge of it. But I started my own business when I was eighteen, making cakes and tarts for delicatessens. I was actually making more money doing that than I was at work. I was working sixteen hours at La Belle, rolling out pastry, making them the next day and dropping them off. My best customer was Valli Little, who is now the editor of ABC *delicious* magazine.

'I did it because I absolutely loved it. It was't about the dough and it wasn't about becoming successful.'

BK: Right.

MM: La Belle was strange. When I was the head chef, the chef had opened up another restaurant that had failed, so he came back. I felt like my long career had been taken away at nineteen. That's when I got poached by Manfredi and I met Peter Sullivan. He is my partner now. He's been my partner for twenty-two years. He was at La Belle, too, and then he went and opened up a restaurant. He was front of house at Armstrong's and I went to Manfredi and I worked there for a couple of years. I loved it. You know, I've learned how to cook at Manfredi's, but I've learned more about produce. It's very different, you know. French cooking is all about style. And Manfredi was–

BK: More simple.

MM: It was simple, but it was the start of the explosion of food in this country. There's no question. That was around 1989, '90, '91. People like Barry McDonald owned the Paddington Fruit Market, a Kiwi guy, John Susman opened the

Flying Squid Brothers who were getting Coffin Bay scallops and fresh tuna, all this amazing stuff, that was in our ocean, but no one would touch sea urchins, mussels. So there was a real explosion of produce, which was the most exciting time to be a chef. So I learned more about produce. And I got very sick of being told what to do.

So at twenty-two, Peter and I decided that we didn't want to work for anyone anymore and bought the Paddington Inn from Steve Manfredi and Barry McDonald. They weren't really working there anymore and it had kind of lost its way a little bit. It had become a very popular restaurant prior to that with Paul Merrony. So Peter and I took it over. Our first foray into owning a restaurant was pretty full on. Pete's a bit older, and he'd done business management, too. But it was all about just doing good food. We got instant recognition with a Chef's Hat the second year we were there. It was all good times, but we lacked the business side of it. We realised that very quickly.

I remember after probably three months, I said to Pete, 'How much money have we got in the bank?' We were rich, but we hadn't actually paid anyone. And then, after about eighteen months, we nearly went broke. We had to put some more money back into it because we just didn't care about costings. We didn't care about anything. We were young guys, money was great, all that stuff. It was just fun, we were just having a great time. And then, basically, we grew out of it and decided to do Moran's Restaurant and Café so we sold the Paddo Inn and moved to Moran's.

We started doing stocktakes and tightening up and getting reports. We had some hard times there. You learn very quickly when you nearly go broke. After a couple of years, it kind of steadied out. We'd bought another place called Bonne Femme, which we built down in Palmer Street. I had a good mate who always wanted a restaurant. He and I bought the one in the city with my brother. Bad move, it didn't work. Mainly because I wasn't on top of it and my name wasn't associated with it. So I had the three at that point in time. And then the ARIA site came up so Pete and I sold the three of them and pretty much put all the dough into it. Massive risk because no-one wanted to touch 'the toaster' back in those days. But, you know, coming in here, looking at the site we just thought, 'Alright! It has to work.'

BK: Was it a shell?

MM: Just the concrete shell, you know, floor to ceiling view.

BK: And with the Opera House so close. It had to be a no-brainer. But you are quite right, at that time there was a lot of controversy about building 'the toaster', there was a lot of bad rap about it.

MM: Which probably worked to our advantage because it was late 1999 that we opened. We got a big contribution from the landlord for the fit-out because, you know, it was very expensive and no-one wanted it. We completely put our balls on the line. We had another partner who came in on it. He is still my partner. I don't want to talk about him because he doesn't like being in public, but he is not a backer. Never has been a backer. He is an equal partner. He is a very good businessman and negotiator. He has been my biggest mentor when it comes to business. All of a sudden we really learned about business. I suppose that's when we grew up.

So we negotiated a great deal. We didn't pay rent for a long time and we had the Olympics and it was just massive, we had a massive start. So, for a couple of years, ARIA went nuts. It is a very different business now to then. We started with sixteen chefs in 1999. We have nearly thirty now, it's a much bigger business. Then a couple of years later we tendered at the Opera House, the Opera Bar. A lot of people don't know that we own that.

BK: It's fantastic.

MM: It's a good business. It's my best. The whole concept of it was to turn it into a bar and offer good food.

BK: But it was pretty down before that.

MM: I can't tell you the figures but we work it really hard. The idea was, as a restaurant, that someone comes and takes your order and then you get the bill at the end. But here, people have got a theatre ticket and they're running out of time. They'd just throw us their credit cards or they would run away and not pay. So the idea was that you paid at the bar and the food comes out to you. You've got a large older demographic going to the Opera House so we weren't sure it was going to work but we tendered and we won it. I was always conscious of putting my name behind it because I was worried people wouldn't come to ARIA. Now, I don't really care because they're polar opposites.

BK: They're two completely different experiences.

MM: I don't need to have my name on every business. I'd rather be running the business. It just didn't make sense having the name Matt Moran everywhere. And you know, without table service anymore, that older demographic didn't come back. So, we took a big hit the first year. I remember saying to my partners, 'I'm sorry. All the money we're making here, we're pouring into there.'

But my partners agreed, they said, 'We believe in this business, let's push on, OK?' and it became a phenomenal business. People love that. We got the younger generation and they're eating and kind of kick-starting the Opera House. The Opera House became something groovy and funky rather than an old people's place.

BK: The Opera House has also done a lot of marketing. They're trying to attract other people.

MM: I think we were a big part of that in the beginning. A couple of years after that, we bought The Truffle Group out of the Opera House. We actually own all the catering rights in our group, which has been renamed ARIA Catering. It was called Opera Point Events when we originally took it over. Same thing again, I was a little bit worried about the affiliation but I suppose that the brand actually brings more people now. We've owned that for six or seven years and it's getting better, but it is a tough business. We started ARIA Brisbane three years ago.

BK: And what was the drive there?

MM: The ARIA brand was so strong that we wanted to put it in another state. It is a hard challenge. It has made my life much more interesting, much busier. I catch over a hundred flights a year. I've got five, six flights this week alone. I go to New Zealand on Sunday. It's a challenge but I love the challenge. I love having another ARIA and it has been very successful.

The problem with us is that over the years, you breed great staff. You either lose them or you do something with them and you grow. That's the celebrity part of it, too. It has made us grow. People want us, people want our brand. And then, this year we opened Chiswick in Woollahra. I haven't actually signed so I can't tell you too much, but we're about to open another big place in Brisbane that is similar to the Opera Bar in style. Having two businesses in one city is much more cost-effective than having one. They can feed off each other. I've started ARIA Catering up there also, which we are doing out of ARIA Restaurant. That's going gangbusters. I am building a big kitchen at the new site and then we will move ARIA Catering down into that site.

BK: So doing more of the same thing and not diversifying off into things you don't really know about?

MM: I've learned from that.

'The problem with us is that over the years, you breed great staff. You either lose them or you do something with them and you grow.'

BK: So what are the dumb things you've done and what have you learned?

MM: You know, I remember many years ago, I went to my bank and I wanted to build six houses in Coffs Harbour. I'd bought a block of land there and I remember their exact words were, 'You're a chef, a restaurateur, you're not a property developer. No.' And I said, you have twenty-four hours to change your mind or I'm moving banks. They called my bluff so I moved banks. And you know what I learned? I learned that you invest in yourself and not what other people are telling you to do. Hence, stock markets and you know, I have done a bit of property stuff over the years and some of it I've done right. I've still got a couple of houses in Coffs Harbour. They pay rent and I didn't lose dough on it.

BK: But this concept of investing yourself and doing what you're really great at?

MM: Yeah, my restaurants, that's what I do best. You put money in the bank and get a 6% return? I could probably open a restaurant bar and beat that a little bit. So, it just makes sense to keep doing that. I think that's what I will keep doing, definitely.

BK: So, you're married with a couple of kids? How do you prioritise and make a successful and busy business work with a relatively young family?

MM: It is really tough, you know. Tougher in the beginning because I was working incredibly hard. Harry was born and I opened the Opera Bar a couple of months later. I suppose it comes down to time management, it comes down to someone who is very understanding, who knows me, knows what I want and knew me before I did all that.

You know, I am incredibly ambitious and a little bit competitive. I like to succeed. She knows that so it is a very good balance. She is very independent, too. She is very successful in her own career, in her own right. She is not sitting at home waiting for me, doting. It's a balance. Kids are hard, you know. It is hard when I travel. I travel all the time. It is about making sure that I do try and take holidays. She helps them understand why I am doing it.

Actually, we just went away on holidays for a nice trip. I'm not going to say where or what we did but it is just – it is probably a little bit more decadent than most people do in the holidays but the kids understand that we are doing it because Dad works so hard and we can afford to do it. The fact that I work for an airline doesn't hurt, either.

Look, it's tough but it is a balance. I am looking after the kids at the moment, and it's hard. Especially when my boy says to me, 'Dad, I don't want a lunch order today. I want you to make me lunch.' 'Alright, buddy, but it is just easier if I give you ten bucks.' He says, 'No, I am sick of buying food. Just make me something.' So I did. I had to do something! My kids are foodies and that's fair enough. Not that they cook, and they love to eat out.

BK: So tell me, how did you become a celebrity chef? Do you like being called that?

MM: You know, I don't worry about it. To be really honest, you're always going to be labelled that whether you like it or not. You know, chef, cook, I don't really care. It's not something you set out to do.

BK: How did it happen, then?

MM: I think it started with a couple of shows early on like *My Kitchen Rules*. Someone came to me, stuck a camera in my face and just spoke to me. Then when they came back, they offered me a part. When I said no, they asked me why and I gave them all the reasons why I didn't want to get involved. They were interested in that and the girl who was doing my publicity at the time said, 'You know, it would be good. If you want expand, you've got to do things like this. Your time can't be spent a hundred hours in the kitchen.' It's great, it's a great concept, but you're never going to grow more places.

BK: Was it a challenge?

MM: I think so, but I just fell into it. I enjoyed it, I was learning something out of it, and then it just snowballed. You start one show and then someone else wants you for another show and then a publisher wants you to do a cookbook and then a bank wants you to do a bit of public speaking. It all just came in at once, the endorsement and the airline said we want you to do our food and then it became the business of Matt Moran, I suppose, Matt Moran Inc. But it is a side thing, my publishing, my endorsements and my speaking roles.

BK: What do you do to keep building your knowledge, your innovation?

MM: Food wise?

BK: Yes.

MM: I travel and eat. I tell these kids in the kitchen, I eat out nearly more than all of them put together. I see different things. I just did a trip before my holiday and my holiday was all about food, too.

BK: So you are always working, you've always got your mind on it?

MM: Yes. I just did a trip with a mate and a partner and it's hard work, lunch and dinner every day. We were in London. We were in Italy. We were in Denmark. We went to all the top restaurants. It's about knowledge to me. I come back and I look at the photos and think, 'How did they do it? How can I manipulate that into my restaurant?' All of my things have a little bit of tourism stuff in the middle of it, but it's all food. I am guilty of snails in Paris – basically we go and we just eat.

BK: So this is more than a career, more than a job, more than a business, even. It is an overriding passion, something that's grown from that.

MM: Yes. I have always said that to people.

'I travel and eat. I tell these kids in the kitchen, I eat out nearly more than all of them put together. I see different things. I just did a trip before my holiday and my holiday was all about food, too.'

BK: Of all the people that I have met who are very successful, they are precisely so successful because they found something that they just overwhelmingly loved and couldn't think of doing anything else.

MM: I have been cooking for nearly twenty-eight years. The first twenty years were sixteen hours a day slaving over a stove. There is nothing glamorous about that. Young kids and *MasterChef* contestants ask, 'How long will it take me to learn everything?' Man, I am still doing it, I am still learning. If you don't really want to do the hard yards in the kitchen, forget it. Because food and being a good cook is all about knowledge. You can have your nous about you and you can have good taste and whatever else, but it's knowledge and knowledge is time. You cannot learn everything in a day, it's impossible. It just doesn't work that way. And a kitchen is a highly disciplined place. I never set out to do what I do but I tell you what, I love what I do.

BK: You're having fun?

MM: I'm having a ball. I don't spend sixteen hours a day in the kitchen anymore but I still have my fingers in it. I still have a say in the menu. I still write most of the menus. I oversee our management team. We have food tastings in every business every six weeks. We gather in each restaurant and we sit down and eat everything, which you know sounds great, but it's a lot of food. We pick the eyes out of it and then we have the relationship with all the chefs. A lot of them have been with me for a really long time. We talk about how we should change things and try to get it right. The business side of it is obviously a big thing, we have a lot of reporting. We do full, weekly stocktakes. We do fortnightly grog stocktakes. We know if there's a bottle of wine missing. We know if food costs are down by 1%. That's business.

BK: Do you have internal auditors?

MM: All the chefs. All our offices. We're in charge of our own reporting but it goes back to head office. We get reports every four weeks on every business. A lot of people don't do that. ARIA is a big business, it's a monster. But you could be losing twenty or thirty grand a week and not even know about it. A lot of people do that – and they fall over. We react straightaway. It is one thing to lose money in a business, but to keep losing money is an absolute sin. We've had harder times, but the last thirteen years, since ARIA, have been pretty good.

BK: And what do you think is the key to a good business?

MM: I think you always have to reinvent yourself. You know, years ago we made a TV documentary out of ARIA in Sydney. It's always had two Chefs Hats but about eight years ago, we lost one. The food critic just thought we were trying too hard, there were too many elements on the plate. I was possibly spreading myself too thin. Whatever the reasons, when it happened, I remember I blew up. I was devastated. I wanted to give up the industry. I hated the person who did it. But I slept on it then thought to myself, how should I react? What do I do? How do I come in here and tell the twenty-eight guys in the kitchen that what we are doing is the right thing and not to listen to the critics? I thought about it and you know what? There was probably an ounce of truth in it.

BK: So what did you do?

MM: I thought, I am going to get it back. We're going to better ourselves. During that time we were approached to do the documentary, which I kind of thought was a set up. I rang the food critic and said I will take it all on board and I will prove you wrong. The next year – success. We got it back. Even though I didn't agree with it at the time, it was possibly the best lesson I've learned in life: don't rest on your laurels. And I reckon every year, from that day, ARIA is a better restaurant. All my businesses have always got better and better from when they opened to where they are now.

BK: You describe yourself as ambitious, but what I see is a drive to improve. Your response to adversity is to take it on board, fire up and do something about it. Where does that come from? Your childhood?

MM: I'm the middle child and when I was at school I was told, 'You're never going to amount to anything.' But there has always been that middle child syndrome!

BK: So, what's the future? Is it just constant improvement? Would you go overseas, open restaurants in different places?

MM: Oh, I would never say 'never', because I just don't know. Twenty-one years ago when I opened my first restaurant, I could never have envisaged opening a restaurant, being on TV. I never wanted to write books. You know, when I opened my first cookbook I remember opening it and thinking, 'I'm never going do that again.' – and I've done it three times since. So it's been a progression. And working with Singapore Airlines, we've got a big presence in Singapore. New York is my favourite city in the world. We have family in New York and my partner thinks he's a Jewish New Yorker. He would love to go. Is that the one that would kill us? I don't know. But if the opportunity came along, I just don't know. We get offered opportunities all the time but most don't fit in with my branding. Branding is a very big important thing. I'm not in for the cheap sell, I want longevity. I want the credibility as it keeps going along.

BK: What's your favourite food, your favourite dish?

MM: That's a question I get asked too many times. To be really honest, to me food is all about what is in season, what is fresh. I can honestly tell you that every year when the first figs come in to season, that is my favourite thing in the world. And then, three months later it will be a white peach. Two weeks later it'll be a Bowen mango. Spring it will be spring lamb, so it just changes all the time.

BK: So, really, just eating fresh produce.

MM: I have one meal a day. It starts at 8 am, finishes at midnight. I just continue grazing. I love my food, I love eating out. I love, I love everything about it.

BK: And what about your health? You're a big, strong, fit and healthy guy. A lot of cooks aren't. Do you take the time to work out or look after yourself?

MM: Yeah, I train a lot …

BK: Where did that come from? Is it because you like looking great?

MM: (Laughs). I suppose it makes you feel good. It gives you energy.

'I have one meal a day. It starts at 8 am, finishes at midnight. I just continue grazing. I love my food, I love eating out. I love, I love everything about it.'

BK: You can eat more, too.

MM: And you can eat more! And I love that part in my life. I'm doing Tough Mudder in September. I can't wait.

BK: I see it all the time, business owners that are too busy to look after themselves.

MM: My partners are very conscious of it, too.

BK: Excellent. Last question. Is there a motto, a quote or a thought that best defines your approach to life? Like the thing that you most often say to yourself or to others.

MM: Look, my mind is a sieve. I've said many things over the years, but I keep forgetting them! The thing is, I can't live without my restaurants. If someone said, 'Matt, your media career is fantastic but you don't have your restaurants anymore', it would devastate me. If someone came to me and said, 'Your media career's over, but you've still got your restaurants', I'd be happy.

Imelda Roche AO

Entrepreneur (retired) – Roche Group

―――――

'If it is to be, it's up to me.'

Imelda Roche is widely recognised and honoured as an inspiring businesswoman. She was named one of the fifty leading Women Entrepreneurs of the World. An exceptional woman in her own right, she was appointed by Prime Minister Paul Keating as Australia's representative to the Business Forum of the Asia–Pacific Economic Co-operation (APEC), and subsequently by Prime Minister John Howard as a representative to the successor organisation, the Business Advisory Council to APEC. She is the recipient of two honorary doctorates and the Australian Centenary Medal.

With exceptional passion and enterprise, Imelda and her husband, Bill, grew the iconic Nutri-Metics business in Australia to become the most profitable division of the American company's multi-million dollar international business. The Roche family acquired the entire Nutri-Metics Organisation in 1992 before selling it to the Sara Lee Corporation six years later. While the Roche Group is now largely a property and tourism venture, Imelda's story shines a light on one woman's amazing ability to succeed in business while not losing sight of the important things in life.

www.rochegroup.com.au

Interview

BRETT KELLY: What do you think are the most critical issues facing Australian businesses?

IMELDA ROCHE: Notwithstanding the present decline in employment overall, there are skill shortages in many geographic areas and specific sectors of the Australian economy which will take decades to overcome without more focus on specialised training and skills-based immigration. The high Australian dollar is having a very uneven effect across the economy, the obvious problems being the impacts on inbound tourism and exports, especially for our manufacturing and rural industries.

BK: What are your views on immigration?

IR: In my view, immigration is vital to Australia's future. While recognising the obvious difficulties, ideally our intake should be through managed sources and as large as we can afford to integrate into our diverse communities in any given year. We are a small nation occupying a very large land area. To secure and progress our nation and to keep us economically competitive in the years ahead, we need to significantly expand our population. To do this we need massive investment in new infrastructure, the most critical of which would be in the capture, storage and distribution of water.

Over the years we have heard many times that Australia, being the driest continent, cannot support more than twenty-five million people. It is my view that this assertion is, and has been, largely based on the judgement that without a substantial increase in our national income, we will not, in the foreseeable future, have the financial capacity to make the necessary infrastructure investment for major water capture, storage and distribution projects.

Though much of Australia is subject to cyclical weather patterns, in most years we do have a high enough rainfall on much of the east coast and across northern Australia to irrigate large areas of the continent, if the necessary infrastructure was in place.

Our national ability to invest in or to attract investment for essential infrastructure is constrained by the size of our population. It is rather like the conundrum of the chicken and the egg. Which comes first?

BK: What impact did the GFC (global financial crisis) have on your business?

IR: It depends on which aspect of our business we focus on. We are now largely a property group, however, our portfolio includes three Irish pubs, the Hunter Valley Gardens and two cattle breeding stations.

The GFC had minimal impact on our hotels, the Gardens or the cattle stations, however, it continues to have a major impact on our property business. Compared to the financial sector, the property sector is heavily taxed. There is no stamp duty on share transfers while transactional taxes and stamp duty are levied on the property sector and are significant. We pay annual land tax on our properties and stamp duty for any property we purchase. We believe that there should be a more even playing field between the different sectors.

'We are a small nation occupying a very large land area. To secure and progress our nation and to keep us economically competitive in the years ahead, we need to significantly expand our population.'

BK: What are your views on debt in your business and life?

IR: Conservative in both business and private life, we are continuously assessing our debt, however, we are very mindful of progressing our diverse business entities and the lives of all who work within our business. In my private life I remain financially conservative and have never had a difficulty in recognising the difference between needs and wants.

BK: What is your view on tax and how has it affected you?

IR: Dealing with the philosophical first, paying tax in any aspect of our lives does not usually represent fun. There are, however, moral issues imbedded in our attitude to tax.

There are, and always will be, critics of any tax system and of any changes to it. There are inevitably winners and losers. However, the reality is that no modern society can effectively provide all the services needed and expected, and meet its financial responsibilities without the majority of the population and all business entities paying their fair share of tax – Greece is a prominent example of a nation with an ambivalent attitude to tax. There will always be competing sectional interests and conflicting views as to what is fair and reasonable.

How much do we need to be taxed for? Amongst other things:
- Providing adequate health services for the entire community
- Caring for those in the community unable to care for themselves

- Providing education for young people and skills training for the unemployed
- Maintaining and improving our national competitiveness
- Maintaining and improving our essential services and public infrastructure
- Maintaining an adequate defence force and effectively playing our part in maintaining stability in our region, etc.

BK: Is there one thing that you think that anybody who wants to succeed in business should definitely not forget?

IR: Yes. That it takes work and commitment and usually involves some sacrifice. It helps to have a passion for what you do and to be able to think outside the box. There are of course a few basics. First and foremost is the importance of the example you set.

In any successful business the leadership must maintain a strong work ethic, generate high energy and maintain a constant focus on productivity goals while never forgetting to recognise the contribution of all who work within the business. A successful business must also be well-researched and have realistic, short, medium and long-term flexible action plans.

BK: Is there anyone that you have looked at, who has really inspired you?

IR: The person who stands out to me most in recent history is Nelson Mandela. Here is a man who had a great deal to be bitter about, however, he emerged from his twenty-seven years of imprisonment with his focus on the advancement and wellbeing of his countrymen. It was about his country, his people and his community – with forgiveness in his heart – not about himself.

BK: Imelda, tell us about the business that you started, where it developed and how it was eventually sold.

IR: My husband Bill and I met in Canberra in early 1957. We were both representing our companies at the opening of Canberra's first self-service food department. Bill was with the Kellogg Company and I was with the National Cash Register Company. I was there to train staff in the operation of the store's new-style cash registers.

Within a few months of that meeting, both Bill and I decided we had found our life partner. However, we needed to find a way to earn more than our salaries provided before we could even think about marriage. We started to brainstorm ways to earn substantially more money. (I was already working a second job three nights a week, and had a third working weekends, babysitting.)

As it happened, Australian television had made its first broadcast just a few months earlier in September 1956. It is funny to think about it now, but soon after

TV was introduced, there was a popular theory circulating in the community that if you did not have a soft light on the set while you were viewing TV, it could injure your eyes. Everyone seemed to believe it, including us.

Bill came up with the idea that we could make television lamps and that he could take orders from country furniture stores for them to include lamps in the sale of their television sets. He secured orders with his first few calls, so we set to work creating mini-workshops in both of our mothers' living rooms and co-opted all the female relatives we could persuade into helping us. I laugh when I think about it now; they were awful – coloured raffia or plastic ribbon wound around wire frames.

We continued selling them into country stores until Bill's oldest brother, who had some direct selling experience, asked, 'Why don't you sell them direct to the home?' He offered to organise a small sales team. We decided we would sell them with a deposit of five shillings, then two and sixpence a week until paid off. Bill's other brother, who was a very handsome young man, volunteered to do the collection rounds on Saturday mornings.

I think the ladies quite liked him and did not mind handing over their two and sixpences. He reported to us that while doing his rounds he was repeatedly asked, 'What else do you sell?' That really set us a challenge. What else could we sell? We tried manchester, unsuccessfully, as we could not compete on price with the department stores.

'In any successful business the leadership must maintain a strong work ethic, generate high energy and maintain a constant focus on productivity goals while never forgetting to recognise the contribution of all who work within the business.'

Soon after, we decided to try fashion and with inspiration from *The Australian Women's Weekly* and Vogue, Butterick and Simplicity pattern books, I became an instant fashion designer. We found several small companies who made garments for the trade and they agreed to manufacture for us and advised how many garments we should order, in each size. I selected the fabrics and put the range together with the manufacturers. Not high fashion, just timeless basic designs. We employed several teams of saleswomen to sell Roche Fashions direct to the home and from a modest start Roche Fashions was in business for over ten years.

As we expanded from Sydney to Newcastle and Melbourne, we needed additional finance and entered into an arrangement with Waltons Department Store to sell our newly opened accounts to them. This provided us with working capital, and enabled Waltons to expand its direct-to-the-home business. This worked well for a time, however, as Waltons salesmen took over collecting on the modest debts we had established, they substantially increased the indebtedness of many customers by further selling carpets, lounge suites, refrigerators and washing machines, etc, on time payment.

We had no control over how these accounts were credit rated, increased or managed and when customers defaulted on their weekly repayments, Waltons deducted the full amount of the original debt from the payment currently due to us from new accounts. This made our arrangement with Waltons unworkable, so it was back to the drawing board for us.

By now it was 1968 and I started researching who else was selling direct to the home and how they operated. This was the beginning of phase two of our independent business lives. As I researched the fledgling industry I found there were several small Australian direct selling companies operating in Sydney and two international majors, Avon and Tupperware, both reasonably new to Australia. Whereas Roche Fashions had salaried sales teams who worked for extra commission on sales, all these companies worked on commission alone, which helped control overheads.

Those old enough to remember will recall that in 1968 there were still two afternoon newspapers in Sydney, *The Sun* and *The Daily Mirror*. Coincidentally, during my research, *The Sun* ran an advertisement seeking management for a California-based direct selling company planning to expand to Australia. I responded and, hearing nothing back, had almost forgotten about it, until early one morning, months later, I answered the phone to the most captivating voice I had ever heard. Any mother of small children will know it is hard to be captivated at 7.30 in the morning with two toddlers and a baby in a high chair demanding breakfast.

The voice belonged to Lee Trent, who I later discovered was the original radio voice of the Lone Ranger in the 1930s and early forties. He introduced himself, said that he was staying at the Wentworth Hotel and asked if I would come to the hotel that day for a meeting. I went and was absolutely fascinated. He stood about six feet five inches tall, was pencil slim and had a shock of silver hair.

He told me that he was in Sydney to establish Con-Stan Industries, a company which marketed nutritional products, skin care and cosmetics in the United States and Canada, and that he was in Australia on behalf of the President and owner of the company, a man by the name of Mulford Nobbs. He explained that a deal had been concluded with a Sydney businessman to establish Con-Stan in Australia and that products had been shipped from California. However, when he and the products arrived the Sydney, the man did not provide, as had been agreed, the finance needed to release the products from Customs, nor his agreed share of the start-up costs. I immediately recognised that this could possibly provide us with the opportunity to take on the challenge of this start-up.

I was intrigued by both the concept of the business plan and the products. The business plan gave women who were principally homemakers a wonderful opportunity to set their own flexible work timetable and to contribute to the financial wellbeing of their families. However, it was the product itself that truly captured me. The concept of a totally natural range of skincare products (a first for Australia) was exciting. I was convinced it had the necessary elements to make it a success. The product was unique, the timing perfect, and both subsequently worked very well for us.

BK: So it was very similar to your own situation. You had already been direct selling for ten years at that point?

IR: Yes, and I was anxious to tell Bill about it.

BK: I was going to ask – what did he say when you said you were going to sell skincare?

IR: He took some convincing that this could be a winner in an already crowded skincare market, however, I convinced him it was worth investigating as this product was unique. Bill met Lee the following day and they hit it off immediately. They both had a very relaxed and ironic sense of humour and enjoyed one another's company enormously.

They worked together closely over many years until Lee passed away, a very sad event for us. The decision to take on the start-up of Con-Stan in Australia (Nutri-Metics as the worldwide company was to be renamed in 1983) was made right there at that meeting. We decided then and there to provide the funds to retrieve the product from Customs and to hand over the running of Roche Fashions to Bill's two brothers.

Under Lee Trent's guidance we started from scratch to develop a field force for Con-Stan in Australia. In the first week we attracted five people who came from the business of the man who had originally intended to partner with Con-Stan.

From the beginning we divided the responsibilities. My focus was sales and marketing and front-of-house activities, primarily attracting and training the field force. Bill took on the responsibility for overall management. Within a year or two, we had set up local manufacturing both in Australia and New Zealand and Bill added new component and packaging design and product development to his overall responsibilities. He was always very creative and loved the opportunity to be involved in design.

As we expanded the Australian and New Zealand businesses he personally supervised the design and building of two training and product distribution offices and warehouses in Auckland and Christchurch and in each of our six State capitals, where possible in a garden setting. As you know, he has gone on to develop Hunter Valley Gardens (with the help of experienced professionals), however, it was his vision, his concept and his creation.

Back to the beginning ... In the first few months, three sales trainers came in rotation from the United States to assist and to train me. From the original five people in Sydney, we rapidly expanded throughout Australia, and by 1972 we were operating in New Zealand and Singapore. During the next decade we also expanded to Japan, Malaysia, Brunei, Thailand, Indonesia, China and Hong Kong and later dispatched Australians to manage start-ups in several countries in Europe.

BK: You had the rights to take Nutri-Metics anywhere apart from the US and Canada.

IR: We didn't have any specific or designated rights, however, as opportunities presented, we went ahead and expanded the business. Of course Mulford Nobbs was delighted with the fact that we forged ahead on literally just a promise and a handshake. It was not until 1984 that we formally achieved any percentage ownership of the business. Up to that time, we worked solely on an agreed percentage of sales revenue.

BK: Of the US business too?

IR: No, nothing from the US, just from the businesses we created.

'I was intrigued by both the concept of the business plan and the products. The business plan gave women who were principally homemakers a wonderful opportunity to set their own flexible work timetable and to contribute to the financial wellbeing of their families.'

BK: So, you had been in the business since 1968. Around 1991 you went to the owner of the business in the US, who was then in his mid-eighties, and said, 'We are prepared to buy the worldwide group.' He agreed a price, a price that wasn't necessarily a function of financial mathematics but more, as is often the case, the number that the owner wanted. You guys struggled to raise the money but eventually found a willing banker. How confident were you in the business? How nervous were you about the transaction? Because you are not twenty-one at this point; you guys are in your late-fifties ...

IR: We were taking on a huge commitment, a business operating in sixteen countries. However, we were confident because we knew what the Australian business was capable of and we knew what the international businesses we had established and developed around the world could be capable of and we were already directly managing most of them. And yes, we knew there was considerable risk in taking on a huge debt burden, however, we believed we could handle it and we did.

BK: You then decided that your main focus would be in the markets that you had established and not in the US. Was that because of the level of competition there?

IR: No, not necessarily. There was a great deal more strength in several of the other markets, so we initially focused on building on strength.

BK: What happened then? You sold the business in 1997 ...

IR: Yes, we acquired it in 1991 and sold it in 1997.

BK: Was the plan always to buy it and sell it?

IR: In 1991 the plan was to continue it as a family-owned company. It had been a family-owned American business and we intended to continue it as a family-owned Australian business.

We made what some would regard as a not-too-bright decision. We immediately headquartered the business in Sydney. This involved us in a very substantial tax bill which, had we maintained the overseas corporation, would have been handled differently. However, we had decided that we wanted Nutri-Metics to become an Australian-owned corporation that would be kept in the family. Over the next six years we continued to build the business both in Australia and internationally and during that time, in 1993, I became Chairman of the World Federation of Direct Selling Organisations. It was the first time for an Australian and the first for a woman.

It was then that we came to the attention of several of the major direct selling companies, and one in particular, the Sara Lee Corporation. Representatives of Sara Lee made contact with us at a World Federation Congress in Berlin and suggested it might be interested in buying Nutri-Metics. We told them we were not interested in selling. However, they continued to make contact regularly over the next three years and on several occasions broached the subject of a possible joint venture into India.

They were particularly interested in the businesses we had developed in Asia as they had very little presence in that region. They were also intrigued by the fact that we had a reasonably strong business in France, which is regarded by many as the home of quality skincare, fragrance and cosmetics. We also had modest businesses in the United Kingdom and Ireland and a strong business developing in Greece managed by Greek Australians. From the United Kingdom we were sending product to several European countries including The Netherlands where we had a strong sales team led by an Australian, and from Greece we were sending product into Cyprus.

In addition to the overtures from Sara Lee, it was becoming apparent that not all of our children saw a career for themselves in Nutri-Metics. Two were already thinking about other things and this in itself could have introduced complications down the track. We began to think that maybe the best thing we could do to assist our children, or young adults as they were by then, would be to provide financial support for each of them to develop their own career paths, and not necessarily tie them to something that Bill and I had created.

A direct selling business is very different in character and style to many other businesses. It is more than usually personality-driven and dependent on very committed, dedicated leadership. In direct sales leadership, you become more than usually involved in the lives of the people working with you, as you endeavour to help them set their business goals and priorities.

I would know much of what was going on in the family lives of many of our senior field leaders because it was necessary to understand their challenges to know how to assist them to set and reach their goals, which of course were a vital part of the overall corporate goals. While always recognising they were not employees, rather independent associates running their own businesses. We needed to motivate, encourage and inspire our field force to want to do what was needed to grow their businesses and enjoy all of the benefits that Nutri-Metics had to offer them.

You can give direct instructions to salaried people and expect them to do as you ask them to do. You cannot give instruction in the same way to people who are self-employed. Motivation and encouragement are the key and this requires an enormous commitment of time from the leadership. Recognising those industry distinctions, gave us pause for thought. Bill and I had lived the business, sometimes at the expense of our family life, and we did this, not only because of our passion for the business, but also to create a better life and for our children, as they grew older, the freedom to make their own individual choices about their future work/life balance.

BK: Is Bill the same age as you?

IR: He is a year younger and I have never been allowed to make a secret of it, even if I had wanted too. Bill regularly enjoyed making a joke of telling the Nutri-Metics consultants at our annual seminars that he married an older woman – to which I would respond, 'He needed the wisdom.'

BK: So, you are sixty-three at the time, approaching an age where people do think about these things. There is an opportunity. What happens then?

IR: The decision to sell did not go down well initially, or create total harmony within the family, because for our children, it was completely unexpected. So there were challenges.

'We began to think that maybe the best thing we could do to assist our children would be to provide financial support for each of them to develop their own career paths, and not necessarily tie them to something that Bill and I had created.'

BK: How did you handle that? Did you sit everyone down and have a discussion? Did you say, 'It's our business and we'll do as we like.'?

IR: We would never say to our children, 'It is our business and we will do as we like with it.' That was never part of our thinking. Our major difficulty was that absolutely no premature hint of a possible sale could be revealed to anyone in case the discussions amounted to nothing. That would have been very destabilising.

BK: So the possible sale was a secret from everybody.

IR: Yes, everybody. We could not take the risk of anything leaking until a deal was concluded. So there was no discussion with any members of the family until after the contracts were signed, and that caused some heartache. The thought that we would sell the business without consulting them was hard for them to come to terms with and the decision was both difficult and, in its own way, painful for Bill and for me.

Within that same week we brought together our senior corporate management from around the world, together with the most senior and influential leaders of our field force and made the announcement to everyone at the same time. It was all done very quickly once agreement was reached.

As the shock of it all settled down, we worked to make sure there was a good level of confidence, security and understanding with all of our corporate people and senior field leaders.

As Bill wanted to move on to other horizons, I agreed to stay on for three years as Chairman of the company, primarily to help with the transition from being a still comparatively small multi-national family company, to being part of a very large multi-national.

My role was to assist a smooth transition and to ensure that we would maintain everybody Sara Lee saw as valuable going forward, as obviously there were bound to be changes in the way the business would be conducted. There were of course some people who were not happy with the change and decided to move on. Fortunately, we did keep the most important players at the senior corporate level and all of our senior field leaders, as I knew would be the case, as all had so much invested in their own independent organisations. Many are still with the company today.

BK: They had invested a lot of time and energy in their own organisations?

IR: Yes and that concerned us. We really needed to ensure that the transition to Sara Lee management was as comfortable as possible for everyone and that both our corporate staff and field leaders saw a positive future for themselves going forward. Working effectively with Sara Lee personnel, it all went smoothly.

BK: So, you get through that. Obviously going from the challenge of a situation where you and Bill couldn't get married because you didn't have sufficient money, to forty years later selling a very successful business and cashing a large cheque, that's a very different scenario entirely. What did you do then? Did you have a clear plan?

IR: We had over the years acquired several substantial landholdings that we never had the time or the money to start developing. They had remained just landholdings for many years. In addition, a few months after we sold the business we acquired a property at Pokolbin, that eventually was to become Hunter Valley Gardens. Bill was inspired from the time we first visited the Butchart Gardens in Canada some thirty-five years earlier to create something similar. He had said to me during that visit, 'One day I want to do something like this.' That thought was reaffirmed for him each time we visited the Butchart Gardens in subsequent years.

It was on a drive back from Broke, where we had for some years attended Opera in the Vines, that we passed a 'For Sale' sign on a vineyard in Pokolbin. We saw that the property had a wonderful 360° view of the valley and the Brokenback Range. It was planted with very old Shiraz vines and we thought we should buy it to have as an out-of-town retreat for the family.

Within weeks of acquiring the vineyard, the property next door, which is now Hunter Valley Gardens, came up for sale so we added that too. Then Bill discovered from an old map of the district that there had been a slice of the original property cut out on Broke Road, which housed the only pub in Pokolbin, and suggested we should also acquire the pub, as it was built on part of the original land grant, and this would enable us to put the original property back together again.

He gutted what was a very 'ordinary' hotel and converted it to a family-friendly Irish pub. We have since gone on to build two more Harrigan's Irish Pubs in two of our residential community developments – one on the mid-north coast of New South Wales and one in south-east Queensland. So there are now three Harrigan's Irish Pubs. They are all family-friendly; absolutely a pleasure to be in.

BK: One of the challenges I regularly see that people have is how to live together and work together. How did you guys do it?

IR: Well Brett, my first response to that would have to be, 'With difficulty!' You would know, it's challenging enough to stay married for over fifty years and raise four children without, at the same time, being in business together for most of those years. I would have to say that you manage through compromise and by separating responsibilities, and by trying not to second-guess one another.

Bill's approach to many situations is very different to mine so we needed to give one another space. If the issue was important enough we would talk it through until we agreed or agreed to disagree. If it involved his area of responsibility the ultimate decision would be his and vice versa. We each understood enough about the overall business that if Bill was overseas and a decision needed to be made in his area of responsibility, I could handle it and he could do the same with sales and marketing. In most instances we avoided second-guessing one another and discouraged staff and the field force from going from one to the other if they didn't get the answer they wanted.

———

'My advice to the women who worked with me, and to any I spoke to who wanted to succeed in business, was to employ as much help as they could afford. It is not possible to maintain being a wonder woman indefinitely.'

BK: How did you manage the domestic end?

IR: In the very early days my mother filled in for me whenever I needed her, especially when I was away from Sydney, and I always supported her with as much domestic help as we could afford. What I really needed from her was for her just to be there with the children when I was away. She would see them off to school, cook dinner at night and tuck them into bed.

I had a number of people help with the house cleaning, the washing, the ironing, the gardening, the window cleaning, whatever! My mother was not a young woman at that stage and she had raised six children of her own and worked hard all of her life. She made it possible for me to work and to travel while retaining peace of mind, knowing our children were well cared for. I was deeply indebted to her.

My advice to the women who worked with me, and to any I spoke to who wanted to succeed in business, was to employ as much help as they could afford.

It is not possible to maintain being a wonder woman indefinitely. You can't be all things to all people all of the time and you cannot meet all of the expectations of family life while continuing to do everything in the home yourself. It is just not possible. You must prioritise what is important to you and your family.

It is good to remember that your husband really doesn't care who irons his shirts unless they are not done to his satisfaction; your children don't care who cleans the oven and scrubs the floors as long as you don't ask them to do it. So really, it is a matter of proper organisation and delegation. 'A happy wife is a happy life'. It is OK to provide paid work for someone else, to do the jobs around the house you do not have the time or the energy to do – it all helps to spread the wealth.

BK: Did you have live-in help after your mother could no longer do it?

IR: Yes, from time to time I did, mostly when my children were young. As they grew older, they all went to boarding school for a period of time, which they mostly enjoyed.

BK: So, you were the public face of Nutri-Metics, Bill was working in the business with you – what was the domestic scenario? Who was the boss?

IR: Bill usually made the major investment decisions both in the business and for the family. I tended not to become too involved because it was not necessary.

He has made good decisions over the years.

Brett, there were times when I wouldn't have known exactly what the business was earning. That wasn't my focus. My focus was marketing and sales, recruiting, training and expanding our consultant base – developing and working closely with our field leadership, travelling constantly to consultant reward and recognition meetings and arranging local and international sales conferences. Cars and travel were a very important part of the Nutri-Metics achievement reward program.

Bill made all the investment decisions as he saw appropriate. Of course he did consult me from time to time! One of the happy aspects of our married life is that we have never had an argument or even a disagreement over money, even when we had very little. There have of course been a number of other issues we could find to disagree about, but never money. As long as we had what we needed to educate our children, live in a comfortable home and pay the bills, I was happy. We have never been particularly extravagant.

BK: No private jets or fast cars? What about boats?

IR: Well, boats are quite a different story. Bill has been known from time to time to be a small fleet owner, which is something of a family in-joke. There is the large family catamaran which he bought as just a hull over twenty-five years ago then designed and had built. He still loves that boat. Over the years he has acquired other smaller boats and has spent next to no time in or on them. However, he has always loved boats, they are his main recreational interest.

BK: But other than that, not a lot of trinkets?

IR: No, not really. The family still has the car Bill bought for me in 1979 which I am reluctant to ever sell (one of my daughters-in-law currently drives it). The car I now drive most of the time has been in the family for twelve years.

BK: Would you describe yourself as frugal?

IR: On some levels I suppose it could be said that I am. One of my sons once described me to his mates as having a Depression-era mentality. They were watching me flatten out brown paper bags, as I had seen my mother so often do, to use again for school lunches. I saw her re-use everything. She rarely threw anything out.

The lessons you learn and the things you observe in your early life are hard to shake off – and in truth, I really don't want to shake them off. I would say, though, that overall I think I am more financially conservative than frugal, and I tried to raise my children to have those same values.

BK: You have four children and they are all well-adjusted and happy. You were committed to raising your children and you built a business – those two things are not normally as compatible as they have been here. What are the values you have tried to give your children?

IR: In a nutshell, to lead wholesome lives.

BK: What does that word mean for you?

IR: It means being a person of integrity, being trustworthy and truthful, with a goodness of heart and a purity of mind and spirit. A healthy self respect with good moral standards and values; nothing contrived or superficial.

BK: How do you guard against a sense of entitlement in children, where there is financial capacity around or there's success right in front of them?

IR: Setting an example is more important than anything else. Expressed in another piece of homespun wisdom I value, 'Your actions speak so loudly I cannot hear what you say.'

'For most people, something unearned is rarely valued.
Something produced with your own hands or earned through
your own effort creates a healthy sense of achievement . . .'

BK: Do you give your kids things, or do you let them go and earn it themselves?

IR: I have to admit that none of our children had to earn a dollar for themselves until they had left school or finished studying at university. I sometimes reflect on this, as Bill collected bottles at the local oval as a kid to earn a few pennies and we both left school and started working at fifteen.

However, our four children have all turned out to be really good citizens, wonderful parents and have all chosen excellent partners in life. We have four very stable young families and much to be thankful for. I would think that my best advice to parents would be to really safeguard against an automatic or unrealistic sense of entitlement. For most people, something unearned is rarely valued. Something produced with your own hands or earned through your own effort creates a healthy sense of achievement and a legitimate sense of entitlement. Somebody said to me when I was a very young woman, 'Remember this: "If it is to be, it is up to me." Keep that in your mind. You are not entitled to hand-outs, what you want and need, you need to go earn.' That thought has influenced my attitude to life. I have also learned along the way that if you are prepared to give more than you expect to receive, you will rarely if ever be disappointed.

BK: Your whole life?

IR: Well, for most of my adult life those two things have guided my attitude to life and business. I don't believe I felt that way as a child or young adult. In fact, I am sure I didn't. These attitudes and thoughts developed over time with experience and maturity.

BK: OK, how is the family business run now?

IR: After we sold the Nutri-Metics business (Sara Lee later stylised the corporate name to Nutrimetics), over time we had a number of family members involved in what became the Roche Group. We had a brother-in-law, two sons and two sons-in-law. By that time the girls were all busy with babies or young children.

When Bill and I decided to retire, our sons were forty-ish and more than ready to take over. It was time for us to stand aside and not wait until our boys were well into middle age. It was not easy for Bill to decide to hand over the reins. Brett, I'm sure you've heard it said many times, that it is easier for a woman to stand aside than for most men.

BK: Yesterday's man. It's a difficult concept.

IR: Yes, it is difficult. Particularly if sons might say, 'Dad, we've got it, we discussed that last week; don't need to go over it again.' During most of his business life, Bill worked with a personal assistant and never had the need to use a computer. Nor did I for that matter, although I have since learned to send emails. Bill was very used to spending time in regular face-to-face meetings with the people who worked directly with him. Personal computers have introduced to business a whole new world that we did not grow up with.

BK: Now you are happily retired and have thirteen grandchildren. Does Bill have a current work focus?

IR: He is focusing a lot of his time on the Hunter Valley Gardens. He loves it.

BK: He's got a passion for it.

IR: A well-kept garden of any size is always a work in progress; that is especially true of a large tourist garden.

BK: It is never finished?

IR: Bill loves that garden and loves being involved in its continuing development.

BK: So your business and personal life have been an extraordinary journey; an example to many.

IR: Brett, in my life I have been fortunate to visit many countries, to see many amazing things and to meet and work with many interesting people. With a little personal discipline and some measure of sacrifice and hard work – and with a fair share of luck thrown in – we have managed to achieve a few things. Though it is interesting to note, like so any others, the harder we worked, the luckier we were.

'We all have responsibilities, we all have abilities and we all have opportunities in many different ways to make a contribution, to make a difference. And it is up to each one of us to make that difference.'

BK: What's next? I mean, you're only seventy-eight!

IR: Thank you for remembering, Brett! Happily, there is a lot of 'next' to look forward to, on many fronts …

BK: So keep going?

IR: Yes certainly keep going, but learn from where you've been. As people and as a nation, we must embrace change and innovation, value productivity and maintain a positive work ethic and we must always remember to give recognition and value the work of others.

BK: Compassion, fair play, wholesomeness–

IR: Where we are all going together does matter. We all have responsibilities, we all have abilities and we all have opportunities in many different ways to make a contribution, to make a difference. And it is up to each one of us to make that difference. While little of lasting value is accomplished alone, we need to remember in leadership, 'If it is to be, it is up to me.'

Andrew Simmons

Entrepreneur (Fitness) – Vision Personal Training

'Getting results, that's what retention's all about. You actually build a great culture and help people get great results so they stay around. We form the culture inside the gym.'

School didn't do it for him, neither did accountancy – but then there was this thing called personal training. Andrew Simmon's passion has helped so many people take greater control of their health and wellbeing, and has resulted in a business enterprise with almost fifty studios, four hundred personal trainers and nearly fifteen thousand people training with his group each week.

www.visionpt.com.au

Interview

BRETT KELLY: Andrew, where did you grow up?

ANDREW SIMMONS: I was born and grew up in Perth – I am a sandgroper at heart. My father was transferred there with his work from Victoria, but when I was ten years old we were transferred to Sydney. I came across with my family to the Sutherland Shire. We moved into a motel, my mum, dad and my sister and me, for the first three months. It was no bigger than your office here, Brett. Then we grew up in Sylvania.

BK: What did your dad do?

AS: He was in industrial chemicals.

BK: An industrial chemist?

AS: He's got a background in that field, mainly operations.

BK: So which school did you go to?

AS: I went to Sylvania Heights Primary School then I was accepted into Trinity Grammar School at Summer Hill.

BK: What happened after school?

AS: After school? My whole life was mapped out for me. I was told what to do during school – I was told to go to swimming, athletics, water polo and rugby and train before and after school for those sports.

BK: Who told you to do this?

AS: The school, but I loved it. The time between nine and three was basically a recovery session for me so I could train and play sport on the weekend. Needless to say, my grades were very ordinary, but I was actually OK at maths and economics.

BK: So what personal general attributes did you get out of sport and training?

AS: It was commitment. I wasn't a natural sportsman. I was OK. I mean, I wasn't poor, but I was OK. In order for me to be good at sport, I had to train my butt off.

BK: So when you finished school what happened then?

AS: I went to work in a chartered accounting firm.

BK: That would have been exciting.

AS: Riveting.

—————

'It took two years to realise that while I could probably make some money being an accountant, I just wasn't passionate about it.'

BK: Were you at university at the time?

AS: I didn't get the marks to get into university. I only got into St George TAFE. I went there for the first twelve months and I worked in a chartered accounting firm in Strathfield. I used to go to TAFE at night, four nights a week. Then I would train in the morning so I could keep playing rugby.

BK: So, how did you get from being in a chartered accounting firm to being in the fitness industry?

AS: It took two years to realise that while I could probably make some money being an accountant, I just wasn't passionate about it.

BK: So there was no drive for it. What did you do then? Did you go and do a course in something?

AS: I just left my job and started working in a gym. I would also train in the gym and I met a lady there who was a registrar at the local uni. I knew it would be hard to get into uni because my grades weren't the best but I managed to get myself into the University of New South Wales. I studied sport science at the Oatley Campus – ten minutes down the road from my house! I was only going to be studying twenty-five hours a week face-to-face with a bit of studying on top. I thought, plenty of time, got to get a job. So I went to the gym and said I wanted a job. I'll do anything. So, they gave me one. I told them about my background in sport and they said they thought I'd be a good circuit instructor.

BK: So, training circuits.

AS: 'You can teach a class here in two weeks,' they said. I sat in the back of every circuit class I could for that two-week period. That threw me off the cliff. I was lucky when I was at uni, I was going through with a girl who was a world aerobics champion. She taught me how to do the basic aerobics moves in the class so I managed to get through my first circuit.

But getting paid between thirty and forty-five bucks a week to teach certain classes wasn't going to cut it. So I asked, 'What else can you give me?' They gave me some reception shifts before uni and I worked three mornings a week behind the reception desk. When I finished uni, I was fortunate to have had three years' experience in every part of the gym.

BK: So you liked the gym?

AS: Loved it. I loved the gym. I was teaching aerobics, circuits. I was working reception, I was working the gym floor. By the time I'd finished my uni degree, I'd had all this experience. I was frustrated though because I was writing all these programs for people on the gym floor, but no-one was getting results because I was just writing my program. I thought, 'I want to be able to help them some more.' Then I heard about this thing called a personal trainer.

BK: Now, what year are we talking about at this point?

AS: We're talking the beginning of 1995.

BK: OK, so 1995. No-one's got a personal trainer unless you're Jennifer Lopez. What happens then? You start doing personal training in the gym you're working at?

AS: I started doing personal training and as I got busier with my personal training clients, I dropped my gym floor shifts. I kept circuits, I kept my aerobics and I just loved it. I loved getting out there in front of people teaching classes.

BK: What were you charging for personal training sessions?

AS: Twenty bucks an hour.

BK: Whatever you could get?

AS: Twenty bucks an hour, mate, I was pumped.

BK: How many years did you do this for? What year did you start Vision Personal Training?

AS: I started Vision in August 1999. So, I had been doing personal training for four years by then.

BK: And then Vision for a good thirteen years. So you opened your first gym and now you've got forty-seven. How did that build up? Where did you get the concept? At the time there were only big, ugly, stinky gyms and you came up with a small format, two hundred and fifty squares with personal one-on-one training. Not the cheapest thing in the world. Was that the beginning?

AS: I was fortunate that I became a Les Mills national trainer. We were one of the first gyms in Australia to pick up a product called BODYPUMP from New Zealand. They'd systematised good training with the barbells. So, I was teaching the barbell class. It was really simple, really effective. You got great results and people loved it.

When I was working with fellow national trainers on teaching the BODYPUMP program to trainers, I felt that I was part of a team. But when I was doing my personal training class in the gym, I felt like it was dog eat dog. It was me against all the trainers rather than working with them, like I was with my Les Mills' experience. So I figured if they could do this with group exercise, if they could systemise group exercise, why couldn't it be done with personal training? When we first started Vision in 1999, I was still based in the gym. I was working in the gym while we built a steady team of, probably, eight trainers.

'I thought, "I want to be able to help them some more."'

BK: In Caringbah, your current head office?

AS: No, it was actually in Club Physical at Sylvania which in August 1999 or 2000 became Fitness First Sylvania. We built up a little team over time. I actually merged my business with Geoff Jowett who was a trainer at the gym as well. We figured we were on the same page and thought we could merge his business and my business together by running a body transformation challenge. His clients versus my clients. At the end of that twelve-week challenge, we had an awards night and launched our new business together, 'Vision'.

BK: I've always understood Vision to mean a vision of a better life, better fitness level and all the things that come from the discipline of strength and good health. Was that what you guys thought? What was the idea behind Vision?

AS: It was just about results, mate. We were the culture of that gym. We built the culture and we were helping people get amazing results.

BK: It's a hard sell. People drop off every five minutes, everyone knows that. People who bought your memberships were there to get results, though.

AS: Getting results, that's what retention's all about. You actually build a great culture and help people get great results so they stay around. We form the culture inside the gym.

BK: So, what is that culture?

AS: Basically, it's a culture of people having a great time, feeling like they're made to feel special inside the gym and they're getting great results.

BK: What was your view of the results that people would get?

AS: I think it's a holistic approach. It's massive. It transcends every aspect of your life. People become better lovers, better fathers, better mothers, better workers, better employers, better employees. It just transforms their lives. People just feel better. Some people might say we're in the health and fitness industry. I believe we're in the feel-good industry. We're helping people feel good about themselves. And there are a number of ways in which we help them feel good.

BK: OK. So, you've built up this feel-good business, you're really changing people's lives. Where does franchising come in? Where does turning this into a business come in and how important is that?

AS: Fitness First decided to change the rules on personal training – that really was the catalyst for the whole thing. We'd heard of a gym called Harper's Personal

Training in Melbourne – Craig Harper was doing a thousand sessions a week in three studios. I thought, wow, this guy's doing really well, we ought to find out what he's doing. So we went down to Melbourne to suss his studio out.

We came back and figured we were going to make ours bigger and better. He had a thousand square metres in his biggest studio in Brighton in Melbourne so we thought we'd try and find a site that big. Unfortunately at the time, but fortunately now, we could only find a spot which was just under five hundred square metres.

'Some people might say we're in the health and fitness industry. I believe we're in the feel-good industry. We're helping people feel good about themselves.'

BK: OK. You start to find the benefit of a scalable model in a small format, high turnover per square metre. So, from a business point of view, obviously, that makes a huge amount of sense – even if by accident.

AS: By accident, purely by accident.

BK: Because you were still in the mindset of, let's just have a huge gym.

AS: Let's just crank out a lot of personal training sessions. Let's try and go a thousand sessions a week in one studio. Then we realised, there's nothing personal about doing a thousand sessions a week and having so many people like a lot of other gyms have these days. They have over a thousand members to be financially viable, I suppose.

BK: Massive churn.

AS: There's nothing personal in that. So for me, then, it was a case of OK, let's try and find one, which I now realised would be small. The franchising thing came about because I realised that unless I gave my trainers the opportunity to grow, they were just going to leave, become competitors and grow their own businesses.

BK: Many people have said to me that to grow a business, you need to be able to offer great opportunities to your best people. Essentially, when I look at your business, these studios have grown out of the trainers – your best trainers and your best studios.

AS: Yes. We call it grow and go.

BK: Who are your biggest inspirations? Big companies or big people?

AS: I'd say Bill Phillips. He's an inspirational dude, transforming people's lives in America. He'd already told me how to get great results in his *Body for Life* book. I also got a lot of inspiration from my old man. He worked his butt off. Then my ex-girlfriend's father, Phillip Trivett, was a great inspiration to me, building the Trivett Classic Car Empire. Craig Harper was a big influence though. He gave me the drive to go and open my own studio.

But the biggest inspiration that really changed Vision into a franchisable model was when I went to the States. I met a guy named Rick Sikorski from Fitness Together and saw his business model. He shared his mistakes way back in 2003. All the mistakes that we were making, he'd already made, and he gave us a couple of tips that really transformed me.

BK: What were those tips?

AS: 'As the big gyms keep getting bigger and bigger in America, we're getting smaller and smaller,' he said.

BK: And more personal?

AS: More personal.

BK: More bespoke.

AS: And also getting people to commit to programs. We're getting people to commit to themselves.

'People have got to commit to themselves.'

BK: To commit to results.

AS: People have got to commit to themselves. The word contract in the gym is deemed to be a nasty term that's counter-productive to people getting results. The difference with us is–

BK: It's not a contract with you. It's a contract with themselves.

AS: Absolutely. We're holding them accountable to that contract. What happens with a lot of people when they go to the regular gym is it's a contract, but nobody's holding them accountable and actually saying, hey, you're not coming.

BK: So, the gyms are just after their direct debit.

AS: Absolutely.

BK: They never ring to say, why aren't you turning up? In fact, often it seems that they prefer that.

AS: Mate, the models can't work.

BK: The model may well be broken. It can't work without a commitment to an individual and transforming their life.

AS: That's right.

BK: OK, so Rick Sikorski's done well. Have you ever found that people at the top are easier to talk to than people in the middle range? That they're more generous with their knowledge?

AS: Absolutely.

BK: How much did he charge you for this life-transforming knowledge?

AS: Nothing. Zero. He was great. We went over there and spent a good day in his business, maybe a bit longer. Then we spent three days looking around his little studios. I think he wanted us to bring his model back to Australia. We realised how much we had learned from Les Mills in terms of systems, so we decided to build our own model.

BK: So, tell me about people outside the fitness industry that have inspired you and continue to inspire you.

AS: I have to say Sam Walton. It's amazing what he's done with Walmart. Guys like Brian Tracy, John Maxwell–

BK: Inspiring guys?

AS: And Tony Robbins, I idolise the guy. I just can't get enough of personal development.

BK: I've noticed a common pattern among the people that I've interviewed. They're not necessarily academic, but once they find something that engages

their passion, they suddenly read books, attend seminars, study in an area that they never would have before. You were an average student who didn't get the marks to get into anything, but you found the thing you were interested in and you got into the University of NSW. It seems a common pattern–

AS: If you're not passionate about it, don't even bother, that's my thing. I happened to find my passion. Jim Collins talks about looking at what you're passionate about and what you can make money from, what you believe that you can be the best in the world at.

I'm just totally passionate about helping people with their careers in health and fitness because the average life span of a personal trainer is about six months. That's ridiculous. I'm living out two dreams. I'm helping fitness professionals with their careers and I'm helping clients get the best results.

BK: So, two sets of clients.

AS: Absolutely.

'If you're not passionate about it, don't even bother, that's my thing.'

BK: Let's talk about pressure. You've built a fantastic business. You've got a great wife and she's obviously a lovely and tough person to be able to put up with the stuff that comes with building this type of business. How hard is it on the family? How many kids have you got?

AS: Four kids. I've got an eight-year-old, a seven-year-old, a four-year-old and an almost twenty-two-month-old right now. It can be really challenging.

BK: And Fiona's at home.

AS: She's been always supportive. She's never known me to be any other way. She met me when I was right into starting Vision in August 1999. We got together in April of 2000. So right from the get-go. We opened our first studio in Caringbah in February 2001.

BK: How focused were you when you had your first child? You were starting this business, trying to build it up, spending a lot of time away from the family. What sort of hours did you work?

AS: I train every day at five in the morning. Fiona's into it as well, she also trains every day. So while one of us is at home, the other one's outside training. We're always doing that. I typically finish that between 6 and 6.30 and then have breakfast with the kids. I'm in the office between 7 and 7.30 and then that goes through 'til six, seven or sometimes eight at night. I tend to work at home late at night after the kids go to bed.

BK: And you're travelling interstate.

AS: Yes, Fiona is really very supportive, probably because that's how her father's relationship was with her mother. My father-in-law built his own business so she understands that in order to get ahead that's what you need to do. I've been really fortunate in that respect. I haven't got a wife who has been used to the average Joe working nine to five, she didn't grow up in that environment.

BK: How important is she to what you do?

AS: Well, massively important. She's everything. She's a massive role model.

BK: I want to ask a tough question. How hard is it to run this type of business versus running four kids under eight?

AS: They're two entirely different things, mate. It's like, sometimes I've got to pump myself up. I'll sit in the driveway at night-time and I've got to pump myself up. You know, sit there and say righto, here we go. Round two.

BK: This is the stuff that people don't talk about – raising kids is very hard for a wife who's at home, it's very tough. Often they've got a career that they're modifying during that period, too. You work your guts out all day, you come home and you've got a lot to do with the kids. It's a shared effort and you can't build a business without a joint effort, either. OK, so what's the future? Do we take it to the cloud? Can I log in on my iPhone? What's the future?

AS: A lot of technology. Technology's an interesting thing. It's very frustrating because it's continually evolving. I think that's what I find the most frustrating thing. A lot of people expect you to draw a line in the sand, but don't realise that you can't. I want to make sure that we've got the highest quality of consistency and standards for personal trainers. I don't like what's going on out there at the moment – the focus, for example, just on exercise.

BK: It's fairly unregulated. The standards are pretty ordinary.

AS: I think too much focus has been on getting out there and training someone. Flog them an exercise and they're going to get a result. But that doesn't work. I mean, the equation's pretty simple but I think what trainers do, out of their–

BK: Misplaced enthusiasm?

AS: Maybe even laziness. They just go, 'Oh, I'll just change the exercise. That'll do. That should make it interesting for people.'

BK: Seventy percent of the outcomes that people are looking for are driven by their eating habits.

AS: Absolutely. People wear their emotions on their body and people self-medicate through food, drugs and alcohol, through work or sex – that's a nice one. People self-medicate in a whole lot of different ways and unfortunately the big one is food.

BK: OK. So, talk to me about fatness. I know you've got a passion for helping people be the best they can be. Fatness is an epidemic and fatness is just a symptom. You've got to treat the reasons that are causing it.

AS: I think that one of the best initiatives that this government's taken on is the investment in mental health.

BK: And your bum typically comes from what's in your head.

AS: That's right. So, if you can make a dent in what's driving people to sit on the lounge at night and closet eat, I think that's the right step.

'People wear their emotions on their body and self-medicate through food, drugs and alcohol, through work or sex … People self-medicate in a whole lot of different ways and unfortunately the big one is food.'

BK: OK. So, talking about mental health, obesity and health generally, what do you want? What's the legacy that you ultimately hope to achieve out of the business? Or are you just happy to flip it? Do something else?

AS: A lot of people ask me that. They ask when am I going to sell Vision and what I am going to do then. I love seeing people develop and grow.

BK: This is the right vehicle to see trainers grow, become the best they can be. Clients grow and become the best they can be, too. If somebody gave you a cheque tomorrow and you swapped the money for that, what would you do then?

AS: I really like what I'm doing, but I've still got challenges. Some people don't maximise their potential, some buck the system. You get that in franchising. But we have plenty of amazing people in our network, and that's fantastic.

James Stevens

Entrepreneur (Retail) – Roses Only

___

'I want to be a brand that lasts forever. I want to be like Coca-Cola® and I want the goodwill of this business to be the most valuable thing on its balance sheet – always. Because you can't buy trust, respect.'

With the hard-working heritage and business knowledge forged in the family business, James formed Roses Only in 1995. His extensive track record in high traffic retail enterprises (fruit and vegetables, fast food and flowers) and a strong focus on branding has transformed the business into a successful market leader. With an exceptional online presence, Roses Only delivers throughout Australia, New Zealand (Auckland) the United Kingdom (London) and beyond.

www.rosesonly.com.au

Interview

BRETT KELLY: James, I'm interested in the way you grew up in Sydney, and a little bit about the business that your dad had.

JAMES STEVENS: I grew up in Randwick. My father was a migrant, he came out in 1950 or 1951 from Greece. He lived and spent his early working life in the Randwick area. In 1954 he went into a partnership in a milk bar, the Winning Post Café, on Alison Road. I attended a Catholic school here in Randwick, Our Lady of the Sacred Heart in Avoca Street. Then in 1973, Mum and Dad decided to move back to Greece. The family was uprooted and we were taken back to Athens.

I was placed in a French Lycée in the middle of Athens. It was quite a nice school, quite an academic school and I did third class there. It was the end of the dictatorship, back in 1974, and then there was the imminent war against Turkey when Turkey invaded Cyprus, so in April or May 1974, perhaps around June, we decided to move back to Australia.

The house was still here in Randwick, a nice semi that my parents had bought themselves. A couple of years later, in 1975 or 1976, I think, they bought themselves a block of dirt up in South Coogee. I think there was a land release and they built a house there, which we stayed in from about 1977 through to about 1990. Then, subsequently, Mum and Dad bought a home in Point Piper. So the last couple of years, we were there. We've always been in and around the eastern suburbs.

BK: How did you get into the flower business?

JS: My mum and dad had a flower shop. Dad set up a little flower business with an uncle of mine, my mum's brother, in 1967 in Town Hall Station. He ran that shop quite well, it was quite a successful cashflow business. He actually maintained that even when we were overseas, he would actually commute.

BK: How long was that there for?

JS: Well, from 1967 through to either 2005 or 2008 – don't quote me. Dad's business model was always pretty simple – high passing trade. No brand. It was all about good quality flowers at a fair price and amazing service. He had to be quick because people could miss a train. I say that because that stuff is still engrained in me culturally, when I'm thinking about service and so on. The next thing was Dad's shop at Wynyard. So again, close to a station. He had a store on

George Street, just as you exited Wynyard on George Street, on the left-hand side, heading down towards the Rocks. We had a little kiosk-type stand there. He also had a shop at Central Station and a store at North Sydney station, and subsequently a store at Milson's Point station. So that was his basic business model. Volume and good service.

BK: What sort of hours did he work? Was he always at the shop or did you have good staff?

JS: I remember Dad leaving every morning to head out to the markets. Initially, it was Haymarket up until about 1974 or 1975. So I saw my dad getting up at the crack of dawn most mornings. I always felt sorry for him. That was because the market then opened at 6 o'clock and our stores were pretty close by, being in the city. But then, in about 1974 or 1975, the markets moved out to Flemington. Again, I remember crying. I felt sorry for my dad having to trek out there. It felt like it was the sticks back then.

'So that was Dad's basic business model. Volume and good service.'

BK: He would take a truck out there and get the flowers?

JS: Yes, a van, with my uncle. Then it went from one van to two vans to three vans and so on over the years, but really doing the hard yards pretty much every morning. Buying fresh produce was really, really important and they pretty much did it five to six days a week.

BK: The shop opened every day?

JS: Yes. All the shops were open, particularly the Town Hall store. Back in the days prior to the Queen Victoria Building and all those other buildings connecting into a station. So at first there were a couple of things that ran off Town Hall. It was the St Andrews Arcade that ran off to the west. Then, heading north, you had the Queen Victoria Building established. South, you had the HSBC building, but back then it was the Cooper's and Lybrand Building. Woolies was always open, that all sort of came about, but prior to that, stores used to close on a Saturday, even the old department stores, like Farmer's which was where Myer is now. David Jones would close at 12 or 1 o'clock on a Saturday.

I recall as a kid running around with Mum on a Saturday. She always helped Dad at work pretty much five days a week so she would do her running around with me, going down to the food hall in David Jones, collecting stuff for the weekend. We'd have the afternoon off, obviously, because the shops were closed. I've got an issue with seven-day trading. I think it's broken what was a beautiful family time. It doesn't exist anymore. We're all running around like crazy and if you think about it, the mere fact that all these stores and businesses are actually open, it means there is somebody on the other end of those counters that has to work

BK: Many of those jobs are casualised as well. It's hard to imagine that they actually stack up, working at three o'clock on a Sunday night anywhere!

JS: I don't believe we eat any more because of the seven-day trade. Some very powerful landlords have used it as a way of saying, well, now you're turning over more because you're open seven days a week, you're more accessible. I think it played into the hands of the much larger retailers, in particular, who could afford to do an Enterprise Bargaining Agreement (EBA) or have some sort of employee structure that a little business probably couldn't afford unless there was an owner-operator. But, as I said, we used to go home on Saturday afternoons to rest and play. Saturday night would be family time again, possibly a meal out or meal at home. The next day traditionally was either going to church or a family picnic. But again, it was family. There was the baked lunch. That was the special treat on a Sunday. I find it quite sad that it's all sort of disappeared. Quite a sad state of affairs.

BK: Yes. Because in a family unit, whereas once you would have come together for a meal, now someone's at uni, or working a part-time job on a Sunday.

JS: Yes, it's all quite disjointed now. So, going back to the business, just so you know, we took some other tenancies or space down at Town Hall Station. We ran a food outlet, which was quite a big food outlet there. And also another one at Central Station. These were very, very busy businesses with obviously a huge throughput, as you come out of Woolworths.

There was this really long sandwich and 'greasy Joe' shop – it had everything. It ran from Woolworths right through to the Commonwealth Bank. It was massive, fifty to sixty metres long. It was a big, big frontage. We ran that business for a long time. In fact, I actually set that up in 1985 whilst in my second year at uni.

BK: What was your path? Out of school into the business?

JS: No, out of school into uni. Uni was what you did on the side. Work was actually what we did day-to-day. Uni, even though it was full-time, was, in my father's opinion, something you did part-time because you were only there for twenty hours a week at most. That is, Dad considered my full-time uni commitment as only being a part-time commitment, in his opinion.

BK: So what degree did you do?

JS: I did a commerce degree. I majored in accounting with a sub-major in finance.

BK: While working full-time in the family business.

JS: While working, so doing the twenty hours at uni and the forty hours at work, pretty much.

BK: So then your first thing was to set up that business.

JS: We already had the flower businesses going. In 1985 we set up a food bar down there at Town Hall Station, the one at Central had already been going for ten years. Obviously, I tried to improve it a bit when I got involved. There were two tenancies side by side down at Town Hall Station. I bought the adjoining food tenancy to the one we had, and made it that big long one, so I was involved in the purchase of that.

'One of the reasons I set up Roses Only, one of the big drivers, was no longer wanting to deal with landlords.'

BK: Were they freeholds or leases?

JS: They were all leaseholds with State Rail. One of the reasons I set up Roses Only, one of the big drivers, was no longer wanting to deal with landlords. It was something that my parents spoke about, if not every night, then every alternate night around the dinner table.

You know, how every three or five years, you had to fight for your tenancy. You had to convince the owners that the rate that they were charging or were proposing to charge was ridiculous. Just because my parents were good retailers and good workers, working their guts out and being able to pay that rent did not justify the sort of rental levels that these guys were after.

You replace that amazing tenant with an average tenant and their ability to pay the rent suddenly drops. So Mum and Dad always felt cheated. The only thing they had in these businesses was the goodwill of the business as a result of where it was located. There's no brand being built. So when Joe Blogs comes along suggesting that a particular large dry cleaning outfit really wanted your space, it's, 'We're sorry to say, but we will be requiring your space.' There was not even an opportunity to match the rent. We had no choice, we had to get assistance from politicians. We weren't asking for any favours. We were just asking for whatever was fair. You know, someone that had been in a business over five years in one instance, sixteen years in another, fifteen or twenty years and then having to fight off someone that could come there and just take over.

The other thing that you don't have as a tenant is you don't have any value. You've got zero goodwill when your tenancy or your term of tenancy is up. So it's too easy for someone to come along and take over. Just because another tenant can actually afford to pay more in rent if you really think about it because they're not building any goodwill. And where a business might be worth $100 000 or $200 000 as a flower shop, they don't have to pay that. They just sort of step in and just take over your business and also have a tax-deductible rental. They could possibly afford to pay 20%, 30% or 40% more in rent.

BK: Yes. Absolutely, because there's no tax deduction on the goodwill if they had to buy goodwill.

JS: So, these are all things that played on my mind, things that I would come across. The other thing was, we ran a flower business. A business that traditionally consisted of a lot of designer, arty people. And we found them very hard to come by and very hard to keep. They could put their hand up and get a job at the next flower shop tomorrow where they might be paid an extra dollar or two an hour. We're talking thirty or forty years ago now, so it was very hard. I've seen my parents accosted by three upset florists just before Mother's Day.

BK: So essentially, blackmail.

JS: Absolute blackmail.

BK: I see it all the time in business.

JS: I've seen three florists not show up in a little flower business on the day before Mother's Day. That is your worst nightmare. So that was another aspect of why I created Roses Only.

BK: So when did Roses Only start?

JS: 1995.

BK: And how old were you?

JS: I would have been thirty.

BK: OK, you've seen all of this, you're married. You've watched your parents put up with all of this.

JS: I joined the business full-time. No university after 1988. I joined the business, persevered, did as much as I could with the structure of the existing situation, but was always looking.

Our first foray out of a high, passing-trade location was this little store where Price Waterhouse Coopers is now in Darling Park. We ran a store there from 1993, thinking what we'll do is try and create a little bit of a brand, do a bit of function work. Just try something different. In 1995, I had a girl working with me and I said, 'Look, I've got an opportunity to take a tenancy that has been proposed to us up at Chifley Plaza. They've approached us.' Back then, if you recall, they were very, very tough retail conditions in the early nineties. They couldn't lease a property up there for love or money and we were, I think, the third tenancy to go into Chifley Plaza. Tiffany's had already been signed up as a tenant. That was Tiffany's first foray into Australia. I think the Oxford Shop was going in there too. Now, I said that I would do it, but I wouldn't just create the same old thing again. I saw it as an opportunity to create a brand because I always felt that that building was never going to get the flow of traffic. But if I created a brand …

BK: There are influential people there, thought leaders? Among other brands?

JS: No, it wasn't leaders. It was more about the fact that if someone heard about it on the radio or saw it in the press, you needed a physical address to seem credible. You couldn't just appear out of nowhere. People don't trust you, and certainly didn't trust you back then if you didn't have some level of bricks and mortar, so we created that initial store up there.

Now this girl had actually said to me that she'd seen an idea in New York where someone was just selling roses. I don't know, it was almost the minute she mentioned that, I thought, that's it. That actually resolves all my issues like what will the brand be about. Roses were always the most aspirational product that a male would come in and buy. You'd only see men walking into the store a few times a year. I thought, you know what, we're going to be, Roses Only.

BK: So you came up with that name straightaway?

JS: I knew I wanted the word roses first because I thought that anything else may not be remembered.

BK: It's all about the roses?

JS: You know, if it's going to go into a white pages listing, it's got to be roses first. So we thought of 'only'. At the time, I remember a couple of friends had actually said the word 'only' is one of the most powerful words in the English dictionary. These guys were in advertising and marketing so we went along with that and created Roses Only. It was all about quality, service and something that could be measured. Because one of the biggest issues that you've got in any flower business is there are no internal controls, zero internal controls.

BK: You cannot duplicate the product, no barcodes, dealing with arty people etc. You cannot measure wastage.

JS: You cannot do a lot of these things, but with roses, it was all a numbers game. I knew that if I sold a thousand dozen a day, I needed twelve thousand roses. It wasn't that hard and at the end of the day, short of half of 1% or 1% spoilage or whatever …

BK: You could actually measure–

JS: Yes, there was a science there. It became a business. It was a business that, in time, an investor – not that I was ever thinking that – but an investor could actually get their head around how it works. This notion of, 'Oh, we'll create a fancy mixed arrangement or mixed bouquet of flowers,' means nothing, that you can measure.

'It was all about quality, service and something that could be measured.'

BK: Other fancy mixtures that are less expensive.

JS: But 98% to 99% of what we do is all about a number of stems going into a box.

BK: So a duplicatable product.

JS: Yes. Twelve or twenty-four tulips, six lilies, whatever. Even a Wow! Hundreds of Roses Arrangement is a hundred roses or multiples of two hundred or three hundred roses in an arrangement.

So there is a number behind everything and that is 98% of our business. So that was one aspect. The other thing is that you didn't need to be a flower designer to be able to lay three rows or four. So short of understanding quality, which is not that hard to learn, we believed that we could …

BK: Begin a scalable system less reliant on specific individuals.

JS: It is interesting to watch your own mind work through the issues that, from a very young age, you watched your parents dealing with. And start to try to knock out the weaknesses of the former model. Then the other thing was to create a brand that would never, ever, be at the mercy of a landlord. That was probably my biggest hook.

BK: Yes, you can feel that.

JS: So this brand is transportable …

BK: And this was 1995, pre-internet–

JS: Pre-internet. It was all about a telephone call to the brand. It had been done before. I mean, there were other businesses that you'd call in, mail-order houses. There is all this other stuff that did exist, but no-one was really doing it for flowers. So it was all about pushing the brand, being at a location that didn't cost as much in terms of rent.

BK: So you had that credibility, you had a location.

JS: And then basically substituting ridiculously high rents for a nominal rent. Then whatever we were saving in rent was being put into advertising and marketing with a product that wasn't as hard to produce.

BK: On a good scale.

JS: Scalable, and lastly, with staff that didn't–

BK: Who were unable to blackmail you in the way that staff can.

JS: Correct.

BK: What I find interesting is that even today, seventeen years down the track, the idea of a box of roses has still got real wow about it. There are plenty of imitators around today, but talk to me about the box because my first interaction with your brand would have been when somebody was delivered these roses to an office. Tell me about the thought process, because to me, now, it's your product. Where did that come from?

JS: OK, to the credit of the lady that was involved with me right at the begining, I thank her for what she initially brought to the business, which was the look and feel. That hasn't changed, it's still the same, even the logo. I liken our business to Tiffany's. They don't go changing their gift bag, it's the Tiffany's blue that everybody knows. It's the same cardboard box, it's the same bag. There have been some subtle changes but the product is essentially the signature product from day one. And I did want a box. Traditionally, everybody else had created bouquets, but you can't stack them. Couriers are limited by how many they can take, so there was this scalability, which didn't just go towards the production of the product, it was also in terms of what could be delivered.

BK: My observation is also that people could pick up these boxes and take them home from the office and without feeling self-conscious about carrying a big bouquet on a train.

JS: Yes, but at the same time, I also feel that you know the brand is established enough when you see a woman walking down the street with a Tiffany's bag or a Chanel bag or a Cartier bag ...

BK: I am sure there's a whole bunch of other women there that are envious of that person walking down the street.

JS: That's a really good observation because the box replaced the flower. Everyone that sees a woman walking with a Roses Only box thinks wow, she is lucky. A bunch could be from anyone, it might have been a gift, but the market we play to is obviously the one where the husband or boyfriend is sending a box of roses to someone they really love. So as the owner of this business, I feel so proud when I see someone walking down the street with one of our boxes of roses because she is actually telling the world that she is loved by someone. And to me, that is absolutely huge. I have actually touched her emotionally.

BK: Because what people feel is so much more important than what they think most of the time.

JS: One hundred percent. And it is not just the commodity, it is like when someone has gone out of their way and gone to Tiffany's. They haven't bought the diamond or the jewellery from the wholesaler, where they may have saved possibly 20, 30, 40 or 50%. They have actually gone to Tiffany's, they have gone out of their way to impress and they haven't cut corners. We're not any dearer – in fact, a lot of people don't know that – but we are probably cheaper than most of our competitors for the amazing quality that we produce. But furthermore, it is the feeling you get when you get it from Roses Only. I think we have stamped that ground and I don't mean to sound arrogant when I say that.

BK: I think it's amazing that the brand that you built in the local market is real. It carries a cachet, it makes people feel something. It has that specialness which is an amazing achievement.

JS: That's what I set out to achieve. Why the box? Because, it's special. When you open a box, when you open a bag from Tiffany's, it's special. No-one is walking along holding the necklace or the bracelet or whatever in their hands showing it around. They've actually got it within a box and within a bag and it's like you are almost undressing it to expose it.

BK: At Apple, Steve Jobs actually patented a lot of his boxes and the way that his iPhones are packaged and how they unravel because he and his chief designer said that if I am unpacking something, it should be a beautiful experience and a ritual, and make people feel something great.

JS: Correct. The wow factor that we want to create is once the ribbon is untied, once the lid is lifted, once the paper is parted and then a dozen of the finest roses in the world are exposed. And what do I want Roses Only to be globally? I'd like Roses Only to be the place that you go and source the finest roses in the world. Ideally, ultimately, anywhere in the world.

'I'd like Roses Only to be the place that you go and source the finest roses in the world. Ideally, ultimately, anywhere in the world.'

BK: What is a great rose?

JS: Look, a lot of people put it down to the size of the heads and the size of the stem. I actually put it down to shape, you know, if the proportions are right and the head looks good, the stem looks good. If it is clean, it is polished, those are the things. It is about quality. It is about beauty. It is about the wow factor. What we want to do is create a wow factor. So what I'd like to see with Roses Only globally, although I may not be here in fifty years time, is a brand that is globally known as the place that you go to get the finest roses in the world for someone that you love. That's all. It's pretty simple.

BK: Where do the roses come from?

JS: They come from all over in the world but invariably, the biggest growers are in Ecuador, in Colombia, and other parts of South America including Guatemala and Central America. So that sort of area in the Andes, due to the elevation. Obviously, elevation is important, and close to the equator is helpful where there are a lot more hours of sun, consistent temperatures as opposed to deviating temperatures, so Kenya and Ethiopia. But you know, that could vary from having a large-sized head to a small-sized head, which is more the supermarket type. Market as in a volume sort of market versus product that is produced at elevation, you know three or four hours out of Nairobi, up in some amazing mountains that are invariably six to seven thousand feet above sea level at a minimum.

BK: So a consistent temperature and sunlight?

JS: That would get the production of a decent-size head and a thick stem. The rose actually grows a lot slower in a colder climate. It's no different to anything else.

BK: How long does it take to grow a great rose?

JS: It takes ninety days in the Andes. And on average fifty days in Australia.

BK: How many crops do they do per year? Can they replant in ninety days?

JS: I think the bush keeps going, but you've also got to rest them as well. You can't just keep on cutting them. I'm really not an expert when it comes to that, you need to get a grower to explain!

BK: Are there any issues around the ethical supply of flowers?

JS: Yes. We don't import directly, we buy through an importer that we've got an association with. We're also buying through other importers and wholesalers. I have seen the farms, I have seen the product. I know that they treat their people well. They're part of Fairtrade and various associations around the world. I have seen the hospitals and the schools that they run within these locations and the businesses from Kenya, Ecuador and Colombia. I've seen how the people are treated who look after the farms. From what I can see of the culture that they are working with, there's a real respect.

BK: So, the growing culture?

JS: Correct. I think that they're respectful of the land and respectful of the people that work within it. I just intuitively know that the sort of person that's treating people badly is invariably the sort of person that you're not going to want to do business with because if they're treating others badly, they'll treat you badly as a customer. I like doing business with people that I like, that's important. I couldn't stomach it if I knew or found out that someone was doing the wrong thing by someone. But look, there are also amazing roses being grown locally. We've got our work cut out because we obviously don't have the climate and the elevation that these roses grow in.

BK: Where are most of the local roses grown?

JS: There are roses growing on the outskirts of Sydney. Some are grown in the Dandenong area in Melbourne and east of Melbourne, seventy to eighty kilometres out. In the north of Adelaide as well as north of Perth, there are roses being grown. There are a few growers in parts of Queensland. So they're all over the place.

Roses Only has obviously gone outside of the flower concept, because what we realised is that we're actually a bit of an expert when it comes to delivered gifting. That's our core competency. So there is a marketing side to our business, and there is also a logistics side to our business.

'I like doing business with people that I like, that's important. I couldn't stomach it if I knew or found out that someone was doing the wrong thing by someone.'

BK: I guess if you can get a dozen roses to somebody in good shape, that's a task in itself, and that gives you a competency that you've now been able to extend across other lines.

JS: We've got Hampers Only and we've got Fruit Only. Fruit was our first foray outside of flowers. It began after my wife gave birth in 1998. One of the nicest gifts came from our son's godparents. They sent the most beautiful basket of organic fruit. My wife has always said that was one of the nicest gifts that she ever received, it was so nice to have a beautiful basket of organic, healthy, fruit.

I thought at the time, wow! Where would you go if you wanted to do what we are doing with flowers with fruit? Who do I call? Online hadn't started. Oddly enough, I went up to our local fruit shop one day to get some fruit and I was charged a lot of money for what was really just couple of punnets of strawberries and six oranges. I thought, you know what, there's obviously enough margin in it. We're already in the perishable game. We're already doing deliveries. Again, it is a product that doesn't need to be stored in a refrigerated environment or transported in a refrigerated truck, which is a massive issue in Australia.

So what we'll do is we'll create a box. And within that box you wouldn't know what you're going to receive. So, when you lift the lid, there had to be the wow factor again. It was all about the finest quality fruit. You don't have to be a genius or have a designer there to place beautiful fruit and make sure that you don't put two pieces of the same fruit next to each other.

BK: You just started up and did it?

JS: But again, it had to be gifting. What were we going to do to make it special? It had to be special, the quality had to be special. But it also had to be able to include a bottle of champagne as we do with flowers, or roses, or some chocolates and perhaps a little baby gift. And in 2008, I had a real cynicism for every hamper and every gift that I received at Christmas time. For the last fifteen, eighteen years prior, we were sick of seeing the same shortbread, the same chocolate, pasta or whatever that I would never open. There wasn't anything that I would keep and I know that some people must have spent a reasonable amount of money. There was nothing memorable.

And when it is not memorable, you won't be remembered by the customer or the person that sent it to you. Invariably, it was a big corporation that spent good money on something that they thought would buy them loyalty or awareness. I thought, 'You haven't bought anything, it looks mass-produced. It doesn't look special. I'd rather you gave me two or three nice items. That would be more memorable than twenty that were rubbish.' So then I thought, 'Who is out there?' I did think of David Jones, but they only set up once a year at Christmas-time. What I wanted to create was something like a school case. Something you actually opened up. Again, it could be reused and had a wow factor.

BK: So, there's a permanence about it.

JS: Yes, and sure enough, we hear people keep their tax receipts in there, put photo albums in there. It is something you don't feel right about throwing out.

BK: So you get to leave a little bit of your brand with people and the person who sends it gets to leave a little bit of themselves with that person, too.

JS: That's one aspect. Then you open it up and you hopefully get a wow from opening it up. Then the other thing is the quality of the products that were going to go in. The most obvious one is Christmas. Of course you're going have to do some food, but when it comes to it, I want it to be all the things that I want to take home. That was the over-riding thing.

BK: I can see that in your hamper, you have these really high-quality things that you've clearly thought about.

JS: Yes. I am cynical about no-name brands. There's no legacy there. So these are all thought processes going through my mind. Lastly, I wasn't going to create a hamper business that was just for Christmas. We wanted a business that was an all-year-round business too, like baby. I think that our baby hampers are as good, if not better, than any others.

BK: From a business point of view, ascertaining your core expertise and leveraging out that expertise and your core rules is interesting. We have talked through your model and I have seen how you have addressed, over twenty years, issues your parents faced for thirty or forty. You've got the building in the city as well as others over time. Tell me about property and the role that has played in your business, because property is huge for people in Australia.

JS: It's really just a very passive thing. It's not an active strategy. If you have got a bit of spare cash, you may invest, but the properties that we have been involved in are just properties that we have used.

BK: So, you don't rely on the landlord.

JS: I wouldn't buy a property unless I thought it had upside in terms of capital. Some redevelopment potential, possibly a great location that is just going to go up anyway. You see, buying anti-cyclically, you can house yourself in there and make it work from a numbers perspective to start with. This particular office here, we may have paid over the mark a tad, but I could make the numbers work and in time it will be perfectly fine. But this particular office suited me from a number of perspectives. It wasn't just about fitting in with a business, it actually fitted in with my lifestyle. I am ten or fifteen minutes away from work if I need to come in urgently. I am close to school. If I wanted to save a lot of money, I probably would have gone a lot further out. But then I think, what sort of staff am I attracting?

BK: Yes, how do you get quality people?

JS: Well, obviously, this is not about being a florist now. It is about accounts people and e-commerce people and they've got to be able to get to public transport. I don't think you should subject someone to having to drive to work if they don't have to.

BK: So access to talent is huge in terms of location.

JS: Yes, I think so.

BK: Let me ask you about the internet. What role has it played in transforming your business?

JS: In 1998 we'd registered a URL and in 1999 we went online. We should have done it a lot earlier. A lot of the media strategy that I had prior to going online was maintained. We had ads in the *Australian Financial Review* on a daily basis, going back to the fact that we targeted professional men. I visualised time-poor men reading the *Financial Review* who picked up the phone and called Roses Only to get a dozen or two dozen roses delivered to their wife for their anniversary.

Similarly, on radio, our first radio ads were with 2UE and Alan Jones. I attribute a lot of our success to being with a trusted and respected voice in the community. There were other people that we used at the time, but Alan stands out. He is also not one to stick his hand out for freebies. So, I am very respectful of Alan and what he did for us. He does a lot of giveaways, involved with a lot of charities. I think that people on the other side see that, and are willing to help you if you're willing to help others. So that is actually part of the ethos of this business and you can see that as you look around.

BK: Yes, you can see all the organisations in this room that have helped with contributions.

JS: The ones that really resonate are the National Breast Cancer Foundation and the Leukaemia Foundation that I served on the board of for almost ten years and acted as vice president towards the end. All those, so the mass media or the media is still what I used when we kicked off online. All we did was add the URL. And persevere with what's working. It takes a lot of time for people to switch over. At the same time, you've got to remember that we've almost clinically closed stores. We didn't just rush in there and say, bang! we're online, this is a new business.

BK: When did you close Town Hall?

JS: It mainly happened in the first part of the 2000s. Town Hall was the last. There was also a little shop that was down in the Price Waterhouse Coopers Building at 201 Sussex Street that closed on 24 February 2012.

BK: So there are no retail outlets now?

JS: There are no retail outlets. You can come to one of our warehouses to buy things if you really want to, but we deliver to you. The most important thing that going online gave us is a way of getting to the market nationally. By virtue of the medium, it was a national business. We were naively doing a lot of things before that. For example, we were paying over the mark for those ads in the *Financial Review*. It was a national newspaper so I'd get someone in Perth asking me to set up a shop. So, a lot of naivety on my behalf, including not knowing that I could just buy advertising for New South Wales alone.

BK: It's interesting though, that when you went national, you found that you'd created a national brand.

JS: We had already created a bit of a brand without even knowing it. So, we did do that. All I had to do then, from a distribution point of view, was to be in the second largest city in Australia. Up until then it was just in Sydney. So, we created a store in Melbourne and subsequently we've got a warehouse and have a distribution store there. Now it's closed down and it's just a distribution warehouse. We found the best people around the country and oddly enough, all of them came by word of mouth.

It was just that people wanted to be part of this and we found the best operators in Brisbane, the best operators in Perth. Best of the best in every other part of Australia. I can tell you, we failed when we first started in Adelaide, we had to move operators there and we also failed with our first operator in Cairns. In fact, our second operator in Cairns, and to this point we haven't found a good operator in Cairns. We haven't opened in Darwin. The reason is it's just too hot up there. We've got to look after the product.

BK: So the ability to say no if it makes sense is important.

JS: Very, very important. That being said, we found the best operators. We've become a significant part of their business. And most of these associations or connections are all being done without a contract, just on a handshake.

BK: Yes, and how does it work? They've got all the equipment and packaging, they fulfill all your orders? Do you go around and check they comply with your standards?

JS: Yes, we mystery shop. But the most important thing is that we also put a response card in every box so the recipient can write in. If they choose to do that, they can also write to the md@rosesonly.com.au. That is managed by me and also the customer service department. I get copied in on everything. I think I probably see 70–80% of those emails, at least. Sometimes I act on it before my customer service people do.

BK: So you are still close to the customer?

JS: Yes. I'm close to the coalface. The reason I like to do that is because I learn so much from my customers. I learn about the things that don't work, and actually, it's driven innovation. There is no better place than your staff and your customers' trust. I mean, obviously, we had a little flutter with trying to do Roses Only in the UK. And that business is still ticking along in London.

The other thing we learned is that the brand needs to be city specific. When it comes to a brand, it's Roses Only and globally will be all about Roses Only being connected to a city's brand. That's really, really important to me. This is not about becoming Roses Only England or the UK even though the URL in that scenario is all about that. It's a bit different in the Australian scenario because we're controlled by or dominated by four or five major cities. In the case of London, London itself is a brand. Paris is a brand. New York is a brand.

BK: So do you mean to extend Roses Only in London?

JS: Correct. And I can't help but go back to the Tiffany's analogy. Tiffany's didn't open Tiffany's, England. They opened Tiffany's, London. Any luxury house that opens is connected to a city. They do not open connected to a country.

BK: Very interesting. So you'll see on so many luxury brands like Cartier in the old days: London, Paris and New York.

JS: Correct, and to this day they still do it. They could be selling globally and they could be selling in cyberspace. Cyberspace itself is a branded city. And it's cool. It's a cool place to be. It doesn't belong to a particular country. It sticks out there on its own.

BK: And they market it as an online presence, as an online destination.

JS: Correct. But you still feel that it is coming out of a city.

'I learn so much from my customers. I learn about the things that don't work, and actually, it's driven innovation.'

BK: OK, I will ask you about the role of debt in a business. We saw a lot of pain during the global financial crisis, especially for early stage businesses. You have grown into a very strong business, but it has taken time.

JS: Well, is it the time or debt! You could drive a lot quicker. But I did have a philosophy – I did not build this business or create this business with a view to making a quick buck. In fact, it doesn't play in my mind. And even if I was thinking about doing that, I couldn't hand over a business to any investor or to anybody, be it the next generation, that was not built on solid foundations. So apologies for all the analogies, but I do see the business as a Tiffany's again.

BK: You want to be an enduring, great company?

JS: I want to be a brand that lasts forever. I want to be like Coca-Cola® and I want the goodwill of this business to be the most valuable thing on its balance sheet – always. Because you can't buy trust, respect …

BK: Track record.

JS: Or track record by throwing twenty or thirty million dollars at something. That doesn't work.

BK: Over the course of the business, what have you used debt for and what is your philosophy on it?

JS: We've used it for infrastructure and various other bits and pieces. I don't like debt. I fundamentally hate debt. I think it's a cancer. I would rather not have it. There is this notion that if you don't have a bit of debt in your business, you're not driving your balance sheet hard enough. I think if you've got an inspirational or passionate person heading your business, it's not going to be lazy just by default.

BK: Business is defined more by its people than by its balance sheet, you would hope.

JS: Yes.

BK: One of the reasons I'm doing this book is because I believe that businesses can make people in communities better off. Do you think, as I do, that we should celebrate our business people as much as we celebrate our sports people as they probably make a much broader contribution?

JS: Well, they definitely employ people and feed people.

BK: I believe the role of work adds so much dignity to people's life and it's so essential to everything. I know you've been involved in many things, but tell us about the things that you've been involved in trying to promote in terms of enterprise and entrepreneurship and just getting off your bum and doing something.

JS: I am an undergraduate from the University of New South Wales and now sit on the advisory council for the Faculty of Business which encompasses the Australian Graduate School of Managment and the Faculty of Commerce, which is where I went through. So I feel that I give back in that way. I am also involved with the Centre for Innovation and Entrepreneurship at the University of New South Wales and we've started some entrepreneurship classes that are really people sharing experiences about being entrepreneurs.

And there are people getting involved in doing things like Pitch Fest, where they pitch their business to you. So, we're involved with that and the sponsor of Pitch Fest is actually Dr Peter Farrell, as in ResMed, you know, the amazing entrepreneur. There are some other great entrepreneurs involved too, again some pretty passionate people. I enjoy going in there and talking to the students, some sixty to two hundred students in an auditorium. Telling them a little about my business and then allowing them to ask questions.

BK: What would you say to young people, particularly in places like Greece, Spain, Portugal, where 40% of the unemployment rate consists of people under twenty-five. Should more young people make their own jobs?

JS: Look, not everybody can because there isn't enough demand, but yes, if you're passionate.

BK: OK, final question. What is a motto, quote or thought that summarises your approach to life in business? What's your favourite saying in business?

JS: I know no investor wants to hear this, but no business is about the money. It's not about the money, you know!

BK: There's got to be a bigger reason?

JS: Yes, it's not about the money.

BK: I understand.

JS: So, that's one. Also, I've just engaged someone and she said, 'Keep it simple.' Simplicity. And when it comes to gifting, make sure it's something you'd want to receive yourself. Don't think that you can just get away with sending someone something you wouldn't want.

Peter Stutchbury

Architect – Peter Stutchbury Architecture

———

'I think it's a common story, but you simply believe in what
you're doing and you do it as well as you possibly can. You work
very hard. You have some degree of talent, you persevere …'

One of Australia's most renowned architects, Peter Stutchbury originally enrolled in a commerce degree at university. When an anonymous woman at the position of registration in the queue asked what he wanted to do for the rest of his life, he knew business wasn't it. An intuitive decision to study architecture transformed the direction of his life and, combined with a new-found passion, it all started to make sense. It still does, as an ever-increasing suite of clients 'return home' to one of the outstanding and iconic projects that now comprise his incredible corpus of work.

www.peterstutchbury.com.au

Interview

BRETT KELLY: Peter, where did the interest in architecture and design come from?

PETER STUTCHBURY: My dad was an engineer. As a kid I went to building sites with him and we built things in the garage together. I actually built cubby houses with him. He was also a tech drawer, a wonderful drawer. So I spent a lot time drawing technically rather than artistically. That was one important influence in my education.

The other influence was my mother's family. They were farmers out in the desert, but we used to stay with them regularly. You learned the meaning of the word survival, you learned the meaning of the word function and you learned the meaning of the word efficiency. You also learned how to observe animals in the landscape because you had to move them through it effectively. But you didn't realise that you were learning, you were merely exposed to it at an extreme level. The desert is a tough environment. You need to have a really comprehensive and sensitive understanding of it in order to manage it.

So I think those two influences created an interesting core of thinking. It wasn't until I explored that core seriously that I found architecture. Up until then, I had no real driving force.

BK: Did you go straight from school into architecture?

PS: No-one ever talked about architecture with me. When we were young, artistic endeavours were not encouraged. It was more a business world, and it was uncommon for a middle-class student to take on an artistic profession. Having people like the architect Harry Seidler on the front page of the newspaper was seen as remote thinking, not real day-to-day life.

BK: Not mainstream?

PS: No, not mainstream thinking! I had been admitted to Commerce at the University of New South Wales but I came back from a surfing trip to the north coast of New South Wales where I'd been thinking a lot about what to do in life. I think one of the main gifts my parents gave me was to dream, to be able to look forward to a future of possibilities rather than probabilities. I stood in the queue to enrol at the university for two hours – this is a nice story – and when I got to the front of the queue, a little placid lady, probably about the same age as I am now, looked at me and said, 'So, what do you want to do for the rest of your life?' I looked at her and said, 'Not Commerce.'

You know, that was a really helpful question. I'd been away surfing, freewheeling, and I walked away, quite confused. A nearby table was piled full of books and I just reached across and grabbed a green book. I opened it, and dare I say it, it fell open at Architecture. I thought, 'Why hasn't anyone told me about Architecture?' It was like I was able to breathe properly. From that very moment on, it was clear. It's like a perfect meal, you can't fault it at the end. You may not choose it next time, but for that particular moment, it's exactly what you felt like.

BK: You're a well-known architect now, tell me about your journey into architecture.

PS: I think it's a common story, but you simply believe in what you're doing and you do it as well as you possibly can. You work very hard. You have some degree of talent, you persevere and you have some wonderful chapters along the way that are indelible in terms of how they affect you.

BK: Did you realise at the time that those chapters were happening?

PS: Only subsequently – it could be tens of years later, couldn't it? For instance, my uncle was a missionary in Papua New Guinea, the second white missionary in the highlands. He used to come back on furlough every four years and we'd sit around in the living room. My mother's family used to play a lot of music. We'd play the piano and sing. And then he'd tell stories about Papua New Guinea – cannibalism and tribal matters, fighting, hunting, ceremonies, village life – because he lived in the middle of one of the most remote villages in Papua New Guinea. I was intrigued. I'd sit there with my mouth open–

BK: Wide-eyed.

PS: Listening. It was always inside me to go there and experience what he'd experienced. There were a number of false starts, but after I'd been working for two years in Sydney, he came down one day and just said, 'I need you to come and build a church with me in New Guinea.' So I went to New Guinea.

I also organised post-graduate studies on the long house, which is a traditional highland building. I lived in New Guinea for a year and I went back several times. I knew I was there to learn about the essence of architecture because in a place like that, they built buildings to last, as opposed to Australia where the indigenous architecture is far less permanent. Papua New Guinea is about the closest neighbour with permanent architecture or permanent buildings. Everything about them is absolutely accurate – their size, their form, their structure, their social qualities – everything has evolved over thousands of years. There's no nonsense.

BK: Can you elaborate on this difference between the permanent and the impermanent?

PS: Well, Australian aboriginal people were semi-nomadic. Their shelters were incredibly refined, but they weren't built to endure permanent habitation. Whereas in Papua New Guinea, the villages were designed to last anything between three and twenty-five years, depending on where they were, the fertility of the ground, travel, warfare etc. The villages down in the lowlands of the Fly River are twenty-five-year-old villages with long houses for up to three hundred people – remarkable structures, just incredible. As I said, no waste. That was a great lesson about what the essence of architecture really is, a great lesson.

BK: What is the essence of architecture?

PS: I think it's probably honesty. If your work is honest, that is, it comes from your own understanding and interpretation, then it's accurate. Whereas if you start trying to take all these other things that aren't part of what you adore, then you'll always be a little bit abstract.

BK: So if an architect is an artist who is coming from their own experience, their own honesty, what obligation is there on that artist to inform themselves before expressing themselves?

PS: Well, being a professional, I think obligations are fundamental. There are building and monetary obligations, obligations to the client to satisfy a brief, obligations to a site, obligations to society. Minor to major obligations. What you try and do is start with the things you know. We've just had two weeks talking about land, for instance, sites and climate and weather. I mean, I know that. I was a surfer and a country boy. It's pretty easy.

BK: It's helpful.

PS: People are the other thing. People are very important. One could say that people are 70% of architecture. Understanding people, the way you sense people and understand what they can accommodate and what they can't. I think in thirty years of practice, only two or three of our houses have changed hands, which is not many.

BK: Why is that?

PS: Well, connection is a really important word. Connection in terms of how we relate to all the aspects of a building – place, people, context. Connection is a part of the explanation of our work. It's hard for people to let go of something that's so honest to them, you know.

One of the frequent comments we get about our work is, 'We love returning home to that building.' So there are two words there: 'home' is a very important word and so too is 'return'. If those two words apply, then why would one sell? We tailor houses for our clients–

BK: Like a bespoke commission? Speaking to the tailor John Cutler the other day, I remember he explained that his job is really to make dreams happen, to understand that he's receiving a commission and that each person has something in them that they want, but that they're relying on him to find it, to draw it out and to interpret it.

PS: You can imagine sliding a suit on and feeling like it's a silk glove. Or an R M Williams boot and feeling that that garment has been made for you, and you feel wonderful. We try to do that with houses, every time.

It's not our purpose to make a work of 'architecture', although that's part of the end result. Our purpose is to groom a building for someone's life and lifestyle and to take them to places they've never been taken to before, to provide them with beauty at a consistent level.

BK: In all aspects of that environment?

PS: Well, from the way you put soap on a basin, to the way you see light come through a wall, there's so much to understand. From how a brick feels in your hand to how the mortar spreads when you put a brick down. And scale, what it feels like to be in a 5 × 5 × 5 room with no windows, or one window, or twenty windows and to change that room from timber to concrete. What that feels like. It takes a long time to get that quality of understanding. You can be like a young painter or you can be lucky and strike it with one work, but you may not find it again.

BK: Because you're not sure how you did it?

PS: Yes. I think with real architecture, your development takes tens of years.

'People are very important. One could say that people are 70% of architecture. Understanding people, the way you sense people and understand what they can accommodate and what they can't.'

BK: Do you believe you can get better and better? Will you ever retire?

PS: No, I'll never retire. I believe you get better and better in different ways. Not necessarily better and better as an architect, but you might get better and better as a person who can help other architects. That's something you might get better and better at, being a teacher. The 'better and better as an architect' is very socially dependent. Society is quite fickle. And it changes with factors more discernible than aesthetic.

BK: Trends and fads?

PS: With whatever's going on. We've been lucky that our way of thinking has overlapped with contemporary social understanding but it may divert again, you never know.

BK: It could change. But it's encouraged you to continue on your path?

PS: Continue and adapt. As Darwin said, if you learn to adapt, you survive.

BK: OK. Now let me ask you about the economics of an architectural practice. What are the major challenges in being in the business of taking on all these commissions?

PS: I think if we as creative architects looked at the economics of architecture, we wouldn't do it, that's the bottom line.

BK: So, how do you survive?

PS: Well, you just have to believe that it's part of a valid position in the world's range of thinking. I can't for a moment ever dream of making money because it would distract me from what I was trying to do. Meanwhile, I've got to manage money because, you know, we've had fifteen people in the practice – it's twelve at the moment – and they have mouths to feed. So we do have to consider that.

At the moment there's more than enough work for twelve people and each in their own way they're all amazing architects. I've created this 'field of practice' that makes things possible for them as well, which is wonderful. Quite often, people will move from this building to their own business and practice in their own way. It's great. In terms of the business analogy, I think we're providing a service to the community if they want it, which is enough.

BK: Which is enough?

PS: It is an artistic service that people would otherwise not have. At any level, from a chair to a table to a light fitting to an addition to a house to a public building, people can decide if they want that sort of artistry in their lives. And that, I think, is not something that's taught to our community, that is, Australian society. Throughout Europe, artists are seen as important people within society, but not so much in Australia, unfortunately. A sculptor couldn't survive in Australia, whereas they can survive as sculptors in many countries around the world.

Connections are also important. How one thing connects to another and another. I remember in second-year Architecture, while I was studying, I met a gentleman who's my best friend to this day. He is a great teacher. He enabled me to see the colour of architecture, the joyful spirit within architecture. As a lesson, that is insurmountable in terms of a contributing to the way you think.

BK: Do you have a business manager to manage the business or do you do it all yourself?

PS: My father was a very reputable businessman, highly respected. I probably learned a lot from him. I've inherited an understanding of business that I've never studied. There's a predictability, I think, to business. If you can understand social trends then you can probably manage a business. Part of being an architect is understanding social trends, understanding society on a broad scale. Running our business is a bit like riding a wave. You don't choose to ride every wave – you choose the one that's right for you and ride it.

So we're following a path that makes a lot of sense, including social sense. Our reputation is for a sustainable base that has a connection with nature. When I asked a very prominent client once, 'Why have you chosen us to do your work?' he looked at me and said, 'Because you connect me with this place.' And that was it. 'In the latter part of my life,' he said, 'I want to go back to nature.' I think there's something very healthy about that, particularly in today's society. There are a lot of people who will get to a point where they think, 'Next year, I'd like to go back and sit on a rock.'

BK: So when the time comes when you can *have* everything, you may not want to *possess* everything.

PS: I think that's a very appropriate way of saying it.

BK: People often describe every sort of modern building as minimalist – when somebody sees your work, what label do they give it?

PS: I don't know. People come from all sorts of different perspectives. We try and do accurate work, like the Papua New Guinean buildings where there is no waste. You shouldn't look at anything on the building and say, 'That shouldn't be there,' you know, 'that's unnecessary'.

BK: Rather than calling it minimalist, is it more accurate to call it not-excessive, because it's not missing anything?

PS: I certainly couldn't say our work is minimalist because, for example, if we design a door handle, while it's not overkill, it's beautiful and sometimes, to make beauty, you need to add something. I mean, a beautiful woman's face may be exceptional to look at, but maybe there's just a touch of eyeliner or lipstick that brings the face alive, like a bright red or something, and suddenly the face changes, the nature changes altogether. In architecture, there's sometimes the need to bring something further alive than what it is, so it's not minimalistic, it's actually activated, you know, activated architecture. It's something that you perceive, something that's incredibly intuitive.

BK: So you can feel it. You might not be able to explain it, but you can feel it?

PS: This building here is just a rough renovation we did, but we had thirty-two students in here yesterday and it felt like home. That was the idea. You come in here as a client or as someone working here, and it feels like home.

BK: Which is the building that is closest to your heart, that means the most to you, that changed your life the most?

PS: I always say I don't have one.

BK: Is it like choosing a favourite child?

PS: Your latest is probably always your favourite, but I must say, we put every ounce of our energy into every building. If there's anything I could pass on in this context, it would be to make sure that every time you do work, you do it properly. I've done one work quickly in my life. It was an office for a timber yard and it wasn't a pleasant experience going back to visit that building. But that was it. That was the lesson for me. I did it when I was twenty-four years old. Everything since then has been done with heart and soul. It has cost money at times, but I think I've been fortunate enough to see that we have a limited lifespan.

I'll never forget one of my friends saying that his father had had two heart attacks and the third one was going to kill him. His father had the third heart attack and my friend held his father in his arms when we were like, eighteen. His father said to him, 'Gary, I wouldn't change anything I've done,' and he died. I thought to myself, 'I really want to be able to say that.'

'If there's anything I could pass on in this context, it would be to make sure that every time you do work, you do it properly.'

BK: When you said earlier about honesty in your work, is it easier to be honest than not have to remember your own untruths?

PS: Yes. The story's always the same, and hopefully, the wisdom's getting better. A great author could write the same story twenty years later and it'd be a different story, it'd be a different way of seeing that story. The same in architecture, you cannot do the same building, but you can perform the same task with a different wisdom. I want to go back to the building question. I go to some buildings that are twenty years old and I see the patina between the client and the building and the place, which is not something you can see when a building is young. Quite often, those buildings only feel complete at that stage.

BK: Once the furniture's in and people are in–

PS: Once the family has a history in the house. Recently built houses are more like works of art until they've been lived in. Our most recent house is the most representative of our thinking, and most remarkable in that way, but it hasn't been lived in yet so it has none of the stories of time within it.

Aboriginal people say that the reason why we shouldn't be digging out the earth is because it has so many stories in it – they've walked over it and put their stories into the earth. I find that a very good currency of thinking. And it's the same in a house. You can go into some houses and they feel naked; you can go into others and they feel fully clothed. It's because they've had so much wonderful history.

BK: They have a wonderful history to them; they've got a vibe in them. When you go through Europe, many of the old churches have such a feeling of just being lived in. It's quite uncanny.

PS: When I was staying with these fellows in Bangalore, I went to a place called Hampi, which is a stone city that is being dug up. It's a thousand years old, maybe? And even the most recent buildings that have been dug out of the ground, you could feel the stone walls, you could almost read the footprints in the stone. I also visited Falling Water in Pennsylvania, one of Frank Lloyd Wright's greatest works, about two or three months ago. You could feel the stories in that house. You could feel the qualities of that building. That's when you get the greatest joy, revisiting buildings once they have been lived in, the stories–

BK: Is it different doing a public building?

PS: Well, I think the difference is there's a greater art to doing public buildings. It's something you need to practise to bring out. You have to juggle different social conditions. There are the different experiences of many people in those buildings, and there's a different scale. There's a different velocity to those places. It's a come-and-go velocity as opposed to the more consistent one you get in houses. I'd love to do more public buildings but you need to have clients that appreciate what you're trying to do.

BK: I was going to ask, what's that image of a building on the wall?

PS: It's the Venice Pavilion. It was a competition. We were one of the three finalists, but not successful.

BK: It's awesome.

PS: That's it, it's so beautiful. We designed it to sit beside the canal. We used a particular roof profile that we were going to develop with BlueScope Steel as a self-spanning roof profile. It would have been quite unique. It was a heat and light collector, all built into the profile itself. It was going to be quite revolutionary and it was clear.

'I think one of the best bits of advice I could give anyone would be to ask yourself who are you intuitively and how does that translate in today's society in terms of a workplace or work ethic.'

BK: All right, we've touched on a lot. Now let me ask you for a motto, a quote or a thought that best summarises your approach to life.

PS: I think one of the best bits of advice I could give anyone would be to ask yourself who are you intuitively and how does that translate in today's society in terms of a workplace or work ethic.

Harry Triguboff

Entrepreneur (Builder) – Meriton Group

'I only like to be involved when there are problems. When there are problems, I come with an instant solution – and it's always wrong, but it doesn't matter. I get all the people around me and I make them all think at once with me and I promise you, our solution is always the best.'

How a child born in China in 1933 and who spent his early childhood in a Russian community south of Beijing ends up as an Australian property legend makes for an interesting story. Trained as a textile engineer, Harry came to Australia in 1948 and drove taxis and owned a milk run before building his first block of apartments and establishing Meriton in 1963 at the age of thirty. A rare individual, the founder and managing director of the Meriton Group of companies has been responsible for the construction of almost fifty-five thousand residential dwellings in Australia.

www.meriton.com.au

Interview

BRETT KELLY: Is there a driving idea or a particular person or event that's had a significant impact on your life?

HARRY TRIGUBOFF: When I came to Australia I was a textile engineer, but I couldn't see any future in it. And that was right. I don't think anybody made much out of it. So I was looking for different things, I was trying all kinds of things when a friend of mine told me that his father had spoken to the boss of Stockton Holdings.

The old fellow told him that his son should become a builder. So he came to me and he said, 'What do you think of building apartments?' I said, 'Terrific idea.' I was already selling a bit of real estate so I knew a bit. I went and bought my first site and I made more money on that site proportionally than I have ever made again. I knew that was where I had to be.

BK: Excellent. So, is there a saying that really sums up your approach to life or a quote or a motto?

HT: I only like to be involved when there are problems. When there are problems, I come with an instant solution – and it's always wrong, but it doesn't matter. I get all the people around me and I make them all think at once with me and I promise you, our solution is always the best.

BK: As a group.

HT: That's it. That's how you do it.

BK: Excellent. I think everyone's read enough about you not to labour the details of your history, but you've bought this block of land. You're not a builder. You don't have any experience or university qualifications but you now have this block of land. How much debt did you have and how concerned were you about the prospect of your first project?

HT: Right. I went into it because I knew that there was a big demand. Believe me, that demand has never changed from the day I started which is fifty years ago. So that's the main thing, there's a demand. You have to have demand. I went to the bank manager in the ANZ and I was lucky. They were training him for big things. His name was Rex Davidson. If you ask anybody in the ANZ bank, nobody had ever heard of him but he ran the bank. And he liked horses. So he told me, 'I'll lend you the money, Harry. And when you reach the roof, I'll come with you. I'll tell you if you are a builder or you aren't. And if you are, I'll give you more money. Then, it doesn't matter. But that's when I'll decide.' So I waited until I got to the roof. I called him and he had a look, this way and that. He said, 'Yeah, Harry, you're a builder. Now I'll give you any amount of money you like.' He became the chief lending officer at the ANZ bank. I don't know if there's such a title anymore, but that's what he was.

BK: Did you stay with him for a long time?

HT: For quite a while, but of course, they sent him to Melbourne because that's the head office. And then, I used to go to him in Melbourne, spend half an hour with him, he'd give me another loan, and I'd come back.

BK: And off you'd go again. You make it sound so simple. Did you hire builders, subcontractors?

HT: I took a foreman. I was lucky he was always drunk. In those days, bricklayers were very hard to get. Then, this young bricklayer came to me, a Scotsman. He was a nice fellow. You see, in Scotland, the bricklayer is the chief contractor. In Australia, it's the carpenter. So, he was teaching me what to do. Every night he would tell me what materials we needed the next day and I'd get them. He'd use them that next day, and that way, I learned very well. I had no other job and nothing else, so I stayed all the time on that site. I was so dirty, worse than all of them. I was dusty and all, but I learned how to work. After that, of course, I started two or three more jobs at once, but I knew from the beginning – I never started the second job until I'd finished the first. So I got to know the whole process, how to get in and how to get out. And that bricklayer stayed with me until he retired. Now, his son works for me, another son worked for me. They've been with me ever since.

BK: Often, as people make money in one thing, they assume that they're brilliant at everything and get involved in other activities. We've seen a lot of people not do so well when they do that. You mentioned that you stayed on the site all the time and, as I understand, in the last fifty years you've pretty much stuck to just building residential apartments.

HT: I think being clever is very good, but you must like what you do. It's impossible to like everything so, if you find one thing that you like, stick to it. And until you find that thing, keep looking. Because the main thing is, you have to like what you do and then the rest will come by itself.

BK: When you started that project, did you intend having your own business and not work in someone else's?

HT: Yes, I wanted to be by myself. I tried to be a public company. It lasted a few months. That was not my cup of tea. I sold the shares for 50 cents. I bought them back for $1.20. Everybody was happy. No problems. Because I was in love with the company, how could I sell it?

BK: Was it love at first sight in the property industry?

HT: Yes. I liked it. That's very important because if you like it, people in the business will like you and they will probably work better than if there wasn't that relationship. It's very important.

'It's impossible to like everything so, if you find one thing that you like, stick to it. And until you find that thing, keep looking. Because the main thing is, you have to like what you do and then the rest will come by itself.'

BK: So, even now as you build seemingly bigger, better, best, you get on top of the project, you're still there very often?

HT: Yes. Every morning, I'm there. I mean, I go a bit later, now, of course.

BK: A bit later than you did. So today, what does the typical Harry Triguboff day look like? Is there one?

HT: Yes. Every day is similar. I get up. I read the paper. When I've finished reading the paper, I take my medicines, I go for a walk. Every day, I go for a walk. Go for a walk, have my breakfast with my dog. Then I go to work. I go around the jobs then I work in the office. I get to work at 11 o'clock or 11.30 but then I stay until 6 to 7 o'clock. I work enough hours. So that's every day.

BK: That's the day. Excellent. What do you think are the most critical issues facing Australian business right now and certainly your business?

HT: Well, we are very lucky that China adores us. I like my business; they like this country. It's not only a matter of money. They like it. So that's good. They help us. But of course, this is still not their home. Their home is China. And even though we are very successful in selling to so many Chinese now, I am always fighting to get Australians into the market. The market is good when the local people are in it and believing it and supporting it. And that's what I want.

That is why I'm always fighting the Reserve Bank – its interest rates make it impossible for people to buy. The governor knows it, but it's not his fault. It's the whole group of them that run that place. He will leave and another will come. It will always be the same. It will never change. So, there's this one problem that we have. It's that we must get those interest rates down.

The other thing is that people have lots of money in super, but they have no money in the bank. And the super funds are not built to help people buy property, so they can't afford to buy property, which they should buy. Instead, the super funds spend money on shares and other things. So, I want that to be changed.

The third big problem here is that politicians run the place. It's very hard to be a politician and run it. A politician wants to be popular with everyone. Well, it's OK to be popular, but there's very little you can do because you want this, he wants that. What does he do? No good. So, more power has to be given to the doers, to the mechanics. And laws have to be made so that they get the power. The politicians must be prepared to let go of the power so that they can do it. For instance, it's much easier to work in Queensland than it is in New South Wales. I think that we have sent ten different ministers from here to Queensland to see how they do it.

BK: There is a lot of talk about immigration. What is your view on immigration?

HT: Well, we are a huge country and we need a lot of people. Unfortunately, our philosophy is very much entwined with what they do in Europe and America and everywhere else. This is different. We are a huge country and you cannot run it with no people. I will give you an example. You talk about mining. If you go to Lake Eyre, you will see that there are no roads. There are no railways. There is nothing there. You cannot develop if you don't have facilities, so we must develop facilities. We won't develop them unless we have people. We cannot do enough unless we have people. People must come. We need them and it is good that we can pick everybody who wants to come here. But it is no good picking them if they understand cricket or they understand something else. They must be useful. They must be workers. So unless we bring them, it is no good. Of course, for housing, they all believe in housing and they all need housing so it is terrific.

BK: Harry, you have the tallest project in Sydney, the tallest project currently in Brisbane and you're about to lose the crown to yourself again. Are you competing with someone else or is it an approach?

HT: Always with myself. I don't compete with others. Others do not exist for me. I do not worry about it. I never diversified. I do not need to diversify. I stick to what I like and I know what I can do. I know what the country needs and what the people want. So I don't compete with anyone and they cannot compete with me because unfortunately, when they go to a certain site, they become public companies and in public companies, they tell them to diversify. So he might have been good at doing what I'm doing, but suddenly he starts doing ten other things of which probably eight are no good. No competition.

BK: Having had the success that you've had, it is understandable that you have that confidence now, but did you always have it?

HT: Probably, always. Yes, no problem. It's very important, very important. All of you must have confidence when you go to a bank. If you don't have confidence, then the bank gets more scared than you are. So always be confident. Now, when you work with the bank, you must make them your partner. They must know everything. Give them all the problems, let them work for it, and then when they know your business, they are your friend. But if you run away from them, you're gone. Absolutely.

'The market is good when the local people are in it and believing it and supporting it. And that's what I want.'

BK: Is there anyone that's really inspired you, whether it was your parents or a friend, someone else in business or society generally?

HT: Well, I look at successful people and I see some of them are still older than I am, they are the ones that give me confidence. If they can do it, I can do it.

BK: The legendary American investor, Warren Buffett, says that he doesn't believe in diversification. He believes that concentration leads to concentration. So you share that view? In terms of your business, I read an article that mentioned many of your managers provide one-page summaries of their projects or business plans or current status of their project. I was intrigued by that. Can you explain that to me?

HT: Every weekend I take home a pile of papers that I think is very important and I go through them. Some things I don't understand and some things I don't agree with, so I make notes. Then, the next week, they fix them, and I look at it

again and so on. I continue looking all the time. Now, the page that you're talking about, that's different. When I first started, I had one page. Now, I have six pages. That is all I have and that summarises all the movements I have to know.

BK: And what's in the six pages?

HT: It says how many units we have for sale, how many we have got deposits on, how many we have exchanged, how many units we are leasing, how many units are up to the roof, how many units are started, and how much empty land I have. That is all. Money doesn't come into it. It's nothing to do with the money.

BK: I've also read that you were very advantaged during the global financial crisis and subsequently because you have little or no need for debt. Can you talk to us about that? You talked about the bank being your friend – it doesn't sound like you need a friend at the bank anymore.

HT: No, no. They need me. I give them money! Best friend. Even easier.

BK: So now you are a good depositor.

HT: Very good.

BK: There is a lot of talk now globally around suitable levels of gearing on all sorts of assets and projects. What do you think is a suitable level of gearing on the types of projects that you run?

HT: It depends. When you start, you need the bank because you cannot start without the bank 100%. So you get from them whatever you can. You should always pay them back because then they will give you more. You pay them back, they give you more. But then when you reach a certain size, you must decide what you want to do. Do you want to work for them or do you want to work for you? That is when you start getting less into debt. Debt means that you will not grow as fast as you could, agreed? But then, it gives you peace of mind because sometimes, when you are over-extended, it is very difficult.

The banks have a very short memory and that is worldwide. It is not only here. We learn from the others, actually. That is what they do. When there is a boom, when things are easy, banks compete with each other. They want to give you more money than you need and you grow very quickly. Then you are in a big hurry and you grow as fast as you can and they give you more than you have asked for from them. Then if something happens – and in today's world, it is nothing even to do with Australia, maybe. Greece, I don't know. Something that is nothing to do with us. Then suddenly a new face appears at the bank and says you owe them money. Seeing that that could always happen to you, you should always be well secured. You should give him not as little as possible, but as much as possible so that everybody is happy. The bank manager deals with you in the beginning but it is not necessarily the bank manager who finishes with you. So these are the things of life. But to start, you need them, grab as much as you can, pay them as quickly as you can and then be comfortable.

BK: Now, Harry, I know that you've got some great cars – when is the right time to buy your first Bentley?

HT: Well, first of all, you must be able to pay cash for it because the moment you take it out, it is not worth half of what you paid, you must understand that. Money must not matter to you. I used to have beautiful American cars when I first started. Oh, yes. It is really a nice one. Drive around the Cross in this car, beautiful, very nice. But we didn't get a Bentley, we went for American cars. I had every type of big American car there was and then I went for Mercedes, but they are a bit dull, you must admit. Good car, but dull. Bentley is a very nice car. I love them, you know. You sit up there and look down on everything. Of course, SUVs now have taken that away, but before that, very nice.

BK: You're the man.

HT: That is how you do it.

BK: Very good. What is the best and worst client, customer or supplier lesson that you've had?

HT: Best time, right. So things were very tough in 1973. Citibank came into Australia. They were going to make a lot of money. Then, in 1974, they decided that I was broke. I proved to them I was not broke. They were convinced I was. I paid them all the money back and around 1975, I think it was, they gave me a cheque for two million dollars because they never believed I would pay them back. So what did they do? They thought that they could stop me from building, but they couldn't. Because I started the buildings on my money I told them, 'Right, it is mortgaged to you, take this half-finished building.' So then they started pleading with me not to do it to them. I said I will do it to you because that is the way I will pay you back. I had a list in my office and every day I showed them how I diminished the debt. Every day I diminished the debt, every day. I built one, I sold two. I built one, I sold two. Every day. They were so happy. That was the best relationship I've ever had.

'I don't compete with others. Others do not exist for me.
I do not worry about it. I never diversified.'

BK: Fantastic, what's the worst?

HT: The worst one I had was with a subcontractor. He was a nice boy, but he was a bit crazy. Now, I have my way of paying. He disagreed with the way I paid him so he came into my room with a gun wrapped up in a piece of paper. It was lucky that the girl who was with me saw him and she started screaming. I had my other fellow there and he grabbed him and took away the gun. His father came to me and he told me that the boy was not right in the mind. He was a good worker, but that was bad – whenever you get a subcontractor, you must be careful.

BK: Alright, talk to us about taxation. What is your view on tax, how has it affected you and how much do you like it. Do you enjoy paying it?

HT: Well, taxation is like this. Tax used to be easy once upon a time. We used to buy loss companies, we used to go into mining. We did all kinds of things, it was very simple. Then they decided to get tough with us and all these big ideas disappeared. As they disappeared, suddenly I owed money to the Tax Department. I think I owed the most money in the country at that time. So they came to me and said, 'You owe us money.' Very good. 'How much money?' I asked and they told me. 'Bull, it's not that much,' I said. So we worked it out and we reduced it.

I learned one thing: I shouldn't assume that I will not pay tax because those days are gone. There were big companies who disagreed with me and they did not pay the tax and they are still fighting them thirty years later, but I paid the tax after we agreed on the price and I became the best friend of the Taxation Department, best friend.

Since then I pay them tax, but what I do is I keep lots of my properties. If you keep the properties in this country and the capital gain is there you don't pay tax, which is beautiful. You only pay tax on the rent. You don't pay all the tax on rent either because you have depreciation. That is the beauty of my business. I build the property, I've already made the profit, and I don't pay tax because I keep it. Then I lease it and I don't pay all the tax on the rent because of depreciation, so I pay very little tax. I do pay tax though on the ones I sell, alright.

So what we do in my case is I buy a lot of empty land because I think I can get a very good floor to space ratio on the land. The government realises at last how important it is to have housing, so if you can explain to them that what you say is right and what they say is wrong, then you make even more money on that. In the meantime, you keep the land and of course it doesn't bring an income, so that's again how you avoid, in my case, taxes. It's all legal, that's how you do it.

BK: It's very interesting. There's a great book that some French academics published on billionaires. They studied thirty-two billionaires and how they became billionaires. They said that there was a great wealth-driving event at one point and one of the ones that they have demonstrated was that tax is a huge driver. Obviously, if you can minimise paying 30%+ tax, the cumulative effect of that over a long period of time – certainly over fifty years – is enormous. Is there one thing that you think that anyone who wants to succeed in business should definitely not forget?

HT: Well, the bigger you become, the harder you work, so if you think that by being bigger you will be able to relax, you're wrong. So decide now if you are prepared to work hard. If you aren't, don't bother.

BK: Do you still sign all the cheques? I did hear that rumour.

HT: No.

BK: How hands-on are you in the business?

HT: Very hands-on. As much as times allows it.

BK: What about the role of your family and spouse in terms of growing this business? How much of an impact does a business that size have on you and your family?

HT: Well, the first two wives, they didn't take much interest. Two daughters, not much interest. Our grandchildren – one, the big granddaughter takes an interest. The other three are still too young, so there is still hope. I hope I will change the daughters first. But, you know, to change them also requires a lot of work from me. It is one thing to make money, it's another thing to make what I do attractive to them. So far I haven't succeeded. But I keep trying.

BK: Now, you are over fifty, what are your future plans? What are your personal future plans? What are your plans for Meriton?

HT: I will keep on doing the same thing. I think I still have a few years left. You know, build seventy storeys now, eighty storeys, maybe build a hundred.

BK: How high can you get?

HT: As high as the councils approve. They sometimes change their minds. The problem with building tall buildings is it's not the best way to make money. You see, when you spread the building over lower levels, say ten floors, twelve, fifteen floors, you can build many at once. When you build one tall one like that, you are limited because you can only build in that little space, so therefore it takes a long time. But we are making changes so that we can make it more quickly.

BK: OK, now explain the changes to how large property developments are approved in New South Wales. Can you talk to us about that and also what happened up at Warriewood?

HT: Well, after many years, the Labor government and the state government, understood that councils would not approve large property developments. And if they did approve, it would be in such a way as to make sure that the developer would go broke. That is even worse because the developer puts his last money in, the bank gives him the money and the rest is history.

So then they decided that the state government would approve big projects. That was going very well, but O'Farrell decided that he would say that the councils should get back the power. Of course, he wanted to control them so he said he was thinking of cottages. You see, where you get approvals and cottages, nobody protests. Everybody is very happy because the councils don't have any money so they approve anything, very easy. What they overlooked is that people don't want to live where we can build cottages. Cottages were built in the wrong place. I said we should renovate, rebuild, fix the old cottages. We have so many thousands of them, hundreds of them, millions of them, just fix them. Big job.

Don't worry about new ones, just fix them. But now we have the problem. What will happen when the councils regain their power? I hope that we will learn how to contain that power, but at this stage it's not sure yet how it will happen. So we might have even less production than before. Even though you can produce cottages, which nobody wants, it will be difficult to get approvals for apartments, which everybody wants.

Now, what happened in Warriewood was I bought some land and they wouldn't approve what I thought they should approve. It had nothing to do with their code so I went to Sartor. He was the minister and he said, 'I can't do anything with these guys because they control the upper house.' McTaggart was a member, he was an independent. Anyway, they got re-elected and now, McTaggart is gone, Labor is controlled and we come up with the same plans, which were approved by the Department of Planning but not by Sartor. They saw the plans again and they said, 'We'll approve it.' I got the approval.

So then the mayor of Pittwater, which is Warriewood, decided he was going to go against us. It was a very interesting case. I had the planning department on my side and the council. Normally it is the developer who is objecting. I love that, you know. It wouldn't even matter who won, but just that picture. Something I waited fifty years for. I saw the picture. That council on that side, not on this side and now I'm on this side I'm like the council for once. I got approval. It was very dangerous what I did, because in their hearts, the planning department would be on their side not on my side. So since I had the approval, I started building and

I built as fast as I could. Then I decided what would the judge do, tell me to pull down the building? Very hard. The council was scared to put an injunction on me because then they would be liable to pay if they were wrong. So, there they are, whingeing over there. Some things are worth seeing in life! They were whingeing and I was building and building and I told them, have a look today, have a look tomorrow. Anyway, thank God the judge decided we were right, 100% right and they have to pay my costs.

BK: What's your best tip for dealing with council?

HT: The tip with the council is this: they have a code. Now you have to decide whether that code will allow you to make a profit. If it does not allow you to make a profit, then leave the development. That is what I'm talking about.

'You must build in the right place. It must be convenient …
you have to be near the transport, you have to be near the city
and you have to be near good schools. If you've got those three
things, you can't go wrong.'

BK: If you look back over your projects, some are more successful, some are less successful. Is there a common theme for the ones that go very well?

HT: Yes. You must build in the right place. It must be convenient. That's the easy thing of dealing with the Chinese. They're very logical. It's very easy to understand what they like. They are the main market and they are the ones who will buy from you. So, you have to be near the transport, you have to be near the city and you have to be near good schools. If you've got those three things, you can't go wrong. The next thing is you have to decide on the size of the apartments. If you go to the local agents they will tell you to build mansions. Don't listen to them. Decide in your mind what you think is the best size. It doesn't mean it has to be the smallest and it doesn't mean it has to be the biggest. Usually, if you go for two bedrooms, make them 80 squares, one garage, you can't go wrong.

Tom Waterhouse

Bookmaker – tomwaterhouse.com

'When you've got an online business you also have other things that you can give your customers … You're not just stuck being an online wagering business. If you want to be, you can be far more. That's the exciting thing.'

Tom Waterhouse is a man living his passion. The managing director of tomwaterhouse.com, his business offers punters around the world an astonishing diversity of wagering opportunities. One of Australia's largest corporate bookmakers, Tom narrowly escaped a career in stockbroking. Coming from some of Australia's legendary bookmaking and horse-racing families, Tom's heritage and flair for the industry has resulted in a company that is reported to have some 80 000 clients, employ over a hundred staff and a turnover in the hundreds of millions.

www.tomwaterhouse.com

Interview

BRETT KELLY: Tom, tell me a little bit about yourself … Where did you grow up and go to school?

TOM WATERHOUSE: I grew up in Clifton Gardens in Mosman, just near Taronga Zoo. I lived in the same house from when I was eighteen months old until I was eighteen. I went to a school called 'Shore' in North Sydney.

BK: What was your first job?

TW: My first job was when I was about eleven or twelve. My mum [racehorse trainer and businesswoman Gai Waterhouse] made me work at her stables on Sundays and for a week every school holiday. I used to hate it once I got a bit older because my friends were going out all the time. I'd go out with them and come home at two-thirty or three in the morning and my mum would say, 'Go down to the track.' I'd go from three until nine in the morning and then come back for the afternoon shift between one and three or two and four. I can remember thinking all my friends were at the beach and it was just the worst thing in the world. But it was a good lesson very early on. She kept saying, 'Unless you work hard at school, this is what you'll be doing for the rest of your life.'

BK: Which I take it was shovelling shit in the stables?

TW: Well, it wasn't actually shovelling shit, because I used to get the shovel and she'd say, 'What are you, a sheila? Pick it up with your hands.' So I didn't like it at all. No appeal for me whatsoever. I realised very early on that that wasn't the career path I wanted.

BK: So you went from school to university?

TW: When I finished school, mum said, 'I've organised a great opportunity for you to go to Ireland for three months to learn how to be a horse trainer.' Everyone was spending the summer in Australia and I couldn't think of anything worse than going to the cold of winter in Ireland to hang out with lots of horses and stuff. Somehow, my dad helped me get out of that and I started university. I did some work experience at Merrill Lynch and I thought I was going to get into stockbroking or finance. But then, six months into my first year at uni, I worked one day out at the track and from that moment on, I fell in love with it.

BK: Who were you working with at the track?

TW: One day I went out with my dad on the bag. I was eighteen or maybe just turned nineteen. It was my first semester at uni or maybe just the start of the second semester. Within five minutes, there was just so much money changing hands. The pace of the environment was so busy. I loved it.

BK: So your dad was a bookmaker on the course at that point?

TW: On course, yes.

BK: You're holding the bag, he's doing the booking?

TW: Yes.

'Six months into my first year at uni, I worked one day out at the track and from that moment on, I fell in love with it.'

BK: And you're starting to work out if you can count $20 bills fast enough!

TW: Exactly. It's funny, my dad and my grandfather both gave me a lecture, 'Now, when you go out there,' they said, 'be very careful of pickpockets.' They remembered back twenty or thirty years before when there were lots of pickpockets around. I've never seen one pickpocket at the races. It was so busy, it was just fantastic.

I was very lucky; sometimes it takes years for people to be given authority, or maybe even never, to run someone's stand for them. My dad went away two months later and he said, 'Oh, Tommy, you run it.' And I replied, 'What do you mean?' I was in my second semester at uni and he said 'You just run it now. This is how I'd do things and this is how I do that. But, basically, you give it a whirl.' It was quite a responsibility.

He was always very good to me as a child. Whether it was driving his car to parties on Saturday nights or driving to school, he just let me. Even from the age of five or whenever, I was allowed to ride my bike to school or catch a bus or just do whatever I wanted. My parents gave me a lot of responsibility and I always rose to the challenge.

I remember, in our first two months of being there, I was like, 'Far out!' People are yelling, 'To win $50 000!' and I was like, 'No … !' But it gave me a great boost. I thought, 'I can actually do this.' Maybe not as well as they could, but I knew the basic principles of what was happening. It was great. I spent the next few years working with my dad and my grandfather and got experience going to all the country racetracks. I also got a licence for the dogs and I kept doing that until I finished university.

BK: So once you went to the track, you knew that you'd be a bookmaker?

TW: I knew as soon as I went there that I wanted to do a lot more of it, so I moved my uni timetable around so I could. I knew I was going to be a bookie.

BK: So then you finished university. Your grandfather had been a bookie for over fifty years by then. Tell me what you learned from your grandfather.

TW: Well, they were so different, my dad and my grandfather. My dad is a form analyst so he assesses every race and the percentage chances and it's very mathematical. Whereas my grandfather is very big picture. He wants to build businesses, build property, take big punters on. He just assumes that by taking the punter on, he'll beat them over a period and doesn't want to get into the nitty-gritty of a particular race. It's more the big picture. So I had two very different influences.

'I knew as soon as I went there that I wanted to do a lot more of it … I knew I was going to be a bookie.'

BK: Two philosophies.

TW: Two philosophies. I thought my grandfather was so wrong for the first few years. I thought, 'This guy has no idea what he is talking about.' But he was actually 100% right over the long term.

BK: So give me a couple of his comments, tell me something of his great lines.

TW: Well, he'd go way over the odds on a favourite that we had marked very short that shouldn't have been that price and he'd say, 'Oh, don't worry. If it wins, we'll get great publicity for betting these ridiculous odds. If it loses, we get the money.' And he was always, 'Just bet that person,' and I'd be, 'Oh, I don't want to lay this horse.' When it got too much he'd say, 'Don't worry, just bet him. You'll get him as a client long-term. Keep him happy and he'll be your client forever. It will pay off in the end.' In contrast, my dad is very much, 'This is how I see the form. This is the view I want to take on this particular race.'

BK: When did you get your own bag?

TW: I had my own licence, but in the city, in New South Wales. I formed a company licence with my grandfather and I worked for a couple of years with him. We worked at all the city tracks together.

BK: So that happened about ten years ago now, around 2002?

TW: Yes.

BK: And your grandfather is now ninety?

TW: He's about to turn ninety-one in February 2013.

BK: Right. So, at that point, you went into business with your eighty-year-old grandfather.

TW: And he was vicious. He was really tough. When I was a child, he was really easygoing. He used to dress up as Santa Claus. We'd play table tennis. We'd go and eat icecream and chocolates for breakfast. He was really easygoing. But at the racetrack, he wouldn't say anything to me the whole day. He'd let me run the show but he knew exactly to the dollar without looking at the computer how we'd gone at the end of the day.

On the way back in the car he'd say, 'Why did you do that? or, 'You're an imbecile for doing that.' I'd be like, 'No! You don't know what you're talking about. This is how it should be. You don't understand.' Because I'd been taught completely different things. I learned very quickly that every bookie at the races works differently. It's probably the same in accounting, you can be very different in the way you approach accounting or getting clients but you can be successful in all of them. Or you could be successful in none of them.

He had a completely different way of doing things to my dad. At the time, I thought, 'Well, that's impossible,' because I knew the right way to do it. But I just knew one way. And there are other people at the races that know different ways and they can all be successful. Over the years I came around more to his style of thinking but at the same time, kept very much that …

BK: … that discipline and being the analyst that your dad is.

TW: Yes.

BK: How did you end up in Victoria?

TW: In 2008, they were changing the taxes in New South Wales so I moved down to Victoria. I realised that not only were the taxes different but the products you could offer to your customer were different, too. So I was able to offer them products that the New South Wales bookies couldn't offer.

A lot of the customers thought, 'Far out! Tom can offer all these products my bookie in New South Wales can't', so I got a lot more new customers. Then I realised that every bookie wanted the smaller, recreational punter. Having dad's form and my grandfather's view on taking the big picture, betting these people big, before the financial crash, I got a small group of punters that wanted to bet very large on racing.

This got to a lot of people; newspaper articles were written and I got a little bit of stuff on racing TV which back then was allowed to cover the big bets I was taking. I got a lot of coverage. Then these companies from overseas came in and did some market research and thought, 'This young bloke is really well-known. He has the second highest awareness besides the TABs' so they said, 'We'd like to buy your business.'

I had a great business. It was making good money, a high turnover, and I knew a few clients really well, but I said, 'Great. Well, that's worth six times, ten times earnings. Is that what you'd pay for it?' And I thought, 'Oh, this is going to be terrific.' But they said, 'No. It's worth nothing. We'll buy your brand for something, but we don't want the business. It's not worth anything because if you leave, how can we keep them? We won't pay anything for the business, but we'll pay for the brand.' And I was like, 'Oh gosh! The brand. I'd never valued that at anything.' I thought, 'If that's worth something, and I've got this business …'

BK: … better build it.

TW: I'll build it. A few overseas companies approached me but so did one of the local TABs. They had a very senior person that was trying to organise a deal with me at the time. Then after that, they were up for sale. At that point he wasn't sure if he wanted to stay with the TAB and I said, 'Come onboard with me and we can build this business online.' He was the first. Every other person I had before then was just a person to collect money or to put the tickets in the operator. There was no real senior management involved in the business. We had a secretary and an accounts person, but no senior management. That was the first time that the business dramatically changed.

BK: Now, was it at that point that you thought, 'The internet is going bananas, let's start an online business'?

TW: No, I knew before then that I was going to build the online business. The whole negotiation with all these people, the overseas people and the TAB was about building the online business. But there was a breakdown in what I saw. I saw that my existing business …

BK: … had some value.

TW: Had huge value. Every year I made good profits out of it. They said, 'We're not actually interested in that. We're interested in this bit.' And I said, 'Well, OK, that bit's worth something, but so is this bit,' and there was a breakdown in price over that.

BK: OK. Your brand is the second most recognised one in the betting space. Tell me about the conversations and the decisions that led to starting an online business.

TW: Well, it was never really a difficult decision because it was just a transition of the business I already had. I already had an on-course and telephone business, but now a lot of the customers were wanting to bet online. So, it wasn't like, 'Oh, this is going to be a brand new business.' It was just a continuation of an existing business.

BK: You didn't see it as particularly risky?

TW: No, not at all. I just thought it was the exact same business except online. But the problem was that the existing advertising was opened up – well, it was a benefit and a problem. Every Australian company, except I think myself and one other, had been bought by overseas companies. They all came in and said, 'We've got to keep pushing the advertising.' They had a ten-year jump on us in terms of technology and infrastructure. So that was where even though the actual betting piece and the actual taking customers online was simple, I didn't realise I needed the ramp-up that they had in terms of marketing and infrastructure. And that was probably the bit I didn't see coming.

BK: So, since then, you've made a massive investment in getting your brand out there and getting your systems right. With great effect, customers come to you. Are you as excited about the space now as you were when you got started, or more?

TW: I think it's more exciting now. You realise very quickly when you're at the races that there are maybe 40 000 people there on a big day. That's huge. Online, Australia is a big market. You've got the whole of Australia, but that's just one little piece of what's out there. The whole of Asia and America are about to open up. India's opened up. Just in our region, you've got so much but there's so much more out there if you do it right. That's one of the exciting things about it. It's not just a wagering business.

You realise once you're online that it's fantastic, that you love betting, and you want to bet on everything. I love it. But when you've got an online business you also have other things that you can give your customers. We take huge numbers of customers out to social activities, events and different things. You're not just stuck being an online wagering business. If you want to be, you can be far more. That's the exciting thing. It's not only the customer base and what you can bet on, once you have a group of customers and you can give them a good service or whatever you want to provide them, you realise that that's also an opportunity.

BK: So now, as you look out, what's the big picture plan?

TW: I think for the next four years, Australia is the main focus for us, but from then on, it's about expanding in our region.

BK: If you look back now, how applicable is the wisdom of your grandfather or the knowledge of your father in the online space?

TW: They've both been so, so valuable. The online business needed the foundations that we call the VIP business to make it run, and without them and their guidance, it just couldn't have been done. They showed me how the business, the core foundations of a bookmaking business, work.

In a broader business sense, my grandfather taught me very early on about the cash flow. I think I've mentioned a punter lost $1.2 million in a day and I won $400 000 of it. I thought, gosh, I'm going to buy a Ferrari. I'm going to have a huge day or a huge trip or whatever – and he didn't pay me for a year and a half. I bet back of the $1.2 million he lost, $800 000 with other bookmakers. I had to pay them on a Monday and it nearly sent me into an awful position. My grandfather instilled in me how critical cash flow is in any business.

When I first moved to Melbourne, we had two or three full-time employees. Within the next month and a half, we'll have about a hundred. If I hadn't kept that thought in mind, we'd be in a very different position.

'I didn't realise I needed the ramp-up that they had in terms of marketing and infrastructure. And that was probably the bit I didn't see coming.'

BK: That's a great lesson. What are the other big lessons you've learned?

TW: Quality of people. I've learned that the hard way. My grandfather and my dad were ruthless. If someone wasn't up to scratch, they'd get rid of them. They had very clear rules. If someone bet while working, if someone didn't turn up on time, they would just say they didn't want them. That was built in to me.

You don't go down the same recruitment path that you do in a bigger business. It's word of mouth, people get suggestions. I remember when our COO came on board, it was he and I and two other people. On the second day he was there we had to get rid of those two people because we caught them stealing. I remember I had to get my girlfriend, who is now my wife, in together with the COO and we basically ran the business for the next month until we got new people in. We were turning over $200 million at the time.

But growing fast, we spent a fortune on recruitment, finding the right people, testing them and going through extensive rounds of interviews because it's so costly if they're the wrong people. Our perspective is worldwide. We do a lot of our recruitment at the moment in the UK and America because they lead the way in IT, especially in the wagering space or gaming space. So that's been a very big lesson. It's important to find the right people.

BK: When we talk to most businesses, there was a long lead-up before an explosion of growth. Do you still consider yourself in that lead-up period?

TW: I think so. An online business needs to get to a critical mass. If I stopped marketing and expanding it, I'd have a profitable business. But I don't see it being profitable for years to come because I see the opportunity to expand it at a rate

to capture market share, not in this market but in the next markets, and I want to keep growing it. So I'm nowhere near that critical mass yet. I need to keep growing it.

BK: So who are the people that inspire you in life and in business?

TW: First, my dad and my grandfather. They're both completely different but unbelievable characters. I also love reading about entrepreneurs who have done stuff, whether it's Rupert Murdoch or Aristotle Onassis, those sorts of people. It's not like I want to follow in their footsteps, I actually enjoy the journey.

I know it sounds strange, but I never viewed being at the races or online as a money-making venture. It's just growing something and building a business and expanding it – the adventure of it. I find that more exciting than saying, 'Oh, I want to make this amount next year.' That's a very short-term goal.

BK: What's the ten-year picture, the twenty-year picture? Can there be one?

TW: Well, people probably look at me and think I must be an idiot when I say it, but I love to be at the place where most people want to bet, whether it's in Australia or around the world. People will go, 'I love betting with Tom, and he knows the kind of products that I want to bet on, how I want to bet, how quickly I want to bet,' and that I have the broadest range of products and groups of people wanting to bet with me. I guess that's a starter, but also expanding and trying different things, whether it's my mum's side of the business or whether it's in a different industry. If you can get that online piece right, it's exciting, all the opportunities out there.

BK: Opens up doors. To finish, is there a motto, a quote, or a thought that best summarises your approach to life?

TW: I never really thought about that. I guess my parents always said to me, 'The woman that you choose to marry will determine if you have a happy life or not.' I guess that's probably number one. You have to make sure the family peace and your family at home is right because all the rest, even if you expand to being the biggest bookie in the world, it doesn't really matter. If you're upset at home or in life with your family, it's a nightmare.

'I know it sounds strange, but I never viewed being at the races or online as a money-making venture. It's just growing something and building a business and expanding it – the adventure of it.'

BK: Let me ask you one more thing, about multi-generational businesses and families. What are the unique pressures of having parents who are very capable people? What is their influence?

TW: Well, I guess they always taught me that you have to work hard. Nothing comes easy. I guess that's true in anything, unless you can delegate to people. You always hear about people that are great delegators. You can delegate, but you also have to say, 'I have to go in and drive it,' because if you don't and you just sit back, nothing happens, or nothing happens the way you want it to. And they always worked hard. My mum gets up at two-thirty in the morning. My dad gets up at three in the morning. They work all the time. Hard work pays off.

Notes

RELEASES

HARDBACK + SOFT COVER / 296 PAGES

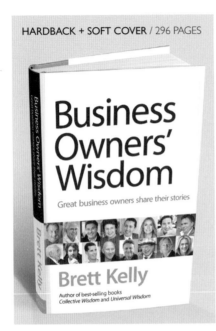

PRAISE FOR THE AUTHOR

"I liked his imagination and chutzpah, it was something quite different … I think he (Brett) is very much to be congratulated."
HON. RJL HAWKE

"(Brett) showed great imagination … persistence and thoughtfulness."
THE RT. HON. MALCOLM FRASER

"An inspiration …"
MIRANDA DEVINE,
THE DAILY TELEGRAPH

"A very determined young bloke."
RAY MARTIN, *A CURRENT AFFAIR*

HARDBACK / 326 PAGES

HARDBACK / 272 PAGES

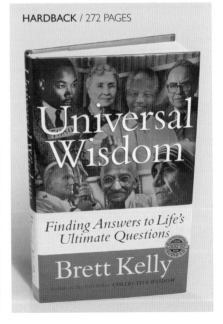

ORDER FORM

TO ORDER YOUR COPIES OF **COLLECTIVE WISDOM**, **UNIVERSAL WISDOM** AND **BUSINESS OWNERS' WISDOM** FILL IN THE DETAILS AND SEND YOUR ORDER BY FACSIMILE, POST, EMAIL OR ONLINE **www.brettkelly.com.au**

PLEASE PRINT CLEARLY

Full Name: _____

Delivery Address: _____

_____ State: _____ Postcode: _____

Tel: ( ) _____ Mobile: _____

Fax: ( ) _____

Email: _____

PAYMENT METHOD

Tick one of the following:

☐ Personal Cheque ☐ Bank Cheque ☐ Bankcard ☐ Visa ☐ Mastercard

Cheques payable to: '**Clown Publishing**'.

Cardholder's Name (as on card): _____

Card Number: _____

Expiry Date: _____

Cardholder's Signature: _____

QUANTITY OF BOOKS

☐	*COLLECTIVE WISDOM* (Hardback) at **$49.95** each	$_____
☐	*UNIVERSAL WISDOM* (Hardback) at **$49.95** each	$_____
☐	*BUSINESS OWNERS' WISDOM* (Hardback) at **$49.95** each	$_____
☐	*BUSINESS OWNERS' WISDOM* (Soft Cover) at **$24.95** each *	$_____
☐	*ORDERS OF 10 OR MORE SOFT COVERS at **$19.95** each	$_____
☐	*ORDERS OF 100 OR MORE SOFT COVERS at **$10.00** each	$_____
	Postage and handling at **$5.00** per book *(Allow 21 days delivery)*	$_____
	TOTAL PAYMENT	**$_____**

POST TO:

Clown Publishing, PO Box 1764, North Sydney NSW 2059, Australia
T 02 9923 0800 **F** 02 9923 0888 **E** brett@kellypartners.com.au
www.brettkelly.com.au

Reno Design 31025_OrderFormGen_V9